Palgrave Macmillan's
Postcolonial Studies in Education

Studies utilizing the perspectives of postcolonial theory have become established and increasingly widespread in the last few decades. This series embraces and broadly employs the postcolonial approach. As a site of struggle, education has constituted a key vehicle for the "colonization of the mind." The "post" in postcolonialism is both temporal, in the sense of emphasizing the processes of decolonization, and analytical, in the sense of probing and contesting the aftermath of colonialism and the imperialism that succeeded it, utilizing materialist and discourse analysis. Postcolonial theory is particularly apt for exploring the implications of educational colonialism, decolonization, experimentation, revisioning, contradiction, and ambiguity not only for the former colonies but also for the former colonial powers. This series views education as an important vehicle for both the inculcation and unlearning of colonial ideologies. It complements the diversity that exists in postcolonial studies of political economy, literature, sociology, and the interdisciplinary domain of cultural studies. Education is here being viewed in its broadest contexts and is not confined to institutionalized learning. The aim of this series is to identify and help establish new areas of educational inquiry in postcolonial studies.

Series Editors:

Antonia Darder holds the Leavey Presidential Endowed Chair in Ethics and Moral Leadership at Loyola Marymount University, Los Angeles, and is Professor Emerita at The University of Illinois, Urbana-Champaign.

Anne Hickling-Hudson is Associate Professor of Education at Australia's Queensland University of Technology where she specializes in cross-cultural and international education.

Peter Mayo is Professor and Head of the Department of Education Studies at the University of Malta where he teaches in the areas of sociology of education and adult continuing education, as well as in comparative and international education and sociology more generally.

Editorial Advisory Board:

Carmel Borg (University of Malta)
John Baldacchino (Teachers College, Columbia University)
Jennifer Chan (University of British Columbia)
Christine Fox (University of Wollongong, Australia)
Zelia Gregoriou (University of Cyprus)
Leon Tikly (University of Bristol)
Birgit Brock-Utne (Emeritus, University of Oslo, Norway)

Titles:

A New Social Contract in a Latin American Education Context
Danilo R. Streck; Foreword by Vítor Westhelle

Education and Gendered Citizenship in Pakistan
M. Ayaz Naseem

Indigenous Education through Dance and Ceremony

A Mexica Palimpsest

Ernesto "Tlahuitollini" Colín

INDIGENOUS EDUCATION THROUGH DANCE AND CEREMONY
Copyright © Ernesto "Tlahuitollini" Colín, 2014.

First published in 2014 by
PALGRAVE MACMILLAN®
in the United States—a division of St. Martin's Press LLC,
175 Fifth Avenue, New York, NY 10010.

Where this book is distributed in the UK, Europe and the rest of the world,
this is by Palgrave Macmillan, a division of Macmillan Publishers Limited,
registered in England, company number 785998, of Houndmills,
Basingstoke, Hampshire RG21 6XS.

Palgrave Macmillan is the global academic imprint of the above companies
and has companies and representatives throughout the world.

Palgrave® and Macmillan® are registered trademarks in the United States,
the United Kingdom, Europe and other countries.

ISBN: 978–1–137–35798–4

Library of Congress Cataloging-in-Publication Data is available from the
Library of Congress.

A catalogue record of the book is available from the British Library.

Design by Newgen Knowledge Works (P) Ltd., Chennai, India.

First edition: September 2014

10 9 8 7 6 5 4 3 2 1

Dedicated to those who have sown seeds,
scattered jades, and given their life
to these traditions, my life, and future generations.

Contents

Figures and Tables

Figures

Tables

Foreword: Historically Embodied Learning

Ray McDermott (Stanford University) and
Jason Raley (UC Santa Barbara)

We had known Ernesto Colín for a few years before he asked us to visit a practice session of a local Aztec *Danza* group. We had followed the frontpage stories in local newspapers whenever the dance group was called on to represent the Latino community at a public function (as recently as March 17, 2014, in the *San José Mercury News*, the morning after we had composed this foreword). We were not uninformed. We even called Ernesto "Tlahuitollini," his taken Náhuatl name that speaks for an identity reaching into prehispanic times. But we had little idea of how things were organized and few specific images of what we were to see.

Colín's book fills the void. After more than a decade of participation and fieldwork, he delivers a rich and thorough account of Aztec *Danza*: its history, its complex layers of organization, its connections to people of Mexican descent, its uses in contemporary American cities, and, perhaps most of all, its power as an occasion for education.

We arrived at a large empty room, about the size of a squared off basketball court. We watched as more than 100 people gathered—all dancers, we were told, but we had to be told. Greetings big and small turned into clusters of people chatting. The people were clearly important to each other, but nothing stood out for a while.

Gradually, without any obvious call to order, things started to happen in the center of the room. Drums were getting set up, some senior men were paying careful attention, and the people started to fall into a set of concentric circles. The conversational clusters slowly morphed into arced lines moving to the right and then to the left in time with the drums. We focused immediately on the outermost ring where children and other stragglers were trying to find their way. The circles had a centripetal force that brought everyone into line. Three- and four-year-old children who had been throwing themselves around stepped into the emerging lines. Sometimes an adult would take a hand or offer a ride. Leadership was distributed among an apparently wide set of participants, from one spur of the moment to the next. Eventually everyone was involved in one way or another: the most serious dancers literally in the middle of things and the rest organized into outer rings by the degree of skill. It seemed almost impossible to not engage.

We wondered where else we had seen such full-bodied, full-minded, everyone-included behavior across generations. *Calpulli Tonalehqueh* seemed to be an educational environment of a type that parents and school teachers dream of, but seldom experience: everyone learning together without bells, clickers, rulers (of both types), screamers, failures, detentions, and dunces. We wondered what held it together, and we wondered what was being learned. Strangely, the two questions became only one question. In the best of worlds, how things are organized and what is being learned are overlapping developments. John Dewey liked to say that learning is something that happens while we are doing something else. Colín's book gives us an account of all the things people have to do at *Danza* while important learning is also happening. By the same line of reasoning, Colín gives an account of the things people might learn while dancing gets done. Perhaps we can use Colín's examples as models for how learning might ideally take place.

One secret came at the end of the two-hour practice. The dancing had grown more intense across the evening: beating drums and dancing bodies becoming more difficult to separate. Everyone was exhausted, but as people began to pack up, a small group of leaders started to convene at one of the exits. The members of *Calpulli Tonalehqueh* had come together to dance, but they had also danced to come together. The formation of persons, what we learn to be the Náhuatl version of "education," emerges from the formation of dance (now, in present time) and the formation of the *calpulli* (long ago, through now, into the future). The leaders talked directly to the facts of life, the facts that they were in some ways responsible for: facts about who needs help with a dying parent, an alienated teen, an immigration snafu, or a lost job opportunity. The problems were ordinary, and easy for the self-important to ignore, but the *calpulli* leaders thought direct action was possible. They talked through the problems faced by their membership, and they made plans for lending a hand directly or through connections with those who might be helpful. Like drum beats and dancers, teachers and learners can be brought together. So too can problems and their solutions. Poets and philosophers know about this, and great teachers can often transform problems into solutions. Now we can add participants in *danza* groups. The problems and their solutions may be ordinary—they may even appear to be theoretically unremarkable—but community groups with an articulate vision for changing the world and lending a hand are unfortunately rare in formal, contemporary educational encounters.

Let us return to the learning of the youngest members of the *calpulli*. Our attention had to be close, easy as it was to lose small bodies in the chest-pounding beats of drums and bigger bodies. No child was ever lost. No child was an inconvenience, nor marginal, nor even just tolerated. Instead, the tiniest dancing bodies had spaces made for them by the adult bodies: hollows carved in the otherwise close-coupled concentric circles of dancers for the child to dance. Occasionally, an adult would appear to model a step or turn of torso or forearm. Rarely, an adult would move a child or reposition a wayward body part. Even in the most frenetic whirls, when individual dancers grew into parts of the whole *danza*, the children were not stepped on, tripped over, or otherwise treated as in-the-way. From this angle, the circle of *danzantes* appeared to be engaged as much in building a moving habitat for their modern children as making and dancing to the percussive music of precolonial Mesoamerica.

The present text offers much more than a description of the kind of *danza* practice we witnessed. The concentric circles of *Danza* practice radiate much farther into the past and future than we could have imagined. It takes Colín five chapters to get us just to the front door! But this time, we get a full account of both the deep (and deeply felt) history that boils behind the *calpulli* and the sharp-edged contemporary challenges it faces. The personal commitments that guide the *calpulli* also animate this book. No less than the day of our visit to *Danza*, we are drawn into the radiating circles of Colín's description. No less than the day of our visit, we are humbled. And moved.

Author's Preface

Organization of the Book

Martha Stone's *At the Sign of Midnight: The Concheros Dance Cult of Mexico* (1975) was a transformative text for me in the journey to this book. It is a piece of anthropology in a well-known format: an outsider moves to México City in the 1940s, spends 25 years living, learning, and dancing with Native Mexican dancers, and writes a text that, in 1975, brought Aztec dance to mainstream American audiences. She was no Margaret Mead or Keith Basso, perhaps, but she did look and listen, immerse herself, and journal well enough to give a breakthrough first-person account of the people and ceremonies that let her in. She spoke to many elders, noted the activity and accouterments of ceremonies, and relayed her own transformation over many years in *Danza*. Stone reached the point where she was appointed to a prestigious position within the leadership of her group. The text became a classic. *At the Sign of Midnight* is illuminating because I am able to see how this type of narrative, this type of direct participation, this collection of voices can be a legitimate and accepted text.[1]

The discipline of cultural anthropology has been critiqued because of its historical complicity with harmful colonial projects and carelessness with researcher bias, not to mention carelessness with local communities. Many aboriginal communities have not been allowed to tell their own stories in academia. It is in the spirit of upsetting this trend, with a model crafted by Stone, and after 19 years in *Danza* (including nine with Calpulli Tonalehqueh) that I provide an account of indigenous education through dance and ceremony, or the building of this *calpulli*.[2]

The focus of this research turned on the following questions: (1) When are environments for a modern Mexica education constructed? In other words, at what times does this group mobilize resources for cultural transmission and socialization? (2) When is palimpsest? In other words, at what times is the metaphor of a multi-layered text with an incompletely erased heritage upon which new text is superimposed apt for group productions?

The concept of a *palimpsest* is a metaphor I use to understand the activity of a modern *calpulli*.[3] Given that, each chapter has the same basic components (see figure 0.1). In each I review historical antecedents and scholarship around one concept in traditional Mexica society (e.g., *calpulli, tlacahuapahualiztli, macehualiztli*) relevant to the environment of indigenous education organized by this dance circle. My intent is to provide the reader with an understanding of the ancient concept and its historical context. The historical information is included because it is material members collect to build their *calpulli*; Calpulli Tonalehqueh recovers and reorganizes each of these practices in the present. After I present the history of the key concept,

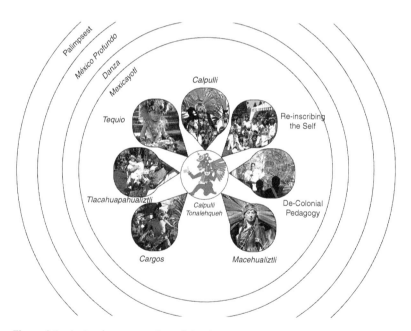

Figure 0.1 A visual representation of the chapter organization and conceptual frame of this book.

Note: I explore seven sites organized for education within Calpulli Tonalehqueh, which is a group that follows the *Mexicayotl* tradition within a larger *Danza* sphere that is a part of and therefore encompassed by *México Profundo*. Intersecting each site is the concept of palimpsest.

I continue each chapter with a description of the ways that Calpulli Tonalehqueh reauthors that concept/tradition using contemporary materials. Calpulli Tonalehqueh builds a bridge between the fifteenth century and the present as they construct their *calpulli*. At the end of each chapter, I discuss the features of the environment created by *calpulli* members in terms of the metaphor of palimpsest. To reiterate, each chapter begins with a historical treatise of a Mexica concept, followed by that concept's reorganization in the present, and concluded with a discussion about how each environment is a palimpsest.

The sequence of the chapters has a scaled logic. I begin with concepts that refer to broad aspects of societal organization (*calpulli, tequio, tlacahuapahualiztli*) followed by concepts that operate at a group level (*cargos, macehualiztli*). I end with traditions focused on the individual level (*huehuetlatolli, in toca in tocaitl*)

Before readers get to the first conceptual chapter (chapter 2, on the concept of *calpulli*), I use an introductory chapter to locate Calpulli Tonalehqueh in the landscape of Aztec dance. I provide background in two main topics crucial for understanding this Mexica dance group: the migration of *Danza* from México to the United States over 400 years, and the origin story of Calpulli Tonalehqueh.

For readers unfamiliar with *Danza* and in order to understand the landscape that situates Calpulli Tonalehqueh, the introductory chapter provides an overview of *Danza* in pre-Cuauhtémoc Anáhuac[4] (Mesoamerica), including as it was portrayed in early colonial texts. Many dancers seek a return to ceremony, dance, and societal organizations that existed before changes occasioned by colonial and postcolonial environments. I discuss the history and features of the main variants in *Danza* that emerged in the last century, focusing particularly on the transition from the *Conchero* to the *Mexicayotl* movements. Knowing to which tradition (within *Danza*) a group subscribes is key to understanding its aims and underpinnings in that field of ideologies. Most groups carefully craft an identity based on a lineage in one of the traditions. Calpulli Tonalehqueh can be circumscribed by the *Mexicayotl* tradition. Next, I provide an overview of *Danza*'s transnational journey back to the United States and into the San Francisco Bay Area. I have been able to trace several lines of ancestry leading to Calpulli Tonalehqueh. Afterwards, I highlight the teachers, evolution, and current make-up of Calpulli Tonalehqueh. Calpulli Tonalehqueh is one of many communities of Anáhuac that engage in a struggle to preserve an indigenous way of life, permeated with the indigeneity of the fabric of Mexican culture.

After the introduction, I move to the body of the book. Each of the chapters explores a site for the organization of teaching and learning inside Calpulli Tonalehqueh by looking at historical constructs and how the members of the *calpulli* reconstruct each of these items. Chapter 2 focuses on the concept of *calpulli* beginning with what scholars contend about the composition of *calpultin* at the *apogée* of classical Mexica society, details how members of Calpulli Tonalehqueh enact *calpulli* social organization, and discusses how these reconfigurations can be understood through palimpsest. Included in this chapter is the story of Gabriel, a young *calpulli* member, and how the dance group mobilized to come to his aid. Chapter 3 introduces a concept, *tequio*, which is central to the functioning of *calpultin* (plural of *calpulli*) and is manifest in the various activities the Calpulli Tonalehqueh achieves through intense collaboration. I discuss how the sustainability of the cultural and political projects of the group requires the same duty and sacrifice that make traditional societies of Anáhuac flourish. Within a sociopolitical institution (*calpulli*) and by way of a social norm (*tequio*) we find *tlacahuapahualiztli*, which refers to the system of formal education in Mexica society. In chapter 4, I explore *tlacahuapahualiztli*, highlight its ideological underpinnings, and then discuss modern learning environments organized by members of Calpulli Tonalehqueh with increasing degrees of intentionality. I discuss how the *calpulli's* contemporary education efforts are positive alternatives to mainstream schooling. Chapter 5 outlines the process Calpulli Tonalehqueh undergoes for designating *cargos*, or leadership roles. The group's decision-making structure is designed around traditional governance systems, yet the leadership roles within it are modernized to fit contemporary needs. I discuss how individuals learn and are acquired by the *cargos*. In chapter 6, the site of palimpsest is the dance ceremony. I highlight the features of pre-Cuauhtémoc dance in Mexica society and then examine the features of contemporary Calpulli Tonalehqueh dance practice, stopping to comment on successful educational components therein. Chapter 7 describes yet another site of education and palimpsest, the public lectures that Calpulli Tonalehqueh organizes for Ocelocoatl Ramírez, an indigenous elder. He is a crucial nexus of education. In that chapter I review the ancient Mexican legacy of the *huehuetlatolli*, the discourses of the elders, and then examine the workshops given by this elder to understand why his pedagogy is so compelling and important for *danzantes*. Chapter 8 is centered on the revival of Mexica divinatory consultation in California, which leads to acquiring a Náhuatl name and having it sown in a public ceremony. This practice is a location for learning, one that involves personal growth, knowledge of Mexica cosmology, and a reinscription of one's personal identity. Together, these sites comprise most of the educational project of Calpulli Tonalehqueh. The project is ambitious and successful in many ways. Its mechanisms, processes, and products are informative to many fields, a topic I discuss in the concluding chapter.

Conceptual Frame

This book centers on environments constructed to transmit culture and ideologies in a group that bridges centuries to institutionalize them. The group with whom I practiced has provocative educational projects and I submit it is helpful to have a lens with which to examine and explain. The metaphor that is taken up as a conceptual frame for this book is palimpsest.

Though it may be ironic in some way, I utilize a term that comes from the Greek (palimpsest) to understand the phenomena in the modern Mexica world. I selected it because it is mutable, interdisciplinary, and multilayered, and because it is helpful for describing dynamic educational environments in the dance group.

Palimpsest

Palimpsest is an extremely dynamic word utilized in numerous academic fields.[5] It has an origin in the seventeenth-century Greek word *palimpsestos*, from *palin* "again" and *psestos* "rubbed smooth." The following are four definitions that together undergird the meaning I employ in this book. I include four because, although they all contain the elemental meanings of the word, each adds a subtle difference that I hope enriches a more nuanced understanding of the concept:

- According to the *Concise Oxford English Dictionary*, a palimpsest is "a parchment or other surface in which later writing has been superimposed on effaced earlier writing; or something bearing visible traces of an earlier form" (2006).
- The *American Heritage Dictionary of the English Language* defines it as "manuscript, typically of papyrus or parchment, that has been written on more than once, with the earlier writing incompletely erased and often legible; or an object, place, or area that reflects its history" (2000).
- A third entry comes from the *Concise Oxford Dictionary of Archaeology* where a palimpsest is a "papyrus or other kind of writing material on

which two or more sets of writing had been superimposed in such a way that, because of imperfect erasure, some of the earlier text could be read through the later over-writing" (Darvil, 2002).

- Finally, the *Merriam-Webster Dictionary* states that a palimpsest is "writing material (as a parchment or tablet) used one or more times after earlier writing has been erased; or something having usually diverse layers or aspects apparent beneath the surface" (2010).

After a review of its use in dozens of academic fields, I am excited to assemble a complex understanding of palimpsest and contemplate the possibilities it provides for the description and analysis of *Danza*. Each of the four selected definitions reveals attractive shades of the word. Common to all definitions are the essential components: original text, erasure, and recomposition. A palimpsest has a past visible and available to the present; a palimpsest's history is layered and retained. A palimpsest has gone through transformation; agents have acted upon it. A palimpsest has been incompletely erased. New writing is present and superimposed.

It is appealing to conceive of *Danza* as a palimpsest. Embodied dance is a text, with a lexicon, syntax, and semantics. It is a living and performative text reauthored by each dancer. Much of the language of *Danza* has been erased, but not all, and *danzantes* gather their heritage and reassemble rites in creative and powerful ways.

As I examine my 19 years in *Danza* while holding present the definitions of palimpsest, I see a match. *Danza* and the cosmo-vision it embodies was and continues to be a ubiquitous part of the fabric of life in Anáhuac. It was taught in the *cuicacalli* and *mixcoacalli*[6] and was part of every day life, both at special ceremonies and as part of the every day. Sixteenth-century European invasion promoted an eradication campaign of the culture of Mesoamerica, restricting dance, burning libraries, disrupting social organization, and imposing language, religion, and a new world order. History and culture were (partially) erased and rewritten with foreign words and worldviews. The extended passage of time, along with a modern-day migration to a completely different context in United States, compounded the erasure of *Danza*. Nevertheless, the genocide and ethnocide were incomplete and the culture endured, strategically and creatively. Syncretic dances emerged (as in the tradition of the *Concheros*), and the keepers of the knowledge waited and protected the traditions (as per the mandate of the *Huey Tlatocan* [appendix A] and other cultural survival strategies).

Nowadays, space is available for *Danza* to blossom. There are growing numbers of teacher-editors and dancer-authors of *Danza*. There are new texts and mnemonics that help reconstruct ceremonies, to various ends and through modern means. Countless dance groups exist in México and the United States, each with their own version of *Danza*—postmodern palimpsests, as such. My intention is to document this phenomenon on a small scale but always referring to the larger historical context layered underneath.

Apart from dictionary definitions, I must acknowledge a set of sources that are primary in my understanding of palimpsest. They are the following:

Daniel Cooper Alarcón's *The Aztec Palimpsest: México in the Modern Imagination* (1997) provides my first encounter with the idea of palimpsest. In the introduction to his text, Cooper Alarcón discussed how "Mexicaness" is a complex palimpsest of interdependent "writings" and goes on to argue that indigenous people's cultural practice and discourses are counterhegemonic texts. He explained how a palimpsest paradigm can be helpful in understanding rapidly shifting Mexican and Chicana/o cultural identity:

> I offer the palimpsest as a theoretical paradigm through which the construction and representation of cultural identity can be foregrounded as an object of study. As already noted, a palimpsest is a site where a text has been erased (often incompletely) in order to accommodate a new one, and it is this unique structure of competing yet interwoven narratives that changes the way we think of cultural identity and its representation, as well as enabling an examination of history, cultural identity, ethnicity, literature, and politics in relationship to each other, providing a new vantage point on the relationship of the United States and México at a time when those two nations are more intimately linked than ever. (p. xvi)

Contemplating the manner in which Cooper Alarcón employed the concept of palimpsest makes it attractive as a term that could describe Mexica dance groups and their ceremonies. The idea of a palimpsest is a generative and apt metaphor for the evolution of cultural traditions and as a framework for understanding *Danza*.

Cherríe Moraga is an accomplished playwright, artist, and scholar of acclaimed works (*This Bridge Called My Back*, *Loving in the War Years*, *A Xicana Codex of Changing Consciousness*, etc.). She holds together art, activism, spirit practice, and scholarship in an admirable fashion. Her teaching and art have been influential in my academic development. In 2005, she led a year-long interdisciplinary programming umbrella and course at Stanford University called the *(W)Rite to Remember Project: Performance and Xicana/ Indigena Thought*. She continues to teach the course regularly. I recognize her influence in my deepening understanding of palimpsest. I have been in indigenous ceremonies, behind the scenes at plays, in on lectures, and at meals with Cherrié, particularly in the spring of 2005. She helped me think about the possibility for scholars and artists to use their work as a vehicle to examine issues of Chicana/o /*Indigena* identity and respond to colonizing forces. One of the callings for scholars who are also what she termed "spirit practitioners" is to stay close to ceremony. She explained that we as Chicanos and indigenous people carry out ceremonies in order to remember who we are, to reinscribe our identity, and ultimately to go "home," where home is a place of recovered values, beliefs, ways of relating, ceremonies, art, holistic health, as so forth, that trace back to indigenous life ways in the hemisphere. I believe that *danzantes* (including me, in the community and through this work) are creating a palimpsest, written with dance, ceremony, performance, education, and community organizing. *Danzantes* come to *Danza* because they want to go "home."

Moreover, as I contemplate the palimpsestic title that Cherrié gave her project—*The (W)Rite to Remember*—I submit it is a helpful mnemonic for thinking about the dynamics of the Calpulli Tonalehqueh. We *write* to remember our history and culture (as I do here, literally. Dancers write, figuratively). In another way, we *rite* to remember (enacting ceremony, embodying ancestral memory). Also, we claim the *right* to remember in the face of colonial history, xenophobia, or other internal and external limitations. The palimpsest of homophones and Cherrié's teaching are a gift to this work because they support the conceptual frame.Finally, I credit Gordon Brotherston, a world-renowned scholar of pre-colonial and early colonial texts in the Americas. His volume, *Book of the Fourth World* (1992), is crucial to my understanding of palimpsest. He saw hemispheric cultural productions as one extensive palimpsest. His expansive analysis of texts from North and South America paid homage to the literary productions of indigenous peoples and made complex the notions of text, cultural grammar, literacy, and cultural imaginaries. He dialogued with and often challenged figures such as Claude Lévi-Strauss who put forth early ideas about the culture of indigenous communities in the Americas from a Western perspective.

The Big Idea and How i Use Palimpsest to Deliver the Account of Calpulli Tonalehqueh's Construction

In the end, this book delivers important news, a decolonial moment: constructing a modern Mexica *calpulli* in the face of centuries of erasure, as Calpulli Tonalehqueh does, is a hopeful and transformational achievement. It involves work inspired by the past, responsive to the assailants of the present, and filled with collectively assembled innovations that move an entire community forward. The collective authorship of ceremony, activism, and cultural diffusion provides materials for personal, spiritual, family, and community health.

This text locates environments that reveal the coconstruction of a modern Mexica palimpsest. Palimpsest creation activities recover ancient Mexica materials—transformed over time—that Calpulli Tonalehqueh interprets alongside new materials to assemble a dance and cultural diffusion group. A significant part of Calpulli Tonalehqueh mission is cultural diffusion and education. The other part involves ceremony and dance. Dancers acquire skills for more full participation in this community through educational spaces that are sometimes intentionally arranged for teaching and learning or at other times inductively educative ceremony and dance activities. By electing this way of life, turning their attention to indigenous practices, affirming their heritage, resisting outside impositions, members of Calpulli Tonalehqueh strive for a postcolonial position.

In the end, Calpulli Tonalehqueh is a thriving and dynamic group where members actively create a communal palimpsest, learning together as they draw from an incompletely erased trove of traditional practice and reassemble modern Mexica life with contemporary materials. This book is an account of that achievement.

Acknowledgments

Nochtin Omecayotzin.

Tlazocamati ometetotl, ihuan ipal nemohuani, in tloque in nahuaque. Tlazocamati nauhcampa chanequeh, nahui ehectatzin, huey tonatiuh, ihuan tonantzintlalli. Tlazocamati moyolotzineh.

I wish to thank all my relations and those who have come before, including the ancestors and all who have given their lives for these traditions.

Agradezco a mis abuelitos, Esteban and Enrique, por sembrar semillas sagradas, por su curiosidad e innovación. Ofrezco gratitud a mis abuelitas, Esther y Rebeca por ser el sustento de nuestro cenyeliztli, la raíz, y depositarias de fuerza, sabiduría y amor.

Con el corazón en la mano, ofrezco energía y gratitud a mi familia y a todos los que me brindaron su apoyo en este camino. A mi tahtli, Rodolfo, por su fuerza y entrega, y su alma joven. A mi nantli, Lydia, por su esfuerzo y cuidado, y su inagotable generosidad. Por la vida que me ofrecieron. A mi hermana Nohemy Huenteo, y mi hermano Rudy por ser espejos y respaldos. A las semillas, Ehuaznequi Natalia y Cuetzquetzalli Robert.

I offer gratitude to Texcallini Doris Madrigal of the Star Nation, for *in iyollotonal, la fuerza de su corazón,* and *yolmelahualiztli,* straightening my heart.

I offer my gratitude to the members of Calpulli Tonalehqueh and *danzantes* who have crossed my path for opening up their circles to me, for their invaluable collective energy and offerings, and for helping me write entries in my own life's palimpsest. There are too many people to name, but know that I thank each and every one of you.

I offer my deepest gratitude to Shane Martin, my *teixcuitiani,* for paving and illuminating my path for over 20 years, for the campaigns we have waged together, for kindnesses I can never repay. This achievement is shared with you.

I offer gratitude to my *huehuetque* and *temachtianitzineh*, Ray McDermott, for scattering jades all along my path. *Ontetepeoac, chachayoac*: there was a good sowing, there was a great scattering of jades. Thank you for inspiring me to look at the world so differently, for saving me so often, for *ixtlamachiliztli*, showing me the red and black ink, and for radiating like the sun. I am so proud to be one of "Ray's Kids." (Also I thank Shelley Goldman for her tremendous support, matching Ray's brilliance, and being his *cihuacoatl*.)

I am so thankful for Jason Raley's sustaining friendship and mentorship, for the way he models an integrated life and for a tremendously positive support of anything I do or imagine.

I offer gratitude to Guadalupe Valdés, my *tezcahuiani*. Thank you for your strength, your amazing clarity, and for putting up a mirror up for me to know myself.

Sincere gratitude goes to Antonia Darder for her spirit, support, works, and energy. This book is not possible without you.

I would also like to acknowledge everyone else who supported this work. To Ruben Ochoa for his art, scholarship, friendship, and help with the revisions; Daniel Ríos for his research assistance and deep friendship; and Amanda Drum for looking over the manuscript. To all the friends who helped inspire or sustain this work.

Also, I would like to thank *everyone* at the School of Education at Loyola Marymount University for nurturing my scholarship.

To all my mentors, friends, and colleagues at the Stanford University School of Education, Stanford Native American Cultural Center, Institute for Diversity in the Arts, and El Centro Chicano.

To everyone I missed and to everyone yet to come. *Tlazocamati huel miac.*

*   *   *

I acknowledge the Loyola Marymount University School of Education, Stanford University Vice Provost for Graduate Education, Ann Porteus and the Spencer Foundation Research Training Grant at the Stanford University Graduate School of Education, and the AERA Minority Dissertation Fellowship for financial support for this research.

A *Danza* Landscape

On May 1, 2006, historic demonstrations[1] ignited across the United States when millions turned out to support the cause of (im)migrant and worker rights in cities large and small. In San José, California, more than 125,000 people marched from the East Side epicenter of the Mexican-origin community to the city hall in downtown toward Guadalupe River Park (which, appropriately, is a sacred site for the Ohlone Nation). Sergeant Nick Muyo of the San José police department was surprised by the attendance and called it one of the largest demonstrations in the city's history (McPherson, 2006). At the head of the serpentine procession were members of a Mexica (Aztec)[2] dance group, Calpulli Tonalehqueh. In full regalia and along with dancers from associated Aztec dance groups, the dancers paced the procession with drums that carried over the shouts of organizer bullhorns. Calpulli Tonalehqueh was invited to head the march by local labor leaders and was placed ahead of the images of Catholic saints, police cavalcades, and the community at large. It was a historic day. Children missed school. Employers closed businesses to allow their workers to attend. Day laborers halted their searches, and counter-protesters organized their platforms. A plane flew overhead pulling a banner that read, "Wake up America close the borders. Americaisfull.com" (Ostrom et al., 2006). Calpulli Tonalehqueh's symbolic place at the head of the serpentine mass that day was a product of their cultural diffusion efforts and community work. They have been invited to head that demonstration every year since that time as a symbolic spearhead in the struggle for human rights, one that has been active for centuries.

I was a 10-year veteran of *Danza*[3] on that day in 2006 and had been a part of Calpulli Tonalehqueh for just over a year. During that

10-year span I had attended many events lying on a political and ceremonial spectrum (e.g., the annual commemoration of the occupation
of Alcatraz Island in San Francisco by the American Indian Movement),
but I had never felt such a vibrant, almost seismic, atmosphere around
Danza in the United States. It was thrilling to reflect upon how in city
after city millions of people would march in solidarity for (im)migrant
rights and that our dancers would be at the head of so many of these
manifestations.

Marching for civil rights in San José was not new. In September
1970, for example, at least 1,000 people marched in San José's eastside in solidarity with the Chicano community of Los Angeles, who on
August 29 gathered in Belvedere Park to protest the Vietnam War and
were assailed by a historic display of police brutality by the Los Angeles
police department. That event is known as the Chicano Moratorium.
The year 2010 marked its fortieth anniversary. The 1970 march in San
José took place a few days after the Chicano Moratorium and was
documented by local public television stations (NCPB/KQED, 1970).
As we fast-forward, the 2006 march in San José can be viewed as an
amplified echo of the 1970 manifestation, carrying a similar message
of solidarity and human/civil rights but multiplying the participation
by a factor of one hundred.

The morning of the May 1, 2006 march, I arrived early to help
Yei Tochtli Mitlalpilli (Mitlalpilli hereafter), the head of Calpulli
Tonalehqueh, get ready at his home in downtown San José. Two other
members, Xochicuauhtli and Don Toño, were loading a flatbed truck
that would carry the drums, water, and banners for the dancers in
the march. The principal banner that Calpulli Tonalehqueh used in
the march was a 10-by-10-foot banner that represents the Mexica
flag. It is a replica of the *pantli* (flag) now expropriated in the Vatican
archives that was carried by Cuitlahuac when leading the indigenous
resistance to the sixteenth-century Spanish invasion of México City.
On a day when hundreds of US and Mexican flags would wave on the
main boulevards of San José, a giant Mexica flag led the way. Calpulli
Tonalehqueh's vision is to study and carry out indigenous traditions
but also position themselves in the community, providing avenues for
cultural diffusion and community empowerment.

At the historic intersection of Story and King roads, human chains of
volunteers tenuously contained the eruption of people in several large
parking lots. I felt like I was in a beehive of white shirts, waving flags,
and horns. I was unprepared for the sensory overload but do remember the crowd parting for those of us who were in ceremonial regalia.

We started dancing and moving the mass. The moment uncapped all the energy the crowd had reserved. Several other local dance groups joined Calpulli Tonalehqueh, including the Tezcatlipoca group and another, Mictlan, the group to which Tonalehqueh belonged before a split. *Danza* groups had collaborated on similar events in the community. Soon we broke into lines and led the mass surrounded by photographers, vuvuzelas, and, in an instance of historical irony, a flank of mounted police.

We proceeded through the eastside of San José, which had the highest concentration of immigrants in general, Mexicans in particular. San José has been an immigrant city since the late eighteenth century. With the whole parade behind us, I felt awe. Streets were closed. Thousands cheered from the sidewalk. Dancers took turns carrying out traditional leadership roles in the ceremony, including drumming, leading dances, and carrying flags and fire. Thousands waited outside the city hall where we formed a large circle and offered several dances before moving on to Guadalupe River Park for some closing dances at the official rally. After the event, dancers from all groups gathered to socialize and then slowly trickled away in cars. The people of the city made their mark. Calpulli Tonalehqueh and I were part of the moment, the living palimpsest.

This book explores how moments like this were made possible. In the twenty-first century, there exists an entire set of resources, ancient and modern, that are marshaled and manipulated, assembled and arranged, as a lifeway for Mexica dancers in a multicultural United States. What follows throughout the text is an account of one group's efforts for indigenous education through dance and ceremony resulting in the achievement of modern palimpsests.

A Landscape that Gives Life to Calpulli Tonalehqueh

The purpose of the following sections of this chapter is to introduce the important milieus and features of dance in México-Tenochtitlan (México City) in the early sixteenth century and trace some historical junctures that shape the landscape from which Calpulli Tonalehqueh was born. Following the details of dance before the European invasion is an introduction of the different expressions of *Danza* that exist in México City today, expressions that emerged in the centuries following European arrival in México City. Next, I describe how *Danza* traditions made their way to the United States and California, particularly in the second half of the twentieth century. This section also includes a narrative of how Calpulli Tonalehqueh was established in 2004. Although the survey of five centuries of dance is brief, the background information is key to understanding the ideals for which members of the group strive and the components they enact in the present.

Danza *in Pre-Cuauhtémoc Anáhuac*[4]

As Sten (1990) has pointed out, there is a dearth of information about the components of Mexica dance before the arrival of Europeans to México. Fewer than 10 of the thousands of books written by the Mexica before contact survive the mass burnings. The friars who did record aspects of dance in Mexica society saw in it the work of the devil, and in the human body, a fountain of sin and vice. It was largely with this lens they interpreted the events they witnessed. Clendinnen (1990) wrote thus:

> The Spanish conquest of México in 1521 was followed almost immediately by the ardent attempt by picked bodies of missionary friars to convert the Mexican Indians to Christianity, or more precisely, given the friars' view of things, to liberate the natives from their miserable servitude to the Devil. (p. 105)

For the most part, the economic and evangelical interests of European monarchies and churches underwrote their chronicles (Keen, 1990). Even with the doubt that must be cast on colonial accounts and the possible imprudence of basing a study of dance in pre-Cuauhtémoc Anáhuac on the descriptions of colonial writers—as many modern scholars do[5]—there are scholarly agreements about the practice I can establish. Additionally, it is important to remember that a fuller picture of the elements of Mexica dance can be gained by examining the paintings, architecture, poetry, musical instruments, ancient murals, and other pieces of the archeological record, especially those that have been guarded in the oral and dance tradition into the present (Sten, 1990, pp. 9–11). The loss of information, or the debated and often contradictory accounts about dance in ancient México, is an obstacle that modern dancers effectively overcome. This achievement is at the heart of the book.

Anthropologists are clear about the importance of dance to every culture in human history. They are also clear about how a study of this art can reveal the entire set of values, beliefs, social relationships, economy, and general life way of any given culture[6] (Hanna, 1979a, 1979b; Kaeppler, 1978; Martí and Prokosch Kurath, 1964; Merriam, 1972; Royce, 1977). Sten (1990) underscored the centrality of dance for Mexicas in their classic period, stating that "in Aztec society, dance forms an inseparable part of the important events of life" and that

> [l]os elementos materiales (vestidos, adornos, pinturas faciales y corporales), elementos espirituales (religión, mito, rito), elementos sociales (estratificación social, edad, sexo, ejercicio del poder), etc., se enlazan en la danza prehispánica a manera de diferentes hilos en un rico tejido formando diversos dibujos que ocultan un sentido no siempre fácil de detectar.
>
> [the material elements (attire, ornaments, face and body paint), spiritual elements (religion, myth, rite), social elements (social stratification, age, sex, exercise of power), etc., are tied together in pre-Cuauhtémoc dance like different strings in a rich tapestry to form diverse images that hide a meaning not always easy to detect.] (p. 23, my translation)[7]

Dance was ubiquitous, and the elements that comprised the dance ceremonies in pre-Cuauhtémoc Mexica society were mutually constitutive and synergistic. Fray Toribio de Benavente "Motolinia" (1971) wrote in the early sixteenth century, "*una de las cosas principales que en toda esta tierra había eran los cantos y los bailes*" [one of the principal things that existed in this whole land (Anáhuac) were songs and dances] (p. 382, my translation). The origin stories and mythology of the Mexica also include dance. The style of dance that Europeans encountered in the early sixteenth century included carryover elements from many predecessor groups of México (e.g., Olmeca, Tolteca, Chichimeca) (see Sten, 1990) that had influence on Mexica culture. Though there is a "baffling hiatus in documentation for the first twenty years or so after the conquest" (Clendinnen, 1990, p. 105), due to the general instability of "New Spain" prior to the arrival of the first viceroy in 1535, early colonial authors such as Acosta, Durán, Ixtlixochitl, Mendieta, Oviedo, Pomar, and Sahagún all described ceremonies of Mexica dance they (allegedly) witnessed. Not one early colonial author excluded descriptions of the frequency and modes of dancing they saw. As I review their text I find mention of the occasions, attire, adornments, structures, locations, durations, pedagogies, politics, participants, instruments, songs, games, theater, splendor, diversity, and pervasiveness of dance. Furthermore, it becomes clear that recreation, agricultural rites, gender norms, collective identities, community service, international relations, commerce, child rearing, and music we all manifest in and through dance. Francisco Javier Clavijero (1780/1987), an eighteenth-century Mexican-born Náhuatl-speaking Jesuit historian, explained that learning to dance in Mexica society was as fundamental as learning the alphabet was in schools centuries later. In the primary grades of pre-Cuauhtémoc Anáhuac at the *cuicacalli*, the house of song, all content was delivered to students through song and dance. Dance was integral to the curriculum of all levels of formal schooling and beyond. There were professional dance instructors, music composers, and musicians. Dance in pre-Cuauhté-moc Anáhuac was unlike other arts and occupations because every member of society participated.

Dance was eminently collective in nature[8] (as opposed to some of the partnered or individual traditions of dance developed in Europe). In his text *The Conquest of America*, Todorov (1995) placed weight on the collective aspect of Mexican dance traditions, explaining that individuals are a constitutive element of a social totality that can be moved collectively and influenced as a whole through dance because every member of society participates whether as a dancer or observer. If changes took place in dance, these changes would reverberate throughout the whole community.

Dance in pre-Cuauhtémoc Mexica society was public and obliga-tory. Vast resources were dedicated to dance and ceremonies that included dance. Mexica people have been called People of the Sun, or People of the Corn. It may be apt to describe them as People of the Dance as well. Dance ceremonies were a time and place to

- pray for fertility and abundance of crops, including prayer for rain (Many dances were tied to ceremonies that were aligned to agricultural cycles.)
- mark astronomical events
- commemorate human events
- tie human relations while demarcating social relations
- show gratitude to community leaders for social welfare
- mobilize communities in spiritual practice
- inculcate discipline in youth and citizens
- exchange news and goods
- celebrate and re-create

In her work "*La danza entre los mexica*," Martha Toriz Proenza (2002) concluded that, above all general human motivations for dance (e.g., enjoyment, courting, exhibition, demarcation of borders, affirmation of identity, and burning calories), producing joy was primary for the clas-sic Mexica. Her work expounds on the ways pre-Cuauhtémoc dance was a repository for such things as the schooling of the young, reinforcement of the governmental apparatus, reciprocity among people and nations, spirituality, ritualized warfare, ideological transmission, social stratification, commerce, control of labor, the cycles of agriculture, and festivity (pp. 305–324). Colonizers took (editorialized) notes on the practices of the people with intent to develop more effective tools of evangelization, and exploit of the extensive reach of dance as a pathway for colonial control of other facets of indigenous life.

Erasure and Rewriting: Christian Impositions on Danza

In the previous section, I established the centrality and pervasiveness of widespread participation in dance for pre-Cuauhtémoc Mexica communities. In the *Danza* palimpsest, the symbiosis between dance and daily life is the original piece of "writing." The second and third requirements of a palimpsest are intentional (but incomplete) erasure and new text(s). This section outlines sixteenth-century efforts to erase *Danza* and impose (rewrite) upon it a new, Christian set of symbols. Later in the section, I outline further episodes of erasure and rewriting that took place in the twentieth century.

Important scholarship on the invasion, genocidal decimation, ethnocide, and colonization of indigenous communities in México is widely available. The literature on colonialism in México is reviewed here briefly so as to highlight its impact on *Danza* and so that readers understand both the context in which modern dance circles are couched and the history to which dancers actively respond.

Benjamin Keen's work, *The Aztec Image in Western Thought* (1990), is an excellent review of the ideologies and motivations behind the writings of the early colonial authors and the voracious consumption of the texts by European audiences during the colonial period. He discusses how colonial authors often fabricated stories about what they encountered in the "New World" in response to aristocratic and popular consumption in Europe. These early writings are the seeds for a multitude of myths and misinformation about the Mexica (and others) that would circulate for centuries, eventually (ironically) returning to México to be parroted by scholars in modern eras. A multilayered palimpsest about Mexica life has been in process for centuries.

Charles Gibson (1964) wrote an indispensible and encyclopedic overview of the tremendous amount of projects, actors, mechanisms, language, achievements, and failures of the Spanish colonial enterprise. He, along with James Lockhart (1999), detailed the concerted and ferocious efforts by colonial and religious authorities to usurp land, liberty, law, and faith. Traditional sociopolitical systems (*calpulli*) were replaced with abusive tribute systems benefitting the manipulative Spanish despots (e.g., *encomienda* and *municipio* systems) and placing the Mexica in impossible conditions of indebted servitude and desperate poverty. Severe restrictions were put on every aspect of Mexica life, including prohibitions on dance, ceremony, and assembly.[9]

Robert Stevenson (1968) examined music in Mexica society at the time of contact and its changes in the early colonial years. He discussed the concentrated efforts by colonizers to introduce European dance forms, instruments, and aesthetics to Mexica music and dance.

Through a different lens, Serge Gruzinski (1996) wrote about the incorporation and survival of Native Mexican societies in the sixteenth and seventeenth centuries (and beyond). He relays the many ways that indigenous life ways persevered, through accommodation or subversion, despite colonial hegemony, Spanish governance, and imposed Catholic systems.

Danza in the fifteenth century was already a palimpsest of centuries of innovation and borrowing from ancestral and neighboring cultures (Toltec, Teotihuacan, Chichimeca, etc.). Fifteenth-century Mexicas built their ceremonial traditions upon a confluence of Anahuacan cultures dating back centuries before European contact, but lasting erasure and rewriting of Mexica cultural productions accelerated as Western and Christian influences entered early after European arrival. In a 1523 letter by Franciscan friar Pedro de Gante, early recognition that dance ceremonies could be a location for evangelization was clear.

Empecelos a conocer y entender sus condiciones y quilates, y cómo me había de haber con ellos, y es que toda su adoración dellos a sus dioses era cantar y bailar delante dellos, porque cuando habían de sacrificar algunos por alguna cosa, así como para alcanzar victoria de sus enemigos o por temporales necesidades, antes que los matasen habían de cantar delante del ídolo; y como yo vi esto y que todos sus cantares eran dedicados a sus dioses, compuse metros muy solemnes sobre la Ley de Dios y sobre la fe, y como Dios se hizo hombre por salvar al linaje humano, y como nació de la virgen María quedando ella pura e sin macula; y esto dos meses poco más o menos antes de la natividad de Cristo, y también les diles libreas para pintar en sus mantas para bailar con ellas, porque ansí se usaba entre ellos, conforme a los bailes y a los cantares que ellos cantaban así se usaba entre ellos, conforme a los bailes y a los cantares que ellos cantaban así se vestían de alegría o de luto o de vitoria.

[I got to know and understand their conditions and values, and since I was going to be with them, and it is that all of their devotion to their gods was to dance and sing in front of them, because when they were to sacrifice some for a particular reason, just as for obtaining victory over their enemies or for temporary needs, before they killed them they sung in front of the idol; and since I saw this and that all their songs were directed at their gods, I composed solemn verses about God's Law and about the faith, and how God became man to save humankind, and how he was born of the Virgin Mary with her staying pure and without blemish; and this two months or so before Christ's nativity, and also gave unto them livery to paint on in order that they dance with them, because that was their custom, according to their dances and the songs that they sang they wore attire of joy or mourning or victory.] (cited in Garcia Icazbalceta, 1971, my translation)

Sometimes slowly, sometimes by force, but assuredly, the language, attire, value sets, spiritual icons, and other elements of Mexica dance ways were (ex)changed in the colonial era. In this period of acculturation, native people were compelled to adopt the vestments of Catholicism in order to guarantee the survival of their traditions (not to mention their persons) and beliefs that always laid below the surface.[10]

All early colonial writers marveled at the beauty of Mexica art, music, song, and dance, but in the end these forms were seen as vile and/or inferior. In 1526, Benito de Bejel and Maese Pedro, two musicians travelling with Hernán Cortez, established the first European school of dance in México. They were granted a plot of land to teach dance for the "betterment" of the city (México City). They would later become land-holding commissioners and tribute collectors (*Actas de cabildo de la Ciudad de Mexico*, 1889; Stevenson, 1968). A constant influx of European forms came in to Mexican music and dance from that point forward.[11] Motolinía (1971) described how around 1538, Native Mexicans were celebrating Christian holy days like Easter, Corpus Christi, and Christmas with songs, language, music, and attire closely resembling pre-Cuauhtémoc dance ceremonies but altered with the assistance of friars.

The Indians celebrate the feast of the Lord, of Our Lady and of the principal Patron Saints of the towns with much rejoicing and solemnity. They decorate their churches very tastefully with what ornaments they are able to get, and their lack of tapestry they make up for with tree branches, flowers, reed mace and sedge…Attired in white shirts and mantles and bedecked in feathers and with a bouquet of roses in their

hands, the Indian lords and chiefs perform a dance and sing in their
language the songs that solemnize the feast which they are celebrating.
The friars have translated these songs for them and the Indian masters
have put them into the meter to which the Indians are accustomed. The
songs are graceful and harmonious…On Christmas night they place
many lights in the patios of the churches and on the terraces of their
houses…The feast of the Three Kings also makes them very happy,
because they regard it a feast which is properly theirs. Many times on
this day they stage the allegorical play representing the Kings' offering to the Infant Jesus…On the feast of the Purification or Candelmas
they bring candles to have them blessed…on Palm Sunday they decorate all the churches with palms. (de Benavente "Motolinia," 1951,
pp. 141–143)

As above, Motolinía chronicled how sixteenth-century friars used
the meter of indigenous songs and wrote new words to them with
Christian messages. Thousands of dancers still attended ceremonies,
the attendance of the ones he witnessed had less than half the number
who would attend ceremonies prior to the invasion. By 1585, there
was mention of dancers using string instruments and also of the 200
former *calpultin* of México City each organizing Christian feasts and
celebrations. Friars recruited artists, made paintings, statues, and banners, and began distributing patron saints to each town they colonized.
People and towns were renamed for saints.[12]

A provincial council of 1555 declared that even though the native
population was strongly inclined to dances and festivals and ceremonies, they should not be allowed to use ancient masks or banners or
to sing songs relating to their ancient histories or religion unless each
of these items was first examined and cleared by religious administra-
tors or persons who understand the native language well. They placed
conditions on the time when dancing could occur and set out punishment for infractions of the decrees. No ceremonies were allowed without the presence of evangelical ministers ("Concilios Provincionales:
Primero y segundo: De México, celebrados en la Ciudad de Mexico,
en 1555 y 1565," 1769). Restrictions on ceremony and dance were
legislated for centuries.[13]

In 1590, Fray Joseph de Acosta (Acosta, Mangan, and Mignolo,
2002) described the manner in which the arts were used as an effective
vehicle for Christianization of native populations:

The members of our society [Jesuits] who work among them have tried
to put things of our Holy Faith into their way of singing and chanting

so much that they can spend whole days listening and repeating, never getting tired. They have also translated compositions and tunes of ours into their language, such as octaves and ballads and roundelays, and it is wonderful how well the Indians accept them and how much they enjoy them. Truly, this is a great way, and a very necessary one, to teach these people. (pp. 376–377)

In the same text, Acosta described the care and beauty he found in Mexica dance ceremonies. In tolerant tones he concluded that it was important not to deprive native peoples of their dance but be vigilant so they did not use it for idolatry.

It is not a good thing to deprive the Indians of them [dances] but rather to try and to prevent any superstition from becoming mingled in them. In Tepotzotlán, which is a town seven leagues from México, I saw the dance, or *mitote*, that I have described performed in the courtyard of the church, and it seemed to me a good thing to occupy and entertain the Indians on feast days; for they need some recreation, and recreation that is public and harms no one has fewer disadvantages than others that the Indians might perform by themselves should these dances be taken away from them. And generally speaking it is good to allow the Indians what we can of their customs and usages (if there is no admixture of their former errors), and this is in agreement with the advice of Pope Saint Gregory, to try to channel their festivals and rejoicings toward the honor of God and the saints whose feasts are being celebrated. (pp. 376–377)

These are a few examples of the manner in which missionaries and vice royal authorities provided materials and arranged conditions for the combination of native and Christian elements in Mexican dance in the first centuries after the invasion.

Beyond written chronicles, there are several works of art and codices that depict the changes undergone in *Danza*. For example, drawings in Duran's chronicles depict changes in *Danza* early in the colonial period. Dancers have new attire and the context holds new elements.

In many pieces of colonial art work, individuals have European attire but dance or fly (*voladores*) with feathered fans and tools in ceremonies that are clearly based on pre-Cuauhtémoc forms.[14]

Underscored in these and many other works is evidence that in the face of centuries of massive change and oppression, native peoples were strategic, resilient, and courageous in the ways they negotiated, mitigated, and undermined a new world order. Native dance ceremonies (along with the ideology, forms, songs, etc.) were so intractable that they persisted for centuries, sometimes with surprising tolerance from vice royal governors and friars. To reiterate, the perseverance of indigenous life ways in the present is testament to achievements of fidelity by indigenous Mexican communities.

After the 1810–1821 war of independence from Spain, México continued to marginalize indigenous communities in the name of social progress and the ideal of Westernization. Beyond the oral tradition, not many records survive of the changes that *Danza* suffered in the period following independence. In general, many Western dance forms and schools arrived on Mexican shores, and traditional dances and aboriginal communities survived on the margins of the society as part of second-class folklore and citizenry. Catholicism was still entrenched in *Danza*, and the original (pre-Cuahtémoc) "text" of *Danza* fades further into the background of the palimpsest. At this point in the description of the changes incurred by *Danza*, I turn my focus to a post-Revolution México.

In the first half of the twentieth century, the most popular, if not the only, form of Mexica dance was the one commonly known as *Conchero*, which was (and continues to be) a form of dance tied to Catholic rites while retaining traces of pre-Cuauhtémoc dance/cere-monial elements. The twentieth century is witness to an adjustment in the world of *danzantes* as some dance circles shifted from a popular Catholic religious version of *Danza* (*Conchero*) toward a version of *Danza* that sought to shed colonial vestiges and return to a native indigenous form. This latter movement has been dubbed *Mexicayotl*, the line that Calpulli Tonalehqueh follows today. This shift was motivated and expressed in generally parallel ways in the United States and México but with differences connected to each context.

Above, I have provided an overview of the erasures, restrictions, and impositions on Danza in the colonial and independence eras, especially in the former. In the next section, I focus on the twentieth century and more pointedly on the *Conchero* tradition in *Danza* and the subsequent movement called *Mexicayotl*.

The Conchero Dance Tradition

The *Conchero* dance tradition arose after sixteenth-century wars of conquest and out of the subsequent context of synergistic/syncretic Christian-Danza cultural productions. In the present day, the majority of Aztec dance circles in México and a smaller proportion in the United States can be circumscribed as *Conchero*. The information provided here is a brief overview drawing upon my personal experience and fieldwork, as well as the notable works of Yolotl González Torres (1995–1996, 1996, 2005), Susanna Rostas (2009), and others (Aguilar, 2009; Álvarez Fabela, 1998; Argueta López, 1998; Armstrong, 1985; Benner, Ellington, and Tauer, 1989; Cruz Rodríguez "Tlacuilo," 2004; González, 1996; Mansfield, 1953; Martínez-Hunter, 1984; Stevenson, 1968; Stone, 1975; Toor, 1947; Velázquez Romo, 1998; Vento, 1994). These publications should be consulted for more extensive information about the *Conchero* movement's history and features.

The term *Conchero* comes from the stringed instrument that the dancers use, which is an armadillo shell or large gourd (*concha*) that has 10 strings and is tuned similar to a mandolin. As González Torres (2005) indicated, this dance tradition has been known by many names and with substantial regional variation,[15] with names such as *Hermanos de la Santa Cuenta*, *Hermanos del Arco y Flecha*, *Apaches*, *Danzantes de Conquista*, *Danza Azteca*, or *Chichimeca*. Oral tradition places the origin of the *Conchero* dance tradition in 1537 (Y. González Torres, 2005; E. Maestas, 1999). The *Conchero* tradition is an enormous movement of popular Catholicism that emphasizes honoring familial ancestors and Catholic saints. It blends elements of indigenous ceremonies with Catholic rites. Dance groups are tied to families and councils, or *Mesas*, which are organized at regional levels. There are dozens of *Mesas* in present-day México City and dozens more in the surrounding areas of Querétaro, Tlaxcala, and the *Bajío* region (these are said to generally predate México City *Mesas*). Many US dance groups in the *Conchero* vein are satellites or have leaders who were students of a *Mesa* in México. Modern *Conchero* ceremonial and dance traditions are the reiterations and the repositories of pre-Cuauhtémoc Mexica dance. *Conchero* groups have a complex regional and local organization, centered around councils and people who hold leadership positions or offices (sometimes inherited, sometimes earned) with the nomenclature of the old Spanish military, for example, *generales*, *capitanes*, *sargentos*, *alféreces*, *soldados*, and *estandartes*. *Conchero* groups hold documents outlining their legitimacy and ancestry in the system, setting out the strict norms of behavior for members and listing the obligations of the group to certain ceremonies hosted by other groups. Each group is "sponsored" by a patron saint. *Conchero* ceremonies are usually held around oratories in homes, in churches, or at (ancient) sacred sites in México. In them, one can recognize indigenous rituals and songs "dressed" in the language, songs, prayers, and holy days of Catholicism (Y. González Torres, 2005, pp. 54–60; see also Rostas, 2009). In any given year, enormous ceremonies to which all *Conchero* groups are obliged take place in churches/sanctuaries in cities that mark the four cardinal directions (e.g., Chalma, La Villa, Amecameca) centered on México City—where a fifth ceremony marks the center. Ceremonies are now held in honor of two Catholic virgins (Remedios and Guadalupe), two images of Jesus of Nazareth (crucified and laying at rest), and Saint James (*San Santiago* in Spanish) the moor-slayer. Some dancers claim each of these personages was superimposed on sacred Nahua concepts originally celebrated at each site (i.e., a ceremonial palimpsest). To restate, these ceremonies seem to follow ancient cycles and occupy sacred spaces that have hosted them for centuries, but are now laden with Catholic rites and symbolism. Missionaries erected churches in the early colonial era at these sacred sites and allowed the continuation of the altered ceremonies in their conversion and baptism efforts. As mentioned previously, similar types of schedules and ceremonial obligations take place in the regions outside of México City where *Conchero* groups reside. The most traditional of *Conchero* families observe strict adherence to elements such as the protocols of the hierarchy of leadership, the rituals, vigils, songbooks, attire, ceremonial obligations, and collaboration with the church. Federico Sánchez Ventura (1963) provided a concise overview of the essence of the *Conchero* variety of Mexica dance:

Para los danzantes el cielo comienza en la planta de los pies. La danza es movimiento y el movimiento es un puente entre el tiempo y el espacio. La danza de los concheros, o danza Chichimeca, ha sobrevivido a siglos, a conquistas, y ha permitido la permanencia del conocimiento original que transmitieron nuestros antecesores. Danza sagrada que, al dar gracias a la creación, realiza el gesto dinámico de integrar cuerpo, mente y espíritu a través del ritmo acompasado de los ayoyotes, del canto de las conchas, del bajo profundo del caracol y del retumbar del huehuetl. Se trata de cantos y danza que datan de miles de años, que han continuado después de la Conquista hasta nuestros días sin perder los rasgos esenciales de la cosmogonía que comparten en las viejas civilizaciones y se han adaptado al cristianismo, en cuyo sincretismo confluyen fuerzas históricas, sociales y políticas de nuestro tiempo. Repartidos por diversos estados en el centro del país y por algunos lugares lejanos del Altiplano, los concheros mantienen vivo el rito del sol, que comparten con otras danzas similares como las de los quechuas, los hoppies, los vascos y los sufís.

[Heaven begins at the soles of one's feet for *danzantes*. Dance is movement and movement is the bridge between time and space. The *Conchero* dance, or Chichimeca dance, has survived centuries, conquests, and has allowed for the endurance of the original knowledge that our ancestors transmitted. A sacred dance that, by giving gratitude to creation, achieves a dynamic combination integrating mind, body, and spirit through a rhythm marked by *ayoyotes*, the sound of the conch guitars, the deep bass of the conch shells, and the reverberation of the *huehuetl*. It is about songs and dances that date back thousands of years, that continue after the Conquest into our day without losing any essential cosmological features which it shares with the ancient civilizations and are adapted to Christianity, under whose syncretism modern historical, social, and political forces converge. Spread out over diverse states in the center of the country and along some far away places like the *Altiplano*, the *Concheros* keep alive rituals for the sun, which they have in common with similar dances such as the Quechua, the Hopi, the Basque, and the Sufi.] (p. 19, my translation)

Before the 1940s, all *Danza* attire was in what Rostas (2009) termed the Chichimeca style and what González Torres (2005) called the *naguilla* style. Heavily influenced by the colonial Catholic church, dancers are required to cover their entire body. Long skirts, long-sleeve collared shirts, scarves, long capes and tunics, stockings and sandals, and imported ostrich and rooster feathers are used along with instruments like jingle bells and mandolins.[16]

Despite staunch resistance from peers,[17] a few dancers in México City began designing *Danza* attire that harkened to a pre-Cuauhtémoc style. Long-sleeve collared shirts, sandals, stockings, capes, and other components were eschewed. Slowly, other dancers readapted indigenous styles for their ceremonial attire and reincorporated native instruments, including the drum, the *teponaztli*. In addition, face paint, iconography, and numerous other ritual items returned after having been prohibited for centuries. These elements had survived either in the underground (meaning they stayed in the oral tradition and were held in secret) or in more rural parts of México where the colonial government had less reach. Dancers studied images from ancient books and stone carvings to design. General Felipe Aranda and others began supporting both the changes and the dancers implementing them in the face of opposition from traditionalists. Furthermore, in the two decades after 1940, a surge in the popularity of modern dance in México and the rise of professional folk dance companies influenced some aspects of *Danza* and dancers themselves. In the middle twentieth century, many *Concheros* began travelling to Europe, the Unites States, and the film industry to dance (Y. González Torres, 2005; Luna, 2011; Susanna Rostas, 2009).

In the present, there are many dance groups in the United States that identify with and follow *Conchero* protocols and traditions.

Present-day *Conchero* groups occupy a position marked by hybrid or popular Catholicism. There are many other groups that occupy a middle space between the groups that practice more strict Catholicism and the groups that practice indigenous Mexica dance focused on autochthonous aspects. The groups in the middle are often designated with the moniker: *Tradición*. Many *Tradición* groups in México are cooperative with US groups that do include Catholic elements in their ceremonies, although a great deal of tension and discussion has emerged about ideology and style. A good deal of variability, exchange, and blending of traditions has occurred transnationally.

The *Conchero* tradition is a centuries-old version of *Danza* that resulted after Christianization of ancient Mexica dance ceremonies. It is still popular today, though many dancers are executing ceremonies without Catholic elements. Included in this group are many *danzantes* who are not Catholic and yet still seek a life inside of *Danza*. The following section discusses key institutions and individuals who were involved in the pre-Cuauhtémoc Mexica recovery and recreation project (called *Mexicanidad* or *Mexicayotl*) of which Calpulli Tonalehqueh is now a part.

A Shift toward the Mexicayotl

From the 1960s forward, changing trends in *Danza* accelerated, influenced by international civil rights movements (including the American Indian Movement, the United States and Mexican Civil Rights Movement, the Cuban Revolution, the Chicano Movement, the civil unrest in México in 1968, and so forth). At this time, an influx of students, scholars, and community activists into the *Danza* community of México called for more indigenous *Danza* forms, resulting in concerted efforts to strip the Catholic and the European elements from *Danza*, as well as to study, understand, and celebrate the language, arts, sciences, and general achievements of the people of pre-Cuauhtémoc Anáhuac. Many dancers in México marked this shift with a change in their naming of ceremonies, calling them *chitontequiza*, meaning coming out of the darkness, or coming out into the light, rather than *obligaciónes* (Totocani Franco, personal communication; Mendoza "Kuauhkoatl," 2007). Some *Tradición* groups attended ceremonies of the traditional *Conchero* groups while also participating in ones hosted by Mexica groups around México City that celebrated sacred days in the ancient day count systems, danced at sacred archeological sites, resurrected native instruments and traditional songs, and uncovered what was underneath that which Mario Aguilar (2009) has called the "surface veneer of Catholic iconography" in *Danza* (p. 126). This movement is known as *Mexicayotl* within *Danza*. *Mexicayotl* can be translated as "the essence of that which is Mexica." Some authors refer to this movement as "*Mexicanidad*" (Aguilar, 2009; Y. González Torres, 1996; Susan Rostas, 1993; S. E. Rostas, 2002). In the United States in the late twentieth century, dance circles with *Mexicayotl* leanings became a viable option for dancers. Various scholars (Aguilar, 2009; Ceseña, 2009; Huerta, 2009; Luna, 2011; E. Maestas, 1999; E. G.-M. Maestas, 1998) have explained that the attraction to transnational, indigenous, cultural-nativist movements within *Danza* paralleled similar currents in the Chicano Movement where many Mexican American youth were politicized and looked for deeper integration with indigenous identities.

Writing in France, Francisco de la Peña (2002) focused on the broader *Mexicayotl* movement in México.[18] At times, he offered a more complimentary view of the movement, though he did critique many aspects, including what he deemed as the movement's "irrationality" and collective and individual "inventions" (p. 285–286). He defined the movement as thus:

> *Un movimiento nativista y una suerte de nacionalismo radical de inspiración autóctona, con rasgos milenaristas y con un importante componente esotérico y profético, cuyo universo ideológico se inspira en el pasado prehispánico, así como en su idealización y exaltación.* [A nativist movement and a type of radical nationalism, autochthonous in nature, with millenarian traits and a significant esoteric and prophetic component whose ideological universe is based on the prehispanic past as well as with its idealization and exaltation.] (p.11, my translation)

In the late 1990s, de la Peña counted at least 40 groups characterized as *Mexicayotl* in México City, citing notable diversity of focus and practice in each. Many of those groups continue into the present day. He analyzed the common activities of the movement, noting that a great number take place in cultural centers and that members are organized in small groups inspired by ancient *calpultin* where education about indigenous languages, astronomy, mathematics, codices, and archeology takes place. He adds that the movement has a series of publications that support the cause and offer articles with a cultural-nationalist lens. Many members of the movement engage in artistic production, Nahua philosophy, dance, traditional medicine, etc. de la Peña assessed two major currents within the movement, one highly politicized and radical, and the other more esoteric and spiritual in focus (p. 13–15).

Though there were many contributing forces in *Mexicayotl*, two substantially influential institutions may symbolize this movement: the *Movimiento Confederado Restaurador de la Cultura de Anáhuac* (sometimes called *Movimiento Confederado Restaurador del Anáhuac*, MCRA) and the *Zemanauak Tlamachtiloyan* (ZT). This section is about the continuation of nationalistic shifts in *Danza* in the second half of the twentieth century and the emergence of the *Mexicayotl* movement as seen through the rise of these two organizations whose histories are summarized below. These histories are included because of their significant influence over the design and implementation of Calpulli Tonalehqueh.

Movimiento Confederado Restaurador del Anáhuac

According to Odena Güemes (1984), the MCRA was founded around 1959 by a charismatic activist named Rodolfo Nieva along with his wife (María del Carmen Nieva Izkalotl, later of ZT fame) and other community leaders sympathetic to the ideals of the group. Early on, the MCRA had aspirations of becoming a political party and executed several community initiatives including a newsletter and various workshops. Followers of the MCRA (estimated at 2,500 by Odena Güemes, 1984) were part of a larger movement in México to restore indigenous sociopolitical, linguistic, artistic, and other cultural practices. In 1930, for instance, a group called *Confederación Indígena* held Náhuatl language, native arts, history, and Aztec calendar classes. Nieva had studied there. And in the mid-1940s, a probilingual newspaper was published in México City with the name of *Mexicayotl* (pp. 103–105). Odena Güemes (1984) detailed how the MCRA's internal governance structure mirrored pre-Cuauhtémoc Mexica organizations. Members began organizing into *calpultin* and embarked on campaigns of indigenous cultural diffusion and research. MCRA members held Mexica naming ceremonies, indigenous coming-of-age ceremonies for young women, as well as ceremonies commemorating the defense of México City against the invasion. They developed guided tours of archeological sites and museums and held Náhuatl language and Mexica dance classes (pp. 21–26).[19] Some alliances were formed with *Tradición* dance groups though there was often tension between the two movements. Some detractors of the MCRA accused its members of distorting history (e.g., their challenges to Aztec polytheism and human sacrifice), being racist and essentialist (e.g., for admonishing *Conchero*

or *Tradición* dancers still adhering to Catholicism), being overly politicized and not following a spiritual practice, and promoting escapism
to a mythic romanticized past (Aguilar, 2009; Odena Güemes, 1984).

Susanna Rostas (2002) represents the strong critics of the
"*Mexicanidad*" movement, arguing that the movement is a generally
incoherent, hypocritical, androcentric, performative, flamboyant, fabricated, fanatical, unstructured, hierarchical, idealist, and urban pro-
tonationalist subculture. Transcending the critiques, the MCRA (and
later the *Zemanauak Tlamachtiloyan*), along with similar groups and
sympathizers, has had a profound impact on the ideology, mission,
and execution of modern *Danza* circles.[20]

In a text published posthumously by his wife, Nieva (1969) sub-
mitted his greatest desires for the *Mexicayotl* movement as allowing
individuals to know their history so they could transcend imposed
cultures and respond to racism and economic deprivation. In the text,
he exalted the advances of millenary cultures of Anáhuac and hoped
Mexicans achieve freedom through a recovery of indigenous identity
and ancestral culture (pp. 19–30). Like many activists in *Danza* and
the *Mexicayotl*, Nieva explained that the time was right for Mexicans
to fulfill the mandate of the last Great Council of the Anáhuac
Confederation of the sixteenth century (see appendix A) that resisted
the Spanish invasion of 1517. Seeing the devastation of the invasion,
the council decreed that all Mexicas should protect their culture by
hiding it within themselves, in an underground movement, or underneath the imposed culture until the time was right to emerge from
those shadows.[21]

The Zemanauak Tlamachtiloyan

The ZT was founded in 1977 by Miguel Ángel Mendoza "Kuauhkoatl"
and Ignacio Romerovargas Yturbide, along with a cadre of
Mesoamericanist scholars, artists, dancers, and community activists
like Leopoldo "Polo" Rojas Tlakololeani, René de la Parra Palma,
Domingo Martínez Paredes, María del Carmen Nieva López (Rodolfo
Nieva's wife), María Teresa Martínez, David Esparza Hidalgo, and
Ángel Tenahuatzin Valladares (González Torres, 2005, p. 164; Luna,
2011; Mendoza, 2007; Ramírez Muñoz, personal communication;
Rostas 2009, p. 196). Ocelocoatl Ramírez joins the ZT around 1980.
The ZT is a continuation of the MCRA in manyrespects.

Kuauhkoatl (2007) explains that the founding of the ZT came
after *El Tercer Congreso Nacional de Bellas Artes y Humanidades*
(Third National Summit of Fine Arts and Humanities) organized in

México City by Kuauhkoatl who invited and hosted scholars, artists, and specialists from all over México. Mesoamericanists who attended the summit decided to form a council to establish a cultural research and diffusion institution in México City. Kuauhkoatl was signaled as head executor of the group, with Romerovargas Yturbide its academic leader and René de la Palma Parra as secretary (later replaced by Tenahuatzin Valladares). Organizational bylaws (*acta constitutiva, lineamientos*) were immediately drawn.

Many schools and community centers predated the ZT.[22] For example, an organization called *Aztecatlamachtlake Hueytlahuile* existed since 1947 in México City, and a Náhuatl school named *Mexica Tlatolcalli* was established in 1960 (Odena Güemes, 1984, pp. 105, 129; 1993). After Rodolfo Nieva's death in 1968, his wife continued the work of the MCRA and helped Kuauhkoatl and his colleagues at the ZT teaching Náhuatl classes. Kuauhkoatl, a colleague of Rodolfo Nieva, had been a journalist and became a prolific writer on Mexica history and culture. His professional contacts and background bolstered the work of the ZT as it continued the work of the MCRA and other cultural centers by organizing dance classes, language and arts workshops, research and publication, archeology, archeoastronomy, and the restoration of native ceremonies.

During its early years, the ZT was involved in activities that factor greatly in the larger *Danza* universe and in the work of *Mexicayotl* groups in México and the United States. Most of the activities the ZT undertook become a framework for and are duplicated in the work of Calpulli Tonalehqueh in California years later. In addition, one of the early members of the ZT, Ocelocoatl, is the principal mentor to Calpulli Tonalehqueh, infusing the group with the ideology, ceremonies, and structures developed at the ZT.

In December 1977 at Teotihuacan, the ZT received a caravan of 16 American Indian nations of the US Southwest that had asked famed *danzante* Florencio Yescas—in Los Angeles at the time—to bring them to Central México to retrace the routes of their origin stories. In May 1978, the ZT received emissaries from the National Congress of American Indians, representing 256 indigenous nations. The favorable meeting resulted in the first meeting of Continental Congress of the Fifth Sun on the summer solstice in June 1978.[23] In February 1979, the ZT organized the first ceremony in honor of Cuauhtémoc (the last *Huey Tlatohani* of the Mexica) in the place where he was raised: the city of Ixcateopan in the state of Guerrero.[24] Later, in 1980, Kuauhkoatl and others were invited to the United States to address the thirty-sixth National Congress of American Indians, a gathering of over 6,000 indigenous leaders from North America.[25] Also, the ZT established the *Toxkatl* ceremony in May 1981, commemorating the massacre of 1520 in Tlatelolco (Y. González Torres, 2005; Mendoza "Kuauhkoatl," 2007). From the late 1970s to the present, the members of ZT organized tours at major archeological sites, major dance ceremonies, Mexica musical groups, and civil actions. ZT members also traveled the world on cultural diffusion and exchange missions. All of these activities (intertribal exchanges, ceremonies, music and dance classes, naming ceremonies, political protests, etc.) are replicated by Calpulli Tonalehqueh in the present day.

In the 1970s and 1980s, ZT did not have many dancers and so they recruited leaders from the *Conchero Mesas* to help execute the ceremonies they were recovering (Ramírez, personal communication). The ZT had conversations with many *Mesas* and with dance leaders, especially with Felipe Aranda, and continued to bring about change in the Aztec dance movement. Aranda's parallel and long-standing reforms in *Danza* would join with those of the ZT. Aranda sent many of his experienced students and officers to work with the ZT, including his lead *sauhmadora* (fire/incense keeper), Miquiztli Franco, and a captain, Totocani Franco (Miquiztli Franco, personal communication).[26]

At one point in the early 1980s, the ZT decided to develop its own dance group instead of relying on other circles for that part of their mission. Kuauhkoatl Mendoza's star pupil, Ocelocoatl Ramírez Múñoz, who featured prominently in the ZT's dance and cultural diffusion efforts at the time, was selected for the task. Ocelocoatl, along with others, rose to leadership in the ZT and became integral to its work with many associated dance circles from the 1980s onward.

The Taking of the Zócalo

The ZT was central in the forceful reclamation of the *Zócalo* in México City in 1982, a monumental and emblematic event in the *Mexicayotl* movement. Andrés Segura, a prominent dancer in México and the United States, was asked to take the lead in the dance at the coup. The ZT asked the generals of the dance *Mesas* to attend but leave the Catholic elements aside. Though there was much resistance, many decided to honor the group's wishes. In 1982, the ZT and many community activists gathered as many *danzantes* as they could and took over México City's *Zócalo* where dancers had been forbidden by centuries of state-level authority. The plan for this civil disobedience was spread through word of mouth, and dancers gathered at the

Metropolitan Cathedral. Many *Danza* generals brought their groups from places such as Xochimilco, Iztapalapan, Milpa Alta, Cuernavaca, Acalpixcan, Atzcapozalco, Mizquitl, Puebla, Tlaxcala, and Querétaro. More than 2000 dancers arrived. It was an epic gathering of dancers working in solidarity.[27] As the mass of dancers grew, Mexican police assembled squadrons of riot police at the Cathedral and around the *Zócalo*. A few of the ZT leaders had radios tuned into the police band. The police targeted Kuauhkoatl and the other organizers who had denied city permits for the event earlier. Panic and hesitation rose within the organizers of the coup as a result of the threats of the armed riot police that demanded the dancers to disband. The student massacre of 1968 was present in the minds of many. While the ZT and *Danza* leaders deliberated, it was the women dancers, many with infants in tote, who blasted out of the Cathedral and went face to face with the riot police. Screaming that they were ready to give up their lives, the women pounded on police shields. Suddenly unprepared to fire upon women and children, police officers were instructed to hold fire. Hearing this on the radio and inspired by the courage of the women, dancers called out with conch shells and drumming to storm out behind the women. The police broke lines and dancers took the *Zócalo*, the center of México-Tenochtitlan (Ramírez Muñoz, personal communication). Before the police could react, Andrés Segura formed circles of hundreds of dancers and launched into the ceremony. Accompanying the dance was an agenda of prayers, invocations, songs, poems, and messages.[28]

From that day on, dancers have been allowed in the most important plaza in México (past and present). The hope of *Mexicayotl* leaders was that the event would be a beacon for unification between the numerous dance groups in México City and the surrounding areas, but that level of cooperation was never repeated. Many *Generales* were reluctant, if not obstinately opposed, to leaving the *concha*, Catholicism, and the traditions they knew for the proposals of *Mexicayotl* leaders. Felipe Aranda continued to support the ZT and made a pact with Kuauhkoatl to keep sending dancers to ZT-sponsored ceremonies (Ramírez, personal communication). The work of the ZT and the dancers in the *Mexicayotl* movement were always seen as political due to their oppositional relationship with governmental institutions and other mainstream cultural institutions.

For years, the ZT would continue its work. For example, in 1992, the ZT and other community leaders organized to host the last leg and summit of the Peace and Dignity Journeys, an event gathering representatives from indigenous nations in North and South America in marking 500 years of resistance from the arrival of Columbus. International representatives were received both at the *Zócalo* and at Teotihuacan. Ocelocoatl helped coordinate the event at the *Zócalo*. There he made the acquaintance of Chicanas/os and many representatives from indigenous nations all over the continent who would host him and the ZT dancers in his future travels abroad to expand the reach of the work being done at the ZT and connect with Mexican communities in Diaspora.

The work of the *Mexicayotl* movement and the ZT was (and continues to be) politicized, and its efforts were done in the name of community empowerment, civil, spiritual, and human rights, and as extensions of a resistance to imposition, carried out by indigenous people on the content for hundreds of years. In a conversation about the topics of this chapter, Ocelocoatl told me, "The *Mexicayotl* is more than a movement, it is a cause." It is a cause still being defined and negotiated today both in México and in the United States.

The Matrix of Danza Traditions

In the preceding sections, I have given historical contexts to explain the *Conchero* and the *Mexicayotl* traditions to orient readers in some of the traditions within *Danza*. Aztec dance groups in México and in Diaspora exist on a matrix with conservative *Concheros* who adhere strictly to *Conchero* popular Catholicism on one side and dancers of the *Mexicayotl* movement on the other—with many iterations in between, including groups in the middle that are often identified as "*Tradición*" or "*Danza Azteca*," for example. One's location on the matrix is determined largely by the amount of Catholic and Western elements included in dance ceremonies versus indigenous and ancestral components (in music, attire, language, spirit practice, nutrition, etc.) coupled with a certain political ideology. Other ideologies/practices on the matrix include various New Age movements that are found in or near *Danza* in México. They have been attractive to many *danzantes* but are not discussed in this book specifically, though other authors do include them.[29]

Danzantes today negotiate the options, tensions, and divisions in ideology and practice that the landscape of *Danza* affords. As in so many other arenas of life, dancers hold fast to the way they were taught or "grew up" in *Danza*, though it is a fluid and complex phenomenon at times. Holding the past and the present traditions together, modern *danzantes* construct various expressions of this sacred life style.

Groups in the *Danza* matrix, be they *Conchero*, *Mexicayotl*, or what-have-you, are operating with the same essence of *Danza*, but variation is inevitable as they practice in diverse contexts, under multiple conditions, internationally, with distinct materials, various entry points, changing technologies and globalization, not to mention histories of oppression, racism, and erasure. It is important to recognize that multiple expressions of *Danza* have always existed, and change is inevitable and constant, especially when *Danza* is constantly introduced to new materials and conditions. This book does not concern itself with authenticity or exalting one form over another. Rather, it focuses on one group, in the *Mexicayotl* tradition, which is undoubtedly caught up in the web of the multiple polemics of *Danza*, but can be celebrated for its contemporary practice, dynamic use of history, positive mission, community development work, and particular expression of *Danza*.

A group's positionality on the matrix helps dictate their dance practices, activities, and associations. In this introductory chapter, I have surveyed the centrality of *Danza* in pre-Cuauhtémoc central México, the type of syncretism that occurred in the colonial era, and the history and basic elements of the *Conchero/Tradición* and *Mexicayotl* traditions. In California and beyond, groups existed all over the aforementioned matrix. Knowing that Calpulli Tonalehqueh follows the *Mexicayotl* tradition and that its community organizing, dance, cultural diffusion, and educational offerings mirror the ZT's provides essential context for understanding their projects and ideology.

The focus of the historical context detailed in this book until now has centered on México. I now discuss more pertinent background of Calpulli Tonalehqueh as I trace how *Danza* migrates from México to the United States.

Danza Migrates (Back) to the United States

The story of the migration of *Danza* to the United States is complex, contended, and not well documented. Given the extensive archeological record of cultural and material exchange between First Nations from what is now Chile to Alaska over thousands of years, it is safe to say that significant interchange and borrowing occurred in all areas of life (language, political economy, technology, art, science) including dance in these lands. I will not say much more about that at this stage other than to signal why I chose to title this section as I have. Even in the present, there is considerable transnational flow of ideas and materials around *Danza* (Appadurai, 1996; du Gay, 1997). Not only are

México and the United States involved, but China, Spain, Germany, England, Austria, cyberspace, etc., are as well. *Danza* is global and can be examined as an element on what scholars of cultural studies call "Circuits of Culture" (du Gay, 1997). It is constantly mediated, produced, consumed, represented, and regulated in transnational circuits of culture.

The history of recent migrations of *Danza* to the United States is reviewed by extremely important academic works including ones by Jennie M. Luna (2011), Mario Aguilar (2009), and Enrique G. M. Maestas (2003). Again, what I offer here is a brief summary, as I have gathered it, with the intent of providing context for understanding Calpulli Tonalehqueh. According to Valencia (1994), many people have been given credit or have taken credit for bringing *Danza* to the United States; others who have brought it may never get credit. The two individuals who are most often acknowledged with bringing *Danza* to the United States are *Capitán* Andrés Segura (b. 1931; d. 1997) and *Capitán* Florencio Yescas[30] (b. ?; d. 1985). By the mid-twentieth century, both dancers were active in the *Danza* movement in México City and both were influenced, to varying degrees, by the surge of popularity of *Danza* in the tourist and film industries, the professional dance milieu, and with government ministries doing national cultural programming during the 1950s and 1960s. Both had professional training as dancers, and Yescas was one of the original dancers in the Ballet Folklórico de México of Amalia Hernández (Aguilar, 2003, p. 258). Andrés Segura was featured in the films *El Es Dios* (Bonfíl Batalla, 1965), *The Eagle's Children* (Lane, 1992), and *Danzante* (Grunstein, 1992), which feature dancers in México and the Southwest of the United States. Maestas (2003) claims that Segura came to Texas in 1967 to bring *Danza* to Mexican American communities and established the group Xinachtli, which is still there. Aguilar (2009) offers that Segura came to the United States for the first time with the White Roots of Peace tour in 1973. Whichever the case, Segura was instrumental in establishing dance circles in Texas and beyond. He worked closely with *El Teatro Campesino* in San Juan Bautista, California, and established a group there as well (that exists today) (Broyles-González, 1994). Luz María Espinoza (personal communication), a student of Segura in California, currently leads a group in Santa Paula, California, and I have spoken to her about how she still diffuses the teachings of *Maestro* Segura. Dozens of groups and generations of dancers who can trace themselves back to Segura exist all over the United States. Throughout the 1970s, *Danza* groups established themselves throughout the United States and can be found today in places one would expect like California, Colorado, New México, and Texas, and in more unexpected places like Idaho, Iowa, Illinois, Minnesota, New York, Florida, Oregon, and Washington.

Mario Aguilar (2009), one of the most tenured dancers in the United States, a recognized *Capitán* by a *Mesa* in México City, and an original US student of Florencio Yescas, has written extensively about Yescas' diffusion of *Danza* with his *Esplendor Azteca* group in the United States. Aguilar remembers that Florencio Yescas had worked in the United States (Chicago, Los Angeles) teaching *ballet folklórico* in the 1950s and 1960s. He returned to Tijuana in the early 1970s with a cadre of young male dancers from México City's Tacuba neighborhood, some of who still figure prominently in the diffusion of *Danza* in California (e.g., Lázaro Arvizu, Gerardo Salinas). After establishing a dance circle in San Diego in 1974, Yescas and his group toured extensively in the Southwest and the Midwest. They ultimately settled in Los Angeles, performing at key landmarks and establishments in the Mexican American community. US-born Mexican Americans, active in the Chicano Movement of the 1960s and 1970s, flocked to *Danza* everywhere it arrived. Yescas and Seguras' influences on choreography, leadership innovation, diffusion, and mediation in the United States and in México can hardly be overstated.[31]

In the coming decades, steady streams of dancers traveled between the United States and México in a circuit of mutual exchange. Established dancers from México continue to migrate to the United States, sometimes establishing residence permanently and seeding various circles (e.g., Lázaro Arvizu in Los Angeles, Gerardo Salinas in San Francisco/San José, Xochitecpatl in Salinas, Macuil Xochitl in San Francisco). Likewise, many *danzantes* who join in the United States travel frequently to México and immerse themselves in the major and minor ceremonies of the hundreds of groups found in all corners of México. In the same way, physical commodities move back and forth between dancers on both sides of the border, so do ideas, styles, and approaches to *Danza*. As a living object, *Danza* migrates transnationally, continuously.[32]

Calpulli Tonalehqueh Is Born

Calpulli Tonalehqueh can claim a lineage to both Florencio Yescas and the *Zemanauak Tlamachtiloyan* in México City. Like all *calpultin*,

Calpulli Tonalehqueh was born when a set of veteran dancers and families converged for community development.

Calpulli Tonalehqueh's leader, Mitlalpilli, danced briefly with Gerardo Salinas, a dancer from the Tacuba neighborhood in México City and one of the original dancers who came with Yescas' *Esplendor Azteca* in 1974. Salinas had danced in Los Angeles with Yescas before moving to San Francisco and then San José to teach dancers. Salinas called his group Xipe Totec (still active). Later, Mitlalpilli coordinated a dance circle in San José in the 1990s with David Yañez, a Xipe Totec student. Mitlalpilli helped coordinate the Yaoyopa ceremony in 1995, a landmark *Mexicayotl* ceremony in Northern California. That ceremony involved a visit from Kuauhkoatl and Ocelocoatl from the *Zemanauak Tlamachtiloyan* who had been in contact with *danzante* activists in San José.

At this time (mid-1990s), a large group of established dancers from the San José area formed a Mexica dance group called Calpulli Huitzilopochtli. Huitzilopochtli was comprised of more than just dancers. Not unlike the ZT, many community activists and artists were part of the collective and lent their efforts to cultural diffusion and community empowerment as well as to spiritual practice. Members made frequent trips to México for panindigenous summits and ceremonies. *Maestro* Ocelocoatl became a key member and advisor to Calpulli Huitzilopochtli. He was invited to California by a dancer/activist, Huitzilín, who had attended the 1992 Peace and Dignity Journeys summit in México City and arranged for Ocelocoatl and Kuauhkoatl to make their first visit to San José in October 1995.

Calpulli Huitzilopochtli soon included dancers from previously established groups in the Bay Area that seceded from those groups and joined Huitzilopochtli, including Tekolpoktli Madrid, Nauhxayacatl Chavira, and Atlaua Hernández. Huitzilopochtli worked for many years in San José from the late 1990s to the early 2000s. The ceremonies that Huitzilopochtli hosted marked the winter solstice[33] and the Mexica New Year ceremony.[34] Huitzilopochtli members endured constant derision from other groups in the San Francisco Bay Area especially for their adherence to the *Mexicayotl*, their alignment with Ocelocoatl, and their decision to exclude the Catholic or religious elements from their practice. Some of its members were charged with having extremist and abrasive views (Hernández, personal communication).

In the early 2000s, internal friction caused Calpulli Huitzilopochtli to fracture in three. Part of the friction is generated when Huitzilín increasingly becomes a lightning rod for controversy in the local civic and dance community. Many dancers grow increasingly concerned about his fanatical views reflecting so severely on the group (Hernández, personal communication). Miztzin, his wife, and a set of dancers left to establish a group called Mictlan. Mitlalpilli and the future founders of Calpulli Tonalehqueh held meetings where they decided to establish a group separate from Huitzilín and stand apart from some of the previously generated controversies. Founding members of the new group (soon named Calpulli Tonalehqueh) included Tekolpoktli and Techicuauhtli, Cuauhcihuatl, and Ollinkoatl. Atlaua, Nauhxayacatl, and others soon followed. Tonalehqueh members retained one of the two practice times (Wednesdays at the Mexican Heritage Plaza in San José) and the New Year ceremony. In a third space, some members of Huitzilopochtli remained under the leadership of Huitzilín. Those who stayed kept their Monday practice at Emma Prusch Park and the winter solstice ceremony.

Membership in *Danza* groups has always had a great deal of fluidity. Even celebrated figures such as Andrés Segura and Mario Aguilar have split from their groups (Aguilar, 2009; Hernández-Ávila, 2005). It is not uncommon for groups to splinter, for members to establish their own circles for any number of reasons, including dissatisfaction with their original group.

Calpulli Tonalehqueh is a new group by *Danza* standards, but members brought significant collective experience to its establishment. Figure 1.1 shows some of the teaching influences traced through some of the founding dancers of Calpulli Tonalehqueh (founding members who were not dancers are not pictured) and then on to me. The lineage traces back to some of the dancers who brought *Danza* to the United States and to founding members of the *Mexicayotl* movement in México City. Founding members of Calpulli Tonalehqueh arrived at the moment of group creation with some clarity about what they did not want to do (based on past experience) and also about the kind of ideology and mission that would guide the group's activity (again, mirroring the agenda established at the ZT).

The name Calpulli Tonalehqueh was not generated arbitrarily. After the Huitzilopochtli split, Calpulli Tonalehqueh continued their community and dance work, though they did so without a name. While *Conchero* or *Tradición* groups traditionally welcomed new dance circles under a *Mesa* through a ceremony called *levantamiento de estandarte* (raising of the banner) during a *velación* (vigil), Tonalehqueh went a route dictated by the *Mexicayotl* praxis.

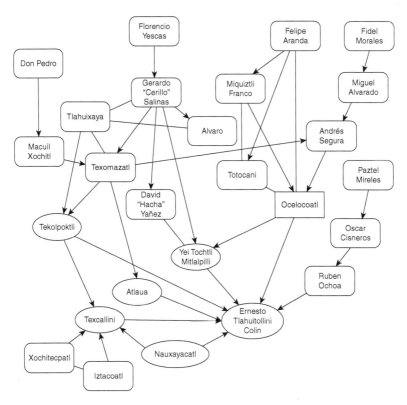

Figure 1.1   The author's *Danza* genealogy (abridged).

Note: The arrows represent teaching relationships. Included are the founding dancers of Calpulli Tonalehqueh (in ovals) who taught me, along with their own teachers, and Ocelocoatl (rectangle) who guides the group. This is but a small subset of an enormous network of dancers who have worked with and/or influenced all the individuals pictured in the figure.

In a recovery of pre-Cuauhtémoc naming rituals, *calpulli* members are given a set of six names to choose from (see figures 1.2 and 8.1), which were generated after a traditional consultation of a *tonalamatl*, or book of energy/destiny, a traditional practice whereby a *tonalpohque* (scholar who interprets the astronomy and reads the day count divinatory books) studies the numbers, signs, and natural elements present at the time of one's birth, which will then be conjugated into one's name and will help determine one's work in the world (what is meant by destiny). Figure 1.2 represents a document that records

Figure 1.2 The *tonalamatl* document produced for Calpulli Tonalehqueh.

Note: It shows the birth elements calculated by Ocelocoatl including day (two caiman), week (one flower), month (*atlacahualo*), year (5 flint), cardinal direction (West), sacred elements, and possible names for the group. Framed by the 20 day signs is a pictographic representation of one of the Tonalehqueh ("followers of the sun") designed by the *tonalpohqueh*, or "s/he who tells destiny," Ocelocoatl. The kneeling (reverent), open armed (ready to receive) figure is tattooed entirely in red (color of the West, setting sun) and attired by a conical paper sun hat (sun), jade stones (sacredness), blue macaw feathers (sky), a jaw bone breast plate (medicine, transformation), braided hair (art), smoke emerging from the head (intelligence, memory), and the imprint of a white hand upon its face (creativity), among other symbols. The symbols designated in the *tonalamatl* ideally guide all members of Calpulli Tonalehqueh.

the results of the consultation with the *tonalamatl*. Ocelocoatl, who stayed allied to the group after its split from Huitzilopochtli, produced this consultation and document. I included the document because it distinguishes Calpulli Tonalehqueh from other groups that select their name through a different process. Calpulli Tonalehqueh underwent a traditional naming process[35] and also received a pictographic symbol for their group.

Calpulli Tonalehqueh was born (formally established) on March 12, 2004, during a ceremony for the Mexica New Year that they were continually hosting in San José.

Components of Calpulli Tonalehqueh

I have been a member of three different *Danza* circles (all in California), and I am in contact with dozens of groups in California and México. All groups do a great deal of community work, activism, intragroup development, intergroup collaboration, ceremony, and/or presentations, but one would be hardpressed to find a group with more "moving parts" than Calpulli Tonalehqueh. It is ambitiously organized. To begin with, not all Mexica dance groups call themselves a *calpulli*. Doing so usually means that the group is intentional about collective community work and usually signals some ideological accord with the *Mexicayotl* movement. Most often, dance circles have a centralized leadership structure, where the primary force of instruction, decision making, and participation runs through one person or a married couple. Though the final decision-making responsibility in Calpulli Tonalehqueh usually rests in Mitlalpilli, the group makes concerted efforts to make decisions and carry out the mission of the group as a collective. The components of the group follow.

Calpulli Tonalehqueh has undergone a traditional process for acquiring its name: *Tonalehqueh*, meaning those who accompany the sun. It has a handbook, which includes the group's guiding principals of *wisdom*, *harmony*, and *culture*, its vision and mission statements, and general guidelines for the components of *calpulli* membership. It holds numerous business and planning meetings and several weekly classes in dance, music, and philosophy. It organizes and hosts an annual indigenous culture exposition and the largest Aztec dance ceremony in the United States in an annual event (Azteca/Mexica New Year). At its apex, the *calpulli* has sent dancers to over 50 ceremonies/presentations a year, even internationally. It is a nonprofit organization and fundraises for events that have a budget in excess of $10,000. It partners with several community organizations, PK-16 schools, musical groups, government organizations, media, and institutions across the United States and México. Recently, Calpulli Tonalehqueh has partnered with San José's School of Arts and Culture. The dance circle has had several Websites (MySpace, Facebook, Aztecdancers.com, etc.), an e-mail listserv with nearly 400 addresses, and several small business and agricultural ventures. Depending on how one counts membership, Calpulli Tonalehqueh has over 50 dancers and over 100 members at large, from infants to elders. Membership and participation is completely voluntary.

These significant undertakings would not be possible without a substantial pooling of resources; the *calpulli* exploits the talents and social and work-related networks of its members for its entire enterprise. The spirit of community is evoked constantly, and members construct a contemporary *calpulli par excellence*.

2

Calpulli (An Alliance of Houses)

The *calpulli* represents the foundation of sociopolitical organization in ancient Central México. Active to this day throughout México (and now the United States), a *calpulli* is an alliance of families, bound by cultural, communal, political, agricultural, and educational ties. *Calpulli* members call on each other to pool their skills and labor for the good of the whole unit. This chapter examines the components of traditional *calpultin* (plural of *calpulli*) using scholarly sources and local definitions. Members of Calpulli Tonalehqueh look to community elders from México for guidelines on how to actualize this ancient organization in the present. This discussion is followed by an example of how a call to *calpulli* can be taken up when resources are marshaled for the family of a dancer with a child in need. It is one of many examples of how *calpulli* members show each other how to be mutual. I present the story of Gabriel, a young *calpulli* member, who finds himself caught in a precarious school situation and whose family receives the collective support of *calpulli* members. The chapter ends with a discussion of the fluid conception of *calpulli* held by group members and the way that Calpulli Tonalehqueh actively calibrates their own *calpulli* to create a modern-day reconfiguration of ancient *calpultin*.

Competing Definitions of *Calpulli*

Agreeing upon the nature and constitution of the *calpulli* is an elusive and factional undertaking for Mesoamericanists. To date over 30 investigations into the sociopolitical structure of Mesoamerican society can be found, starting with two early colonial scholars who portrayed Nahua life in ancient Central México and upon whose work every other scholar bases their interpretation: Bernardino de Sahagún

(1557/1992) and Alonso de Zurita[1] (1565/1963). Centuries later, anthropologists became interested in ancient societies and their placement on an evolutionary scale like A. F. Bandelier (1878a, 1878b), and L. H. Morgan (1877/1964). Alfonso Caso (1959) leads a generation of Mexican scholars including Arturo Monzón Estrada (1949) who writes one of the canonical texts on the subject of *calpultin*. In a review of their texts, authors debate *calpulli* social stratification, fates after the Spanish invasion, caste, land tenure, administration, membership, functionaries, regional variants, labor, occupational groupings, formal education, theocracy, and precursors, among many other things. Since the most vigorous conversations in the mid-1900s, the debate and investigation of *calpultin* reemerges every couple of years as scholars revisit Mexica social organization[2] (c.f. Brumfiel, 1988; Carrasco and Broda, 1982; Caso, 1954; Caso and Wicke, 1963; Chance, 2000; Cuauhtlatoac, 2010; del Solar, 1963; Guerrera Estrella, 2010; Hicks, 1982; Milbrath, 2001; Nutini, 1961; Perkins, 2005; Romerovargas Yturbide, 1957; Rounds, 1979; Van Zantwijk, 1963).

Most *calpulli* scholars rely upon colonial texts, especially those of de Zurita and Sahagún. Reliance upon them for the definition of *calpulli* is problematic. Colonial chronicles were written from a Western perspective, plus they were censored, edited, and translated several times over decades and centuries.[3] Colonial Spanish authors often had no equivalent terms for the concepts and cultural performances described by native informants or observed with their own eyes. I point out the colonial texts and their flaws to make the case for the palimpsest of *calpulli*. Sixteenth-century authors, in many editions, wrote interpretations of *calpulli* that most of the world used for centuries. If in fact they misinterpreted any part of the social organization of ancient Mexica, then part of a more authentic history was erased. Recently, scholars in the *Mexicayotl* vein look to reconstruct a version of *calpulli* sympathetic to contemporary community progress (as I point out below).

Above all, and despite the disagreements about particulars and the *noise* introduced by colonial reporting, is the unanimous agreement among scholars that *calpultin* is the primary institution that organized life in Central México and beyond. I also must note that the scholarly debates around classical Mexica *calpultin* are largely irrelevant to everyday *danzantes*.

One can ask whose definition of *calpulli* does the community use in the twenty-first century? As noted, dancers in Calpulli Tonalehqueh are largely unaware of the scholarly debates, colonial writings, or contemporary Mexican manifestations of *calpultin*. Those debates are markedly inconsequential in everyday conventions. What the members *do* is go to their most trusted source, the primary elder of the group: Ocelocoatl. Ocelocoatl has conducted over 30 years of formal research on Mexica culture, founded several *calpultin*, mentored hundreds of dancers, and had teaching appointments at several academic institutions, including México's most important National Autonomous University (UNAM). Ocelocoatl is the primary force in the group's understanding of *calpulli*—that is, before members take the term and reinterpret it. The definition at hand is delivered to the group at its founding, in subsequent reorganizations, and in public lectures (these lectures, or *huehuetlatolli*, will be visited in a later chapter).

The group's handbook (Colín et al., 2007) defines *calpulli* as follows:

> The *Calpulli* System is the most fundamental social, political, economic, and cultural institution of our native community. *Calpulli* derives from two words in Náhuatl: *calli*, meaning house, and *pulli*, meaning reunion. Thus, *calpulli* stands for the meeting of the houses. The most basic *calpulli* is a nuclear family. A group of extended relatives (in a broad sense) form a larger *calpulli*, and so on. When united, they form a sustainable, mutually supportive, and vigorous unit. Our *calpulli* is a meeting of such families, forming when individuals act as representatives, come together, support each other, share talents, and thereby enable the work of our group.

In a public lecture, Ramírez (2007) used a simple explanation to relay how a *calpulli* is structured:

> The *calpulli* needs two pillars; it needs equilibrium, and everyone's work and talent. The most basic *calpulli* is a family, and then we grow to groups of families. But a family is like the fingers of a hand. The father is the thumb, he supports, he executes the plan, gives his strength. The mother is the index finger. These are the two most important fingers. The mother is like the index finger: she sets the vision, she points the way, she gives direction. And the children are like the rest of the fingers. There is the older one, the middle, and the baby…They are all important, but they are all different. Each has their talent. Separate, the fingers have little strength. But together they make a fist, they are strong. And working together, with each of their talents, they can create. It is the most human thing to do: create. The fingers of the hand work together to make music, to paint, to write, to work, to create. That is the first *calpulli*. Now, what happens when you get two hands? You can make

more things! Remember, it takes two hands to make tortillas. And that is it. Our own body tells us how we should be in the world. We don't have to look anywhere else. (my translation)[4]

Accessibly, and in a manner reminiscent of traditional Mexica *hue-huetlatolli* (see chapter 7), Ocelocoatl delivered (his invocation of) essential aspects of a *calpulli*. Emphasized is the value of each individual in a community and the vital role they realize when leveraging their talents for the good of the many (this is the way the group works to manage the term).

With few exceptions, members of this *calpulli* are not looking through journal articles and books to come to the definition of *calpulli*. Instead they infer the meaning through story, dialogue, immersion, and through the *calpulli* they coconstruct each week. This notwithstanding, scholarly information is available and sometimes circulates among dancers. For instance, after one of his community lectures, I asked Ocelocoatl if he trusted/recommended a written source that defined *calpulli*. He pointed to the work of Ignacio Romerovargas Yturbide (1957). I reviewed over 30 definitions of *calpulli* in encyclopedias, colonial texts, Websites, handbooks, papers, reports, letters, and books, but I extol the work of Romerovargas Yturbide who based his writing on many of the same sources available to the other Mesoamerican scholars, but approached them in a manner particularly sympathetic with an indigenous Mexican point of view. In addition, Romerovargas Yturbide included the oral tradition as a source of his research.

Romerovargas Yturbide[5] (1957) explained that the *calpulli* was the primary sociopolitical institution of Mesoamerica—socialist, sophisticated (and in force today although largely supplanted and corrupted by the *cacicazgo* and *municipio* systems imposed by the colonial and postcolonial governments). There were many types of *calpultin*, but in general a *calpulli* consisted of a collective of families, organized around communal land, and federated with other *calpultin*. *Calpultin* were marked by autonomy whereby each governance structure was tailored to local customs and needs. Each was autarchic and its leaders emerged organically. Every *calpulli* was self-sufficient; by rule, each *calpulli* maintained its own economic, agricultural, and human resources. By and large, a *calpulli* had a general leadership council headed by two figures, one administrative and the other executive (duality being central to Mesoamerican cosmology). The council would establish the other offices on the governance team organically (e.g., treasurer, sheriff, schoolmaster, director of medicine, director of public art, historian). In other words, they were established according to local needs. In addition, each *calpulli* had two general assemblies divided along gender lines that meet semiannually to discuss the particular concerns of men and women. From among the elders of the community with impeccable reputations, the *calpulli* elected two judges to hear the grievances of members and work to maintain communal harmony. Laws were written by consensus. Two representatives were selected to sit on larger regional councils to represent each *calpulli*. The legitimacy of all elected officials emanated from the public, and officers can be stripped of their titles if ineffective (pp. 1–22).

The Story of Gabriel and the *Calpulli*

Because Calpulli Tonalehqueh is a completely nonprofit, community-based organization, every event or activity they organize is a modern manifestation of the *calpulli* system. Readers can examine numerous examples of the marshaling of the collective skill of *calpulli* members throughout this book and may refer back to this chapter, even though those activities serve to illustrate different aspects of learning in a *calpulli*. For the present concept, the following occurrence exemplifies ways Calpulli Tonalehqueh operates as a modern *calpulli*. In other words, it illustrates how the group's collective resources echo traditional *calpultin* activity (and how members invoke the concept of *tequio*, as we will see in chapter 3). This is the story of Gabriel:

One of the members of the *calpulli* had a son in kindergarten (a "*calpulli* kid" as the elders call them) who had a significant outburst in class and toward a classmate, which, unbeknownst to the teachers and school staff, was caused by an allergic reaction combined with general 5-year-old exuberance. The school referred the child to both a doctor and a school psychologist for evaluation. Unfortunately, the child was misdiagnosed on multiple occasions with little or no consultation with parents and ended up in a psychiatric wing of a hospital for a short, traumatic stay. The child's hospitalization and the stress placed upon the family reverberated through the *calpulli*. The child made it out of the hospital, and only negligible apologies were made for the misdiagnoses.

The school scheduled an individualized educational program (IEP) for a diagnosis of attention-deficit hyperactivity disorder with which the parents were apprehensive. Soon, one of the members of the Council of Elders called for an emergency meeting of the *Tlahtocan* (the group's general council; see chapter 5). The *calpulli*'s *Tlahtocan* quickly convened to bring their energy and experience to bear in support of a family of the *calpulli* members. The *calpulli* and *Tlahtocan* membership included social workers, classroom teachers, teacher educators, parents, hospital employees, school counselors (who are experts in IEPs), community activists, city employees, county health workers, students, and dietitians. Through e-mail and in person, the *Tlahtocan* was able to give this member expert advice on the IEP process, point him in the direction of parent support groups for the IEP process (including legal challenges), discuss modifications to the child's diet, workshop ideas on parental rights, play devil's advocate from the perspective of a classroom teacher, and advise litigation for the grave errors of the school and the doctors.

The expertise of the group was mobilized to support the *calpulli* member. The fealty and collective strength of the *calpulli* was in full display just as in ceremony and in the more mundane life interfaces. In a comment that was part of that discussion, a member remarked:

> As in your case and thousands of others the school system, doctors, psychologists, psychiatrists and all other considered professionals drop the ball and are quick to make personal decisions for the WELL BEING OF OUR CHILDREN, which is very wrong in most cases. We as parents should be the first teachers and responsible care takers who make the right choices for their raising but allowing them their freedom to make their own choices. We need to put our children first before ANYTHING…Children need a nurturing home as in our cultura the first kalpulli [sic] is our family. Something we see the school system cannot provide. We will look for actual resources you can turn to that have alternatives to our disinfranchised [sic] school/health systems to give to you. (Nesaualcoyotl, personal communication)

During discussions in/of *calpulli*, members often reference family, culture, children, and education.

Modern Interpretations of *Calpulli*

The manner in which the general membership conceptualizes a modern *calpulli* mediates the composition and function of the group. In this section, I present the most common interpretations of the concept of *calpulli* gathered in my fieldwork. Generally, dancers relay that a *calpulli* is for:

- studying, researching, and learning culture
- learning native language
- examining history
- education and teaching
- *Danza*
- learning philosophy
- songs, prayer, and music
- cultural defense
- community work
- cultural diffusion
- art expositions
- community development

Although largely unaware of the scholarly debates about the constitution of the classic Mexica *calpulli*, members nonetheless articulate clear connections between the classic components of *calpulli* and the one they actualize at present. There is a general match between the formal/classic definitions of *calpulli* and the various types of interpretations of the concept that members discuss. In addition, there is a match between the mission of Calpulli Tonalehqueh (dance and cultural diffusion) and the activities contained by this array of purposes.

When I examine member interpretations of the term, I recognize *calpulli* is not a static term. It is both understood and lived in various ways. There are four main understandings of *calpulli* that emerge from my conversations with dancers: (1) family, (2) community, (3) a form of organizing work, and (4) as a multivalent location.

First, *calpulli* is conceived as family. Once I asked Mitlalpilli, the *calpulli* leader, how he defined *calpulli*. He replied with two words: "Family. Community." Xochicuauhtli (personal communication) told me that for him *calpulli*

> is an alliance of homes/households which as a collective make up a *calpulli*. I believe our *calpulli* has a particular niche in the *Danza* community and it's evolved into a particular group identity. I believe a *calpulli* is a union of families, who share the same values and beliefs and receive support from other members of the *calpulli* when they endure the storms of life.

Members of Calpulli Tonalehqueh are conscious of the fact that networking with and supporting each other in arenas beyond dance is not always common in *Danza*. They recognize that Calpulli Tonalehqueh is unique because of its intentionality to construct *calpulli*.

As we have seen in the case of Gabriel and in numerous other instances, the support and organizing that happens in the group extends to many of life's challenges. Cuauhyohua, a teenage *danzante*, echoed these sentiments. To the same question, she responded, "it [*calpulli*] means family with people you can trust and have your back, people that are willing to be in your life for good causes" (personal communication).

Though the vast majority of informants allude to the idea of family in their definition of *calpulli*, a few recognize a disconnect between the ideal and the real, stating that cohesiveness is not always evinced in Calpulli Tonalehqueh. One *danzante* (anonymous) expressed that *calpulli* is

> family, even though I do not feel I have that in this *calpulli*. I would say that family was the intention—some members do find that sense of family with others—but as a whole, that is missing. I do not feel that this will ever change, but this is not necessarily a bad thing.

Equating a *calpulli* with a family or a set of families is definitely an ideal and an objective of the group, but as with all human institutions, it is not easily obtained and some do not feel included in this definition.

Second, the theme of community is prevalent in conceptions about *calpulli*. *Calpulli* not only provides a space where individuals and families can claim membership in a Mexica way of life, but it comes to stand for the idea of community. People opt in and out of the *calpulli* and often conceive of it as a community, not as in a geographic location, but as a network of people, united in a mutual cause and communally active. Recently, a new member explained, "*calpulli para mí es la comunidad, la unión, el grupo, un hogar donde me siento cómoda y libre con las demas personas dentro de ese calpulli.*" [*calpulli* for me is the community, unity, the group, a home where I feel comfortable and free with the rest of the people in that *calpulli*] (Itexcatlayohualli, personal communication). One of the founding members of Calpulli Tonalehqueh elaborated:

> Calpulli means houses that come together. It means families, groups, or individuals that come together to form a union as in a community. It means family to me. It has more meaning to it then just that. When I say my *calpulli*, it means the people that I love and respect that have the same purpose as I do within our Mexica Ways. (Cuauhcihuatl, personal communication)

The *calpulli* is a group both active in the geographic community and is a group bound by social relationships and responsibilities to each other. A member of Calpulli Tonalehqueh answered my question about how he conceived *calpulli* with the following: "For me it represents a place where community unites to work together on things such as *Danza*, organizing events like birthday parties and dinners, trading things, social networking or traveling to other ceremonies" (Yapaltecatl, personal communication). This quotation brings me to the third main theme in the conception of the term by members of Calpulli Tonalehqueh: the *calpulli* as an indigenous form of organizing work.

The theme of family and community is by far the most common answer to the question of "what does *calpulli* mean to you?," but many members acknowledge a third conception, that the *calpulli* is an institution created for social and communal organization, for the organization of labor and governance. Omicuauhtli agreed with Yapaltecatl on the idea that the *calpulli* organizes group activity and creates a system of social order on large and small scales, saying that a *calpulli* is "the oldest form of order that our people had and continue until today." Calpulli members often note that the *calpulli* provides order and describe it as an organism that facilitates community work. In order for this organism to function at maximum efficiency, members must have common goals and ideals. This is evident in comments such as one from Zihuayaocuicatl who defined *calpulli* as a "circle of like minded people who move in the same direction for the good of the whole."

The fourth theme that members elicit is about *calpulli* as multivalent location, a space that exists on multiple planes that are active at various times. The *calpulli* can have a physical location. It can be the community building where weekly workshops are held, the ceremonial grounds where dancers gather, or the backyard where members gather to work or discuss. The *calpulli* can also be a social space, outside of the physical dimension, existing in the bonds between people or found in the moments people support each other. For example, dancer commented that the *calpulli* is "sacred and safe place to gather and celebrate my indigenous roots" (Pedrizco, personal communication). Dancers coconstruct an environment that is spiritual and allows members to practice their traditions free from many outside threats. This is significant given the centuries of assaults indigenous life ways have endured. Additionally, *calpulli* is conceived as a location for education. One of the founding members of Calpulli Tonalehqueh sums it up when he defined *calpulli*, saying it "represents community and learning to me. It is a place were people come to learn and to teach" (Ollinkoatl, personal communication).

Calibrating *Calpulli*

This chapter presented how calpulli members conceive *calpulli*. This entire book refers to the ways dancers build *calpulli*. Now this section discusses the refining and calibrating of the construction of the *calpulli*, a constant process. Calpulli Tonalehqueh has held many evaluation meetings to assess the work and state of the *calpulli*. For example, in April 2009, members of Calpulli Tonalehqueh held evaluation meeting with a two-part agenda. The first was to evaluate the Mexica New Year ceremony the group had recently hosted (this ceremony is discussed in chapter 3). The second objective of the meeting was to evaluate the mission and vision of the *calpulli*. This meeting was called because group leaders were growing increasingly concerned about the challenges of sustaining the work of a growing *calpulli* and a large ceremony with just a few people carrying a large load of the work. In addition, many members of the *calpulli* had left the group in recent months, and leaders hoped to address the causes.

Members of Calpulli Tonalehqueh were only able to finish the first part of the agenda in one evening, so they scheduled a meeting a week later to finish the second agenda item. This chapter focuses on the content of the second meeting, on members' opinions about the mission of the group.

At this meeting, leaders acknowledged that there was great talent in the *calpulli*, but that it is spread out, often squandered. Also, members stated that it was important to revisit the mission and goals of the group with frequency in order to keep a focus and move forward with a unified vision. As the group and its activities grew, so did the challenges. In the meeting, the goal originally set out by the founders of the *calpulli* was shared: to create a positive place for the *Mexicayotl*. Then, the question was asked, "How do we strengthen the *calpulli*?" The answers varied and included:

- getting a physical location for the group to anchor the projects
- establishing regularity for gatherings (meetings, *temascal*, workshops, etc.)
- deepening the relationship with Zemanauak Tlamachtiloyan
- focusing on short-term goals and stemming the growth of the group

- harnessing the talent of members
- enhancing the focus on children and their education
- strengthening the *cargos* of the group (see chapter 5)
- focusing on strengths and on sustainability (see chapter 3)
- focusing on personal relationships

The fact that the meeting was called and the comments collected reveal the one way that leaders of Calpulli Tonalehqueh sought to overcome the challenges of coconstructing a *calpulli*. Group evaluations also occurred frequently in informal conversation, in personal conversations, and in other meetings. The group diagnosed any troubling symptoms and decided to calibrate. The constant renewal and evaluation of what the *calpulli* was doing, of what a *calpulli* should be, or of what changes could strengthen the group are noteworthy in the modern construction.

Reconfigurations: Palimpsest

The theme that characterizes the palimpsest of *calpulli* in Calpulli Tonalehqueh is reconfiguration. I submit the way members of Calpulli Tonalehqueh reconfigure the constitution of *calpulli* as a space for palimpsest.

All *calpulli* activities are evidence of a palimpsest—the meetings, the ceremonies, the workshops, the lectures, and so on. The *calpulli* is a site for raising children, for cultural transmission, for the curriculum of a Mexica way of life. Whether in the support lent to Gabriel, in the organization of large-scale ceremonies, in the institution of traditional *cargos*, or in any of the various dance and cultural diffusion efforts of Calpulli Tonalehqueh, reauthoring is central to the *calpulli* palimpsest. In all *calpulli* evaluation and planning meetings, not to mention the formal workshops where classic definitions of *calpulli* are received, members establish and refine how they wish to organize their *calpulli*. As in all traditional *calpultin*, the design of the group is organized based on local needs.

Calpulli Tonalehqueh constructs a modern-day *calpulli*, a palimpsest of interpretations and activities that take up ancient manifestations of Anahuacan *calpulli* life and reinterprets them, reactivating them in the present. None of the dancer's conceptions of *calpulli* are mutually exclusive; the fluid definitions of *calpulli* overlap. Family. Community. Work. Spaces. The role the group plays in the personal and familial lives of the members is equally central in the reconfiguration.

Certainly, Calpulli Tonalehqueh enables a significant amount of community organizing, of traditional internal governance, and multiple types of collaborative work. Also, there are multiple spaces for education. The rest of the chapters in this volume bear this out as we look at the community organizing, workshops, ceremonies, and identity innovations of Calpulli Tonalehqueh.

Despite the fact that not everyone feels a deep sense of camaraderie, the laudable achievements of Calpulli Tonalehqueh are signaled by two quotations signaled in this chapter. The first is that people share support for each other to help them "endure the storms of life" (Xochicuauhtli). The second is that the *calpulli* is a "circle of like minded people who move in the same direction for the good of the whole" (Zihuayaocuicatl). And though other cultural and community groups may develop a sense of community and a sense of family, what makes this Calpulli Tonalehqueh different is their particular palimpsest, which is manifest when they look back to ancient Mexica forms of organization and come together to move their collective families forward in a like-minded hopeful vision for the future.

This modern *calpulli* is a palimpsest because most families are neither land-based, nor agriculturally based, nor based in México in the present context. They must negotiate a US context, urban spaces, a complex democracy, capitalism, mainstream schooling, xenophobia, various oppressions, and the loss of ancestral memory. They must find avenues for collecting the ancient ideology and sociopolitical structure to innovate upon them. In other words, as the group fashions a contemporary *calpulli* with new materials and challenges at hand, it reconfigures an ancient concept. The process is generative, culturally meaningful. Members organize around a culturally based vision and survive and resist in the face of important historical and actual challenges.

3

Tequio (Community Work)

The concept of *tequio*, community work, is central to the sustainability of many indigenous communities around the hemisphere. This chapter examines the meaning of the concept and the manner in which *calpulli* members understand and actualize it, particularly as they organize the largest *Danza* ceremony in the United States. The concept of *tequio* is ancient, and it is indispensible for a vibrant, productive, sustainable *calpulli*. At the same time, it is a malleable concept, and members manifest it in complex ways

Tequio Defined

Emerging from the word *tequitl*, or work, *tequio* is the ancient concept that every person has a civic duty, an obligation to contribute to the vitality of the *calpulli* as directed by the leaders of the community. In ancient Anáhuac, every citizen of a *calpulli* was obliged to contribute to agriculture and greater public works. Labor on these projects (e.g., executing large ceremonies, building housing and roads, hosting visiting dignitaries) were rotated among citizens. Guzmán (1989) explained that the duties of traditional *calpultin* were rotated so that everyone had experience in all the vocations. In alternating turns, citizens lent their labor to public works, assisted teachers at the schools, helped the judges in office, merchants at the market, or the keepers at the monuments (p. 45). In order for a community to have streets, lamps, schools, granaries, architectural monuments, mail, firewood, public restrooms, aqueducts, or any public service, public labor was pooled.

Recently, Morehart (2011) examined the ecological sustainability of *tequio*, the large *chinampa* (raised-field farming on water) projects in lake regions just south of México City from the tenth century to the fourteenth century and the human politics that created them and then brought them to a collapse. Among other things, he described the *chinampas* as a place where "people made a living, taught children patterns of knowledge and practice, interacted with their community, and reproduced both the spiritual and physical universe" (p. 9). In addition, Morehart updated readers on the status of *chinampa* farming recently in Central México. He noted that the presence of *chinampas* in the twenty-first century was a testament to sustainability, and the tourist industry, innovations, and general changes that this context has absorbed are evidence of human reconstructions of tradition. I offer this example as a reminder that *tequio*—which is rooted in *calpultin* and agriculture—is ancient on this continent and that the structures, *tequio* requirements, and traditions of *calpulli* are viable and flexible enough to confront a vastly different social, political, and economic landscape in the present.

In the *calpulli* system of precontact México, the education of children and care for the infirm were total community projects. This type of communalism forged strong community bonds and interdependency, from birth to death. *Tequio* was required of all students, and in turn, when students graduated from schools, they were given a home and an occupation and the support of their fellow *calpulli* members. Members of a *calpulli*, through their *tequio*, formed part of an ecosystem where every person was valuable and virtually no one was left behind. Furthermore, individual land ownership was not espoused by this system. Each family could build its home, but the land belonged to the entire *calpulli*. Each family was required to work in the fields or *chinampas* and support each other's agricultural activities (see Romerovargas Yturbide, 1957).

In line with others, Romerovargas Yturbide (1959) exalted the sophistication and sustainability of the *calpulli* system precisely for its brand of socialism. The *calpulli* system that existed at the time of European contact had been refined over thousands of years of trial and error. *Calpultin* were endemic, autochthonous, adaptable, and founded on the pillars of community service and communal economic, moral, educational, and spiritual welfare. Governance by local leadership was checked and balanced. People identified loyally with their *calpulli*, and undoing the ties to family and neighborhood was difficult. With this base, *calpultin* federated with other *calpulli* and scaled governance up to the regional level[1] and all the way to the capital city of Tenochtitlan (now México City), with its grand council (*Huey Tlahtocan*) and numerous *calpultin*.

Tequio Still in Effect Today

The tradition of *tequio* is widespread in modern indigenous communities. Modern materials now support ancient community associations and the obligation to community work. *Tequio* is known with a variety of terms such as *faena, fajina, gasona, el tequil, la guelaguetza, el trabajo de medio*, or *mano vuelta* depending on the particular indigenous community (Programa Universitario México Nación Multicultural, 2011; Saldaña Arellano, 2011). Warman (2003) described the system of *tequio* thus:

> *la obligación de realizar jornadas de trabajo gratuitas para el mantenimiento y construcción de obras públicas como caminos, calles, edificios públicos e iglesias, o para la introducción de nuevos servicios como educación, electrificación, agua potable, construcción de clínicas. Fue esencial para las comunidades marginadas por la inversión publica…el tequio es una de las instituciones más vigorosas para la cohesión y persistencia de la comunidad, incluso está sustentado por un discurso igualitario y equitativo.*
>
> [the obligation to give days of uncompensated labor for the maintenance and construction of public works such as paths, roads, public buildings, and churches or for the introduction of new services like schooling, electricity, potable water, the construction of clinics. It was essential for communities that were marginalized from public investment…*Tequio* is one of the most vigorous institutions for community cohesion and persistence, also it is supported by a egalitarian and equitized discourse.] (my translation)

Tequio obligations exist in hundreds of indigenous communities throughout México. Flores Quintero (2004) described the system of *tequio* in indigenous communities in Oaxaca that do not wait for an incompetent state or municipal government to build roads, classrooms, clinics, churches, etc. Instead, communities pool resources to complete the work. She describes how men who migrate to large cities or the Unites States for work continue to stay in constant contact with their home communities and contribute to the *tequio*. Oaxacans in México City and Los Angeles, for instance, have formed committees to support *tequio* back home and have developed magazines, newsletters, and several Websites (including one called tequio.com) to communicate, coordinate cultural events and share resources in Oaxaca and in their new locations.

In Triqui communities, men above the age of 16 work in agriculture and construction at different times of the year for the good of the community. They are not monetarily compensated, but it is prestigious and the achievement provides access to positions of authority in the community. Failing the obligation makes one subject to community penalties. The *tequio* is institutionalized and highly organized (Triquis de Oaxaca, 2011).

Miguel Angel Mendoza "Kuauhkoatl" (2007) described how members of the Zemanauak Tlamachtiloyan supported an indigenous community building of a bridge through *tequio* after years of requests had gone ignored by the local governments. Regino Montes (1998, 1999), a lawyer working in Mixe communities in México, stated that the *tequio* operates on two levels: inside the family in a personal space and in the larger community:

> *Frente a la globalización en todos los aspectos de la vida indígena, resulta prioritaria la creatividad de la gente en lo individual y colectivo para que puedan diseñarse alternativas de trabajo en el plano familiar y comunitario. Se trata entonces de potenciar y recuperar este tipo de mecanismos dados a nivel familiar, interfamiliar, y comunitario, para fortalecer la capacidad de la gente de potenciar su relaciones sociales y de recrear la naturaleza con equilibrio y armonía.*

> [In the face of globalization, in all aspects of indigenous life, people's creativity on the individual and collective level is primary so that alternative family and community work can be designed. It is a matter of empowering and recovering these types of mechanisms operating at the family, interfamily, and community level in order to strengthen the capacity of people to empower their social relations and recreate nature with equilibrium and harmony.] (cited in Programa Universitario México Nación Multicultural, 2011, my translation)

Members of Calpulli Tonalehqueh understand *tequio* in similar ways. They look to the work of modern indigenous communities in México as models for their own efforts. They activate *tequio* at the individual and at the *calpulli* levels in order to confront a sometimes-hostile context and empower individuals to reconnect with their cultural heritage to care better for their families, environments, and selves and to diffuse this ideology in the larger community.

Large-Scale *Tequio* in Calpulli Tonalehqueh

The Tequio *Formula*

When I asked Ocelocoatl what suggestions he would give a group looking to implement *tequio*, he responded that our *calpulli* was (already) doing it every time people gathered to support each other, bringing whatever tools they had and sharing food (Ramírez, personal communication). As a formula, deeds and food equal *tequio*. Dancers are acquired by this formula through participation in the group.

Where is *tequio* evoked and manifest in Calpulli Tonalehqueh? The presence of *tequio* in the Calpulli Tonalehqueh can be seen in all aspects of the group, as it supports member activities such as births, weddings, graduations, family events, fundraisers, workshops, ceremonies, memorials, and professional work. Innumerable are the occasions of mutual support. As members often say, *Danza* is a way of life, not just an activity or a hobby. In this chapter, I focus on one major Calpulli Tonalehqueh activity that would not be possible without significant buy-in to the *tequio* ideal: the Mexica New Year (MNY) ceremony. Ancient Mexica developed large-scale projects, constructing the largest city in the world and achieving the highest levels of civilization (as evidenced by their astronomy, architecture, science and medicine, agriculture, arts, governance, etc.), using the *calpulli* system and *tequio*. Today, Calpulli Tonalehqueh achieves large-scale cultural productions using contemporary resources.

The annual weekend MNY ceremony organized by Calpulli Tonalehqueh is a remarkable iteration of the *tequio* formula. By *Danza* standards, it is an enormous (nonprofit) event that culminates a year-long planning effort by dozens of volunteers helping with fundraising, dancing, art production, properties, securing space, photography, video production, costume design, organic farming, graphic design, printing, publicity, grant writing, translation, research, babysitting, transportation, sales, resource management, web design, event planning, database maintenance, and so on. Thousands of people, including hundreds of dancers from groups across the United States, attend the event (see figure 3.1).

Similar resources are marshaled when coordinating and executing several other events, ceremonies, and summits headed by Calpulli Tonalehqueh. There are teams of dancers who volunteer time every week, year after year, in service of the *calpulli* ceremonies/events. One can see 20 lead organizers overseeing the efforts of 50 coordinators/ volunteers in service of 500 dancers and 5,000 attendees who will then spread what they take from the ceremony to all their networks. At the heart of everyone's contribution is the deliberate manifestation of *tequitl*, duty, and obligation to the *calpulli*. Remarkably, *tequio* is sustained despite all the frustrations and the fallout that emerge with large undertakings.

Figure 3.1   The photograph depicting a part of the MNY ceremony hosted by Calpulli Tonalehqueh.

Note: At a recent ceremony, nearly 700 *danzantes*, 5,000 community members, a dozen indigenous nations, and numerous artists, activists, merchants, and scholars presented their spirit practice.

There are many *danzantes* who negatively critique Calpulli Tonalehqueh's approach to ceremony, group ideology, and general practice. For instance, in March 2010, the leader of another Aztec dance group in California posted a representative comment on an online blog in response to an invitation he received from Calpulli Tonalehqueh to attend the New Year Ceremony:

> With all due respect, this event seems to grow more and more every year into a corporate-sponsored, Renaissance Fair...for new dancers more interested in showing off their huge *copillis*, and tattoos, rather than praying with compassion, humility, and faith for our agricultural roots of La Danza, Our sacred ancestors, or children and our elders..."maestros" speaking for a price at a corporate-sponsored event...how traditional. Cuauhtémoc is probably rolling in his grave...
>
> Please forgive this old timer, crying in the wilderness of the old ways.
> (cited in Programa Universitario México Nación Multicultural, 2011)

Negative critiques of Calpulli Tonalehqueh and their events are frequent. I have had numerous personal conversations with influential California *Danza* leaders who either boycott or disapprove of the manner in which Calpulli Tonalehqueh conducts their annual ceremony. Criticism comes from groups on both ends of the *Danza* spectrum. For instance, when elements required by the *Conchero* tradition are absent (e.g., a *velación*, or vigil, or reciprocal attendance to other ceremonies), or when elements of the ceremony are deemed to be in excess (e.g., grants, funding sponsors, musical artists, a large marketplace), friction or disparagement ensues. Some lose sight of the dance circle's stated mission or the fact that Calpulli Tonalehqueh is working under a *Mexicayotl* that stands apart from some of longstanding iterations of *Danza*. Calpulli Tonalehqueh forges according to its unique *Mexicayotl* ideology. It strives to reach as many people as possible through their ceremony, touch a huge Mexican American community in the Bay Area, expose the culture to nonindigenous people, partner with community organizations, unite as many *Danza* circles as possible, assemble a huge *tianguis* (marketplace) supporting vendors all related to indigenous culture, organize a workshop series for cultural diffusion, present a concert of conscious-raising musicians, invite numerous indigenous nations to participate, and so on. That strategy is difficult for groups that have operated differently in their tradition. A Bay Area dancer posted her comment on the aforementioned blog to represent these views:

> I have to say, as a *danzante* from another *circlo* in the bayarea [sic], I and many other of my *Danza* brothers and sisters, agree with the general sentiment of his post. Even though this *Calpulli* works hard at putting this *ceremonia* together, a lot of outside *Danzantes* feel that this "*ceremonia*" focuses too much on making a festival out of it. Last year, one of my *danza* friends went to the *Ceremonia* and was shocked to see that the majority of parking was set aside for all the puesto/ vendors. Needless to say, neither [sic], neither she or her famila went this year. Neither did our dancers, but we heard from others that there were a lot of dancers from [sic] of the area, but not many local groups or dancers. I am sorry, but that has to be indicative of something. Although the hosting group is unwilling to admit it, the general feeling among *danzantes* is that it's not a "traditional" or spiritual ceremony anymore. It's just an opportunity to "sell" us *danza*. Mabye [sic] the goal of this ceremony needs to be refocused on just the *La Danza*. (Cuauhtlatoac, 2010)

An undertaking of such ambition is inevitably challenging.

Sometimes the negative evaluations come internally. I certainly have expressed concerns about sustainability. To its credit, Calpulli Tonalehqueh always has postceremony evaluation meetings to discuss opportunities to improve practice. It strives to improve while staying true to its mission.

Evaluations notwithstanding, my aim is to outline the tremendous amount of *tequio* on display in the planning and execution of the MNY ceremony and to argue that this ceremony is a modern-day site for palimpsest. I argue that a close look at everything organized through the MNY reveals a high degree of alignment between the ceremony and the mission of Calpulli Tonalehqueh. It stands as an innovative palimpsest authored by the group. Furthermore, I submit that the reach, scope, and benefits of this *tequio* outweigh any shortcomings alleged by critics of the event.

The MNY Ceremony

I had helped organize and/or attended at least eight of the annual MNY ceremonies.[2] This description focuses mainly on the MNY ceremonies between 2008 and 2012, but includes general components from all the MNY ceremonies Calpulli Tonalehqueh had hosted up to the one on the weekend of March 15, 2014.

It is customary for *Danza* groups to host at least one formal ceremony throughout the year. Most groups host more than one. In California alone, with more than 30 *Danza* groups, this provides year-round opportunities to attend ceremonies. The ceremonies are usually scheduled on Saturdays and are tied to dates established by traditional *Conchero* ceremonial timing (Catholic saint feast days, *4 vientos*), Mexica *veintenas* (20-day "months"), astronomical events, or other established commemorations (e.g., equinoxes, solstices, zeniths, *Día de los Muertos, Despedida de las ánimas, Defensa de Tenochtitlan, Toxkatl, Tlacaxipehualiztli, Xocohuetzi, Cuauhtémoc, Virgen de Zapopan, Virgen de Remedios, Virgen de Guadalupe [Tonantzin]*, and *Niño Limosnerito*).[3]

In the *Conchero* tradition, the concept of obligación is tied to attendance at ceremonies; *Conchero* groups are obligated to attend ceremonies of their *Mesa* (their group) or the allied groups that have supported them in the past. There is a generalized ideal, a generalized norm of reciprocity embedded in ceremony attendance. (You come to my ceremony, I will go to yours.) Each hosting group of a ceremony is expected to provide everything: invitations, space, food, shelter, altar, ceremonial logistics, and so on. Inherent in this cycle of ceremonies is mutuality, *tequio*, and interchange. The effort put in to a ceremony is rewarded 20-fold throughout the year; when each group spends its time, effort, and money to host one ceremony, it will have the opportunity to be guests at 20 or more ceremonies each year. They will be invited, fed, received, and so on. This system has the *tequio* formula embedded.

Apart from their weekly dance *ensayo*,[4] the MNY is Calpulli Tonalehqueh's central activity, their signature event. Calpulli Tonalehqueh plans the entire year for the MNY ceremony they host in mid-March. They organize numerous business and planning meetings, fundraisers, committees, volunteer recruitment, grant writing sessions, and so on. The budget and scale of the MNY ceremony requires a massive *tequio*. No *calpulli* member gets monetary compensation for the great deal of time and energy rendered in service of the *calpulli*. Moreover, the preparation for the MNY ceremony is concurrent to the ongoing management of all other *calpulli* activities, such as weekly *ensayos* and music/dance/philosophy workshops, community performances, and attendance to myriad dance ceremonies. Calpulli Tonalehqueh designs its MNY ceremony around its mission and vision, which centers not only around dance but also on cultural diffusion.

Below I elaborate on discrete elements of the MNY ceremony, remembering that the MNY is multiplex and every component is connected to the sum of the parts. Each of these aspects of the event has a Calpulli Tonalehqueh person in charge of recruiting volunteers and overseeing execution.

Elders. There are *calpulli* members in charge of liaison with other indigenous nations. Elders from as many nations as in the Calpulli Tonalehqueh network are invited to open the MNY weekend with a sunrise ceremony.[5] The MNY ceremony commemorates the beginning of the solar year, which begins the day after the spring equinox. At the MNY sunrise ceremony, Ocelocoatl (the *Tlacatecatl*[6] and elder of Calpulli Tonalehqueh) leads prayers and music in the predawn ceremony and at the greeting of the newborn sun. At that point elders from other nations share messages, prayers, and songs with attendees. Representatives from more than 20 nations typically speak at the sunrise ceremony. For some attendees, this is the most powerful and important part of the weekend. The gathering of elders and the intertribal exchange is closely aligned with Calpulli Tonalehqueh's mission.

Momoztli (**altar**). A traditional altar is erected in the center of the dance circle,[7] next to a fire that has been continuously lit during the four days prior to the MNY. Each year women in the *calpulli* are put in charge of designing, furbishing, recruiting assistants, and assembling the *momoztli*. In the Mexica day count system, reach year is marked on a cycle that combines 1 of 4 "year-bearers" (House, Rabbit, Reed, Flint) and the numbers 1 through 13. Each year a piece of art representing the year-bearer is commissioned and placed at the center of the *momoztli*. Hundreds of flowers are secured for the *momoztli*. In addition, the builders use fruit, dry foods, ceramics, sculptures, cloth, and other materials to create the large work of art/altar. More than 20 volunteers assemble the *momoztli* before the sunrise ceremony and give away its contents at the end.

Arbor. *Calpulli* members design and construct a ceremonial arbor in which the dance ceremony takes place. Volunteers design a circle that has a diameter of more than 104 feet and is made up of rebar stakes, bamboo, reeds, plant bundles, chord, and paper. They harvest the materials and assemble a team of volunteers to construct the arena and the entrance to the arena the day before the ceremony.

Danza. The heart of the MNY ceremony is the Mexica dance component. The whole event, especially the dance, is a reiteration of the large-scale ceremonies that took place in Central México in pre-Cuauhtémoc eras. Calpulli Tonalehqueh makes efforts to invite other dance circles to the ceremony in a formal way. Traditionally, this is done by attending their ceremonies, or *ensayo*, and announcing the invitation and by sending out a formal letter of invitation to other group leaders. Presently, the use of e-mail and social media Websites are utilized to invite dancers and groups. There is a good amount of personal contacting that occurs as well.

Needless to say, the politics around invitations and attendance are challenging, but with those who arrive, Calpulli Tonalehqueh and the *cargos*, or officers in charge of the ceremony, conduct hundreds of dancers over two days of dancing. Five to seven hours of dancing takes place over the weekend. During the dance ceremony, invocations and prayers are made, dancers are placed in multiple concentric circles, ceremonial protocols are followed, dances are passed to the various groups, drummers and musicians play, fire keepers cleanse with incense, and each dance session is completed with an open speaking session called *palabra*. At a typical MNY, more than 25 *Danza* groups from all over California, the United States (e.g., Texas, Illinois, Wisconsin, New York, Minnesota, Washington, and Oregon), and México attend.

Intertribal dance. Before the Mexica dance ceremonies of each day, Calpulli Tonalehqueh invites and sponsors dancers from other indigenous nations to share their songs and dance. The MNY hosts dancers from such nations as the Ohlone, Pomo, Huastec, Pima, Maya, Cree, Diné, Yaqui, and Zuni. These dancers are given space in the agenda and honored as visitors. The presence of other nations at both the sunrise and dance ceremonies aligns with Calpulli Tonalehqueh's mission of panindigenous exchange, honor, and education.

Naming ceremony. In the *Mexicayotl* tradition, the *In Toca In Tocaitl* (naming) ceremony takes place concurrently with the *Danza* ceremony (presently a separate naming ceremony is organized in August). In short, it is a ceremony conducted by Ocelocoatl and numerous volunteers next to the *momoztli*, in the middle of the circle, and during the entire dance portion of the ceremony. At this naming ceremony, dozens of individuals culminate the process of acquiring a Náhuatl name. This ceremony requires its own significant amount of coordination, volunteers, preparation, and planning. Calpulli Tonalehqueh is unique in the *Danza* landscape because it organizes/hosts *In Toca In Tocaitl* ceremonies.

Security. Members of Calpulli Tonalehqueh coordinate volunteers to help keep security at the MNY. The ceremony was hosted recently at the National Hispanic University, San José High School, and Emma Prush Park in San José. Calpulli Tonalehqueh is required to buy insurance, provide security volunteers, and coordinate with the San José Police Department (SJPD) officers. Recently, Calpulli Tonalehqueh partnered with a local community organization working with incarcerated young men looking for a fresh start and a positive path. Calpulli Tonalehqueh has also invited the Harmony Keepers organization as well as the Brown Berets and Black Berets to assist in mentoring and coordination of the security efforts for the weekend. Community leaders as well as some of the young men told me that they gained much from participating in the ceremony.

Workshops. Cultural diffusion and community health are two focal components of the mission of Calpulli Tonalehqueh. To this end, many workshops and educational spaces are included in the MNY weekend. Calpulli Tonalehqueh flies elders in from México and invites local scholars to present various topics of interest to *danzantes*. Workshops take place throughout the weekend, concurrent with the dancing. Topics include drum making, Mexica history, the Aztec calendar, fire keeping, indigenous food and nutrition, human rights violations against indigenous peoples in México, Mexica music, etc. The workshops are well attended, open, and free. The elders are not paid, though they are sometimes offered donations to help them cover their expenses. In addition to these lectures and demonstrations, many children's activities are coordinated. There is an area of the ceremony dedicated to children where Calpulli Tonalehqueh coordinates crafts and other activities with cultural diffusion aims.

Food. Remembering that community work and food equal *tequio*, Calpulli Tonalehqueh makes huge efforts around food design and delivery. At the MNY there are three meals delivered: breakfast for the sunrise ceremony, dinner after the Saturday dance, and lunch on Sunday. Calpulli Tonalehqueh seeks partnerships and sponsors with local food organizations to secure the ingredients and designs menus that are completely organic and indigenous. Over 1,500 plates are prepared and served by teams of kitchen volunteers from Calpulli Tonalehqueh. Anahuacan ingredients such as pumpkin, chia, avocado, tomato, turkey, corn, *mole*, and chocolate make up the menu. Members of Calpulli Tonalehqueh recently leveraged relationship with the directors of a local vocational culinary academy and received culinary student volunteers to prepare food and coordinate the kitchen.

In addition to concerted efforts with the menu, Calpulli Tonalehqueh makes big efforts to manage the waste of the ceremony. It has partnered with the San José Conservation Corps to collect, reuse, and recycle all the waste produced by the ceremony. Volunteers coordinate to sort out the waste. Also, Calpulli Tonalehqueh purchases compostable plates, cups, and cutlery for all their meals. Calpulli Tonalehqueh produces brochures explaining the choices made and the significance of the ingredients selected for the menu and the ways of reducing waste throughout the event. Calpulli Tonalehqueh is conscious of the impact of waste on Mother Earth, and while they host a large event, they take pains to raise awareness and reduce their environmental footprint.

Vendors. Calpulli Tonalehqueh solicits and coordinates more than 30 booths at the MNY. There are generally two types of booths. The first group is made up of merchants selling indigenous art and items. The second is of community organizations promoting health and services in indigenous communities. Calpulli Tonalehqueh accepts the presence of merchants and informational booths only if their business has an indigenous focus or is connected to supporting Mexican-origin community health. Many *danzantes* are local, independent merchants and craftspeople who benefit from having a booth at the MNY.

Music. Calpulli Tonalehqueh coordinates some of the best Mexica musicians to play during the MNY. In particular, Calpulli Tonalehqueh retains Xavier Quijas Yxayotl, a world-traveling, award-winning master musician, who has dedicated his life to learning, playing, and diffusing indigenous Mexican music. At the MNY, he mentors apprentices and showcases instruments, techniques, and histories. In addition to the traditional music of the ceremony, Calpulli Tonalehqueh always invites modern indigenous musicians and artists to play during the meals and breaks in the weekend. Many groups participate, such as Grupo Tribu, El Vuh, Quese IMC, Skylar Wolf, Yaocoatl, Adrian Tepehua Vargas, Fuga, and many Northern drum circles. Calpulli Tonalehqueh has a music workshop that has produced several singers and musicians who are also showcased during the weekend. All the music is a complimentary, educative, and powerful component of the ceremony. In 2014, Calpulli Tonalehqueh hosted the most accomplished Mexica music groups in the world: Tribu. The education initiatives and space carved out for traditional music forms facilitated by Calpulli Tonalehqueh are notable.

Publicity. Calpulli Tonalehqueh, on top of inviting as many dance circles and indigenous nations as they can, aims to have a large general audience attend the event. Calpulli Tonalehqueh leaders recognize that modern Mexicas are a minority even in the Mexican-origin community and that many Mexican-origin individuals are disconnected from their indigenous past. They hope to attract as many Mexicans and Mexican Americans as possible so that they may come and reconnect with their cultural heritage. This is in line with *Mexicayotl* ideals. In addition, Calpulli Tonalehqueh hopes the MNY is an occasion where all communities, other nations, and the mainstream come and learn about these traditions in an effort to promote crosscultural understanding and the dissolution of crosscultural barriers. To these ends, Calpulli Tonalehqueh coordinates large publicity efforts. Dancers design publicity materials and then seek out venues for their deployment. Calpulli Tonalehqueh partners with several newspapers, both small and large, many television stations, radio stations, and Websites to publicize the MNY. Teams of dancers are sent out to give press releases and interviews, put up posters, visit other groups, and invite people to the ceremony. Furthermore, the group prints thousands of high-quality postcards to distribute by hand. The scale at which Calpulli Tonalehqueh does every aspect of the ceremony, as evidenced by its publicity efforts, is striking.

Tequio. Ceremonies come in sizes big and small. There is a general template for ceremonies, but dance circles continually adapt, expand, imitate, and/or innovate the template. Calpulli Tonalehqueh is ambitious with its ceremony, often pioneering its elements. Many of the designs are not well received, and with so many moving parts, there are increased possibilities for mistakes, oversights, and friction between people. To their credit, Calpulli Tonalehqueh evaluates the ceremony year after year. Members are aware of the challenges, the burnout, and the criticisms. Each year they attempt to recalibrate the ceremony. Almost everything they include in the MNY has positive ideals and stem from models provided by the long history of general Mexica, *Mexicayotl*, and *Danza* ceremonies. One of the most important achievements of the MNY is the annual display of *tequio* by members of Calpulli Tonalehqueh.

Calpulli Tonalehqueh's MNY ceremony is just one example of the invocation of *tequio* and the multitude of collaborative efforts of the *calpulli* members. Powerful stories can be relayed about the significant ways that members come together to support events other than the MNY ceremony such as Yuwipi healing ceremonies, Hanblecha vision quests, Sun dance ceremonies, Temascal sweat lodge ceremonies, fundraisers for Autism research, birthdays, graduations, weddings, Powwows, and death memorials. These events and the cooperative requirements of their execution are all locations for active, interdisciplinary, and multimodal learning. With children included, members leverage their talents for the benefit and support of others.

Tequio Understandings

In this chapter, I have discussed the ancient concept of *tequio* and the undertaking of the MNY ceremony by Calpulli Tonalehqueh as an example of the manifestation of modern *calpulli tequio*. I have been in on the meetings, lectures, e-mail conversations, and the casual conversations evoking the word *tequio*. I reviewed all of these occasions and culled the themes that emerged. I provided this information to signal an aspect of the *calpulli* palimpsest, where members recover an ancient concept and reinterpret it in their community efforts.

The first theme I identified in *calpulli* member conceptions of *tequio* is in reference to ancient indigenous community support obligations to public works projects. One dancer said *tequio* is

> *una forma organizada de trabajo en beneficio colectivo. Consiste en que los integrantes de una comunidad deben aportar materiales o su fuerza de trabajo para realizar o construir una obra comunitaria. Siempre trabajar en equipo y para el equipo. Esta es la forma orginial en que nuestros ancestros trabajaban y les funcionaba bien.*

> [an organized form of work in benefit of the collective. It consists in that the members of a community should give materials or labor to

achieve or construct a community project. Always work as a team and for the team. This is the original form in which our ancestors worked and it functioned well for them.] (Fernández, personal communication, my translation)

Second, many dancers talked about the idea that *tequio* can take on many forms because a *calpulli* is more than just dancers. The *calpulli* includes young and old, dancers and allies, individuals and whole families. Each one of these units can contribute. According to Omicuauhtli, *tequio* is

the individual as well as the communal work that one does to continue the work that we have inherited from our parents and great grandparent and so forth. This duty or *tequio* is not limited to *Danza* but also to helping in a way that you bring your experience to the circle from dancing, singing, working, chopping wood, attending sweats, etc. (personal communication)

As Omicuauhtli alludes, *tequio* can operate on two scales: the group and the individual. Yapaltecatl agrees that

it implies community or collective work...it also means your own personal/individual work, like inner endurance and energy while in the circle, but also the energy you put into the circle such as the dance or drum you offer and how fast, slow or graceful you do it, which influences the whole. (personal communication)

Any contribution a person can make is valued, whether it is organizing part of a large event or offering a song, a prayer, a dance, or a drumbeat. Taken together, the small contributions add up to large achievements.

Third, members of Calpulli Tonalehqueh understand not only the multiple levels on which *tequio* operates but also the connection between *tequio* and the larger mission of the *calpulli*. Xochicuauhtli believes that *tequio*

refers more to the specific specialty or niche of work that some people become renowned for. To me it seems like work that is done by a person to achieve the overall mission of the *calpulli* and the people. It can be general like cleaning and setting up, but it can also be specialized like using medicinal herbs or conducting elaborate ceremonies. (personal communication)

On that same theme, Mitlalpilli discusses the communal work of *tequio* in a pragmatic way, explaining it is a means to achieving important work. He adds that *tequio* is also "the ability to use the people power to make something big and beautiful for the community" (personal communication). Buying-in to this ideology can produce momentous results.

The fourth theme involves tying *tequio* to generosity. Often the focus of *tequio* is on community health, on making a positive impact in the lives of others, on remembering traditions, or on the selfless contribution of talents. Ollinkoatl echoes this idea thus:

> For me I see *tequio* and *calpulli* as synonymous. I see people with great love for their community and heritage. This often times motivates them to give much more of themselves than they receive, often times depriving their own personal lives and families so that these traditions and knowledge can live on. (personal communication)

Another member, Cuauhcihuatl, supports Ollinkoatl, explaining that in helping others and remembering cultural traditions, *calpulli* members end up helping themselves. According to her, *tequio* is

> the organizational work that benefits each and every one of us. We work as a team, a *calpulli* to make things happen that benefit the community and ourselves. It means the work that needs to be done for the ones who don't know by the ones who do so we can share what is known. (personal communication)

A former member of Calpulli Tonalehqueh once told me that she conceives *tequio* as a set of "efforts which support, nurture, and bring wellness to a community" (Yellowwolf, personal communication).

Finally, I acknowledge that the quantity and scale of activities endeavored by Calpulli Tonalehqueh can tax members. I had numerous conversations with former and current *calpulli* members who identified troubling trends. They identified a cycle of burnout for many people. Many people who join the group—mainly as newcomers to *Danza*—are eager to learn dance and history, to experience spirituality and ceremony, and to contribute to the planning and execution of the group, but soon complain that the size of the events and the expectations are unwieldy, unsustainable, and they feel exploited. Many veteran members of Calpulli Tonalehqueh experience jadedness. Whenever group decisions are imposed, or group voices are ignored, or workloads are imbalanced, member disillusionment increases to the point that some people leave the group. Speaking to this point, one of the founders of the group discusses *tequio* and vision alignment:

> It depends on people's current level of involvement and willingness to help in which ever way that can. On the negative side of this *calpulli*, the leadership's vision is not shared by all, and that causes people not to participate with the *tequio*, and in fact causes people to feel alienated, as is evident with many past members.

Though many of the members of Calpulli Tonalehqueh are happy to contribute and recognize that the pooling of resources can produce powerful achievements like the MNY, the work of the *calpulli* has to be constantly calibrated and the group must monitor its equilibrium to ensure that its efforts are sustainable.

External and internal criticisms exist, but Calpulli Tonalehqueh perseveres, possibly because of their foundations in millenary structures or the perseverance of leaders who have brought vision into the group, but certainly because of communal goodwill and the energy of collective work.

Sustainability: a Palimpsest

As I contemplate the concept of *tequio* and how it operates palimpsestically in Calpulli Tonalehqueh, the theme of sustainability arises. *Tequio* sustains *calpulli* efforts geared toward cultural, community, ceremonial, and environmental sustainability. If *calpulli* is the form, the organizational model Calpulli Tonalehqueh recreates, then *tequio* is the modus operandi.

Tequio is central to the environments constructed by Calpulli Tonalehqueh. The social nature of *tequio* makes all group activities holistic educational environments, involving cultural transmission and occasions for education. Membership in Calpulli Tonalehqueh requires continual personal contributions to the construction of the *calpulli* and the achievement of the activities. People are acquired by this ideal. The hope is that everyone benefits personally after contributing to collective efforts directed to the benefit of the community at large. In the case of the MNY, the *tequio* is directed at large-scale cultural productions, which are a cultural diffusion for the education of the community and ceremony for a meaningful continuation of cultural traditions.

In the process of pooling human resources year-round, conditions for the education of the mind, body, and spirit are created. Countless educational moments are built when, for example, people collaborate on fabricating attire, work in the kitchen, play music in ensemble, build the arbor, erect the *momoztli*, enter the *temascal* (sweat lodge) together, stand in the drum cadre, follow with the multitude of dancers, support the naming ceremony, mentor youth, supervise the children's area, engage elders, sell wares, write grants, or coordinate the workshops.

As I reflect upon both the multifaceted interpretations of *tequio* and the innovative ways that Calpulli Tonalehqueh organizes *tequio* in events like the MNY, I see another case of palimpsest. In the first place, Calpulli Tonalehqueh is active in their recovery of the term *tequio*. The term is ancient and also used in indigenous communities in México, but it is not a widespread term in the US *Danza* landscape. Calpulli Tonalehqueh, in their construction of a *calpulli* palimpsest, reintroduces the term and promotes it as central to its mission. It fosters a "one for all" mentality, where no one gets monetary compensation and yet there is a payoff—individual to each person—for the enormous amount of time, labor, and sacrifice offered to the events.

Second, it is clear that Calpulli Tonalehqueh marshals *tequio* in service of their *Danza* palimpsest. The MNY is, in and of itself, a multilayered event, but as a whole it presents a modern iteration of pre-Cuauhtémoc ceremonies where thousands of dancers participate, where international dignitaries are hosted and honored, where games and entertainment compliment the ceremonies, where markets and exchange take place, and where innovation is constant. In more recent times, *Conchero* ceremonies have seen change, and the *Mexicayotl* tradition has made an impact on the cultural diffusion, involvements, and ceremonial components of *Danza* circles. Calpulli Tonalehqueh receives those parts of their heritage and endeavors to continue in dynamic ways. Calpulli Tonalehqueh seeks to honor and remember the essence of ancient components of ceremonial gatherings but does so with the materials at hand in their contemporary context. When Calpulli Tonalehqueh make community partnerships, establish an intertribal sunrise ceremony, utilize multiple media outlets and online social networking, partner with organizations for fundraising and sponsorship, provide spaces for vendors and workshops and native musical artists, or dream of making their event the largest Aztec dance ceremony in the United States, they do so by overcoming most of the inevitable pitfalls of ego, politics, and exploitation, but with the noble intentions of helping communities move forward. In the end, each activity of Calpulli Tonalehqueh dynamically produces through *tequio* is another entry in the palimpsest of *Danza*.

Calpulli Tonalehqueh, through events such as the MNY, successfully responds to historical and community needs. Through their *tequio*, they hope to resist the erasure of indigenous life ways. They hope to connect citizens in the larger Mexican-origin community to their cultural heritage. They hope to dissolve some of the barriers between nations and ethnicities through cultural diffusion, inclusion, and education. They support youth in need. They capitalize on the wisdom of elders. They support indigenous merchants and community activists. They claim space in a metropolitan city. They remember environmental concerns, and they help sustain the perpetuation of Mexica ceremonies and spirituality. Calpulli Tonalehqueh innovates, appropriates, and resists. Despite the mistakes, friction, critics, and other flaws in execution, Calpulli Tonalehqueh leverages the vast resources of its membership and moves forward together.

4
Tlacahuapahualiztli (The Art of Educating a Person)

A word for education in Náhuatl is *tlacahuapahualiztli*, meaning the art of raising or educating a person. It refers to the education broadly defined. *Tlacahuapahualiztli* in pre-Cuauhtémoc Anáhuac began at home, was supported by schools, and was reinforced in community living. Today, much of the teaching and learning that takes place in Calpulli Tonalehqueh is not explicit; rather, it is informal and experiential. However, there are several *calpulli* enterprises designed around formal and semiformal education. Intentional about organized cultural transmission, Calpulli Tonalehqueh programs educational environments (e.g., parenting classes, agricultural partnerships, music/art workshops, philosophy classes) with curricula that are supplemental if not alternative to those found in mainstream US schools as they are based in indigenous cosmology, history, agriculture, and art. In yet another way, a palimpsest is written as members of Calpulli Tonalehqueh look back to the schooling systems of ancient México as guidelines for their own organization.

The Classic Mexica Structure of Formal Schooling

All authorities on ancient México agree upon the central role the *calpulli* enjoyed in support of formal education in ancient Central México and the important integration of teachers and schools with the community. The same early colonial scholars who registered the features of *calpultin* necessarily discuss institutions of formalized learning. The most common bases of scholarship on Mexica education are the sixteenth-century Codex Mendoza (Berdan and Anawalt, 1997), the writings of Diego Durán (a Dominican priest who came to the continent as a child, learned Náhuatl, and later wrote about the customs of the people), and the narratives of Bernardino de Sahagún[1] who undertook a systematic investigation of life in México with interviews of native informants in the mid-sixteenth century and published over 1,000 handwritten pages, which included hundreds of images in a 12-volume work.[2]

In *History of the Indies of New Spain*, Durán (1581/1995) offers conclusions about how ceremony was connected to all schooling in ancient Mexica society. There was no separation between art, dance, song, work, school, family, and community. Education in Mexica society was wide-ranging and integrated. Everyone played an important role in sustaining the institution. Durán pointed out that community elders were intimately involved in the teaching and disciplining of youth who generally attended three levels of schooling (*cuicacalli, telpochcalli,* and *calmecac*). In fact, school attendance was strictly compulsory, and foregoing it was punishable by law.

Next, in *General History of the Things of New Spain*, Sahagún (1992) details that parents of a newborn child would meet with teachers, offer gifts, and promise to support the formal education of the child. The place of teachers was an exalted one. He wrote about the strict discipline encountered at school, where children boarded, shared chores, taught younger students as they advanced, and worked in teams on community service projects (a status quo that would have made John Dewey proud). Sahagún highlighted the manner in which education was tailored to gender and how the institutions of higher learning were especially rigorous and expansive in their curricula.

Through another lens, Ignacio Márquez Rodiles (1990) and Jaques Soustelle (1970) wrote about how increasing urbanization changed *calpulli* life by compelling the population away from a connection to land through direct participation in agriculture toward an urban life focused on service to the city and state complex. They argued that schools and neighborhoods (*calpultin*) changed to meet these needs.

Scholars in the past 115 years have debated the elements that constituted the formal centers of learning in Anáhuac, in areas such as ages of attendance, admission policies, single-sex education, curriculum, religious aspects, military purposes, vocational training, proliferation, and urbanization (Damián Juárez, 1994; Díaz Infante, 1982; Larralde Sáenz, 1988; López Austin, 1985a, 1985b; Oltra Perales,

1977; Ordóñez, 1992; Reagan, 2005). There are competing and often contradictory conclusions about these items.

Putting these debates aside for a moment, I focused my review of ancient Mexica schooling on the terminology and organization of the educational program to ascertain ideological elements. I acknowledge that generalizing is difficult given the flexibility of the *calpulli* system where the teleology of each pre-Cuauhtémoc *calpulli* and each school therein employed context-dependent design. That said, there are several findings I submit.

Miguel León Portilla (1980, 2001), a preeminent scholar of Náhuatl life and culture, argued successfully that the official and everyday mission of formal education in pre-Cuauhtémoc Mexica society was to form an individual who was humble, compassionate, well-rounded, and hardworking. The concept and process of *tlacahuapahualiztli* leaves the educators and the location of education intentionally vague. It allows for a person to be formed with everyone, by everyone. Education occurs in all activities, including schools, but not exclusively. Focusing on what terminology reveals, León Portilla (1961, 2001) relayed that schoolmasters in Mexica schools aspired to two specific principals: *ixtlamachiliztli* (the art of imparting wisdom to a person) and *yolmelahualiztli* (the art of "straightening the heart" of another). The ideal individual was one with a strong character and a compassionate heart, expressed in the idea of *in ixltli, in yollotl*, one's heart and one's countenance (read: identity/character). Professors at the schools provided rigorous physical, philosophical, moral, and natural lessons. The elders of the community taught the young with guessing games, idioms, epic poems, songs, and public lectures, called *huehuetlatolli*, venerable teachings from elders.

Furthermore, León Portilla (1999b) performed an ethnolinguistic analysis of the synonyms that Náhuatl speakers had for a teacher in order to arrive at a deeper understanding of the cultural precepts behind the ideology of formal education. He highlighted some of the many words for a teacher found in early colonial texts:

- *Temachtiani*: s/he who knows the canons and measures
- *Teixcuitiani*: s/he who makes others establish an identity
- *Teixtlamachtiani*: s/he who gives wisdom to the identity of others; s/he who makes others wise in their character
- *Tetezcahuiani*: s/he who puts a mirror in front of others
- *Netlacaneco* (*Itech*): (thanks to them) a person's desire is actualized
- *Tlayolpachiuitia*: s/he who makes hearts strong
- *Tlamatinime*: wise elder

Taken together, the role of a teacher was to impart wisdom, be rigorous so that a student displays strong personal conduct. The model citizen has discipline, a strong character, a good heart, humility, self-reflection, carefulness, and knowledge of the natural world through their teachers, parents, and community. This ideal cuts across lineage, status, occupation, gender, and school. The ideology and aims of *in ixtli in yollotl* are consonant with families (*cenyeliztli*) and *calpulli* school aims.

Recently, *Temachtiani* Ocelocoatl has given many *huehuetlatolli* (lectures) on his visits with Calpulli Tonalehqueh, including the ones that coincided with what I heard when I sat down with him in August 2006 and asked him to talk about formal schooling and the "curriculum" of *Danza*.[3] He explained that, starting at birth, parents consulted a *tonalpouhque* (scholar trained in calendar and astrological reading) to name and discuss the personal/professional destiny of the child. They also visited a woman therapist to discuss the child's health and upbringing. With insights from their elders, parents raised the child at home.

Mexica *calpultin* each had several schools depending on population size. At about four to seven years of age, *all* children went to the *cuicacalli* (the house of song), where they learn history, mathematics, physiology, poetry, and cosmology through songs and dance. At the *cuicacalli*, children learned language and ceremony, patterns and discipline, history and exercise, all through vehicles that provided these effectively: singing and dancing. *Danza* was an integral part of all life, from birth to death. It continues to be a vehicle for education today.

At around seven years of age and according to gender, children advanced to one of two places: the *telpochcalli* (the house of the young men) or the *cihuacalco* (the women's priory). The curriculum was rigorous but differentiated. The young men learned astronomy, mathematics, philosophy, and poetry as a base curriculum, as well as a variety of vocational trades such as carpentry, metallurgy, painting, agriculture, animal reproduction, physical education, zoology, archery, hunting, and fishing. In terms of the *cihuacalco*, the young women learned mathematics and humanities as well, but took courses that counterbalanced the curriculum at the *telpochcalli*, such as biology, culinary arts, medicine, botany, weaving, hairdressing, feather work, and reproductive science.

Aside from academic and vocational training, community service (*tequio*) was mandatory at the *telpochcalli* and *cihuacalco*. Young men and women were required to gather firewood for the community, light the public lanterns, help at the *teocalli* (sacred building), sweep streets, participate on public works projects, clean the public restrooms, and care for the elders or infants.[4]

Additionally, young men had a physical education that included sporting and military training. Throughout this adolescence, school officials got to know their pupils well, observed their aptitudes, and recommended further studies in the *calmecac*. The *calmecac* was the institution of higher learning.

I acknowledge that there is much debate in the scholarship about who was allowed to attend the *calmecac*. Some scholars (c.f. Carrasco and Broda, 1982) say that only the children of the "nobles" are allowed to attend. The debate centers around what the terms *pilli* and *macehualli* mean. Some scholars contend that they mean noble and commoner, respectively. Others say that studies at the *calmecac* were open to all and that those terms differentiate graduates of the *calmecac* and those who did not attend because they chose to go back to their *calpulli* to begin their profession. The former position presupposes a deeply stratified Mexica society, one described in Western terms. The latter position stems from the work of *Mexicayotl* scholars like Ocelocoatl (personal communication), Ignacio Romerovargas Yturbide (1957, 1959, 1978), and Eulalia Guzmán (1989) who argued that ancient Mexica society had much flatter hierarchies and democratic and socialist governance. They also argued that students who emerged from the *telpochcalli* or the *cihuacalco* did so with a significant set of skills and a specific vocation. These graduates would be marriage-eligible and would receive land and a home back with their *calpulli*. Meanwhile, students who wished to continue higher education and were recommended by their secondary teachers could go on to the *calmecac*. With this as a framework, it follows that *calmecac* studies would be open to any student who desired to attend and had demonstrated scholarly achievement in specific areas of study (for more information about governance in Mexica society, see chapter 5).

Ocelocoatl argues that doubt must be cast on any schooling conclusions based exclusively on incomplete and skewed accounts by Sahagún and Durán: "They did not fully understand the terminology, cosmology, traditions, structures, and systems and their accounts are brief and incomplete" (personal communication). For example, no Spanish colonial authors mentioned the *cihuacalco*, the secondary school for young women, and yet we know from other sources, including the oral tradition, that it existed. Schooling for women did not fit the Western paradigm, and some argue they had neither eyes to see it nor ways to describe it. This is replicated for many aspects of Mexica society including schooling. I believe that education was public, compulsory, and open, and we will continue the review of ancient Mexica schooling with these assumptions.

Each *calpulli* fed into at least one *calmecac* supported by the whole community run by professional educators. Students in the *calmecac* specialized in one of four areas that corresponded to the four parts of Mexica cosmology in a similar way that today's higher education students select a major area of study. Generally, there is (1) a college of humanities that includes poetry, art, history, and music connected to the concept of wisdom, *Quetzalcoatl*; (2) a college of psychology with studies having to do with a person's personal and internal self, or the science of *tezcatlipoca*, the mirror's smoking; (3) a college of natural sciences that includes the study of medicine, agriculture, botany, astrology, and so on, or the sciences of regeneration, or *xipe totec*; and (4) a college of political science with its branches of administration, business, resource management, leadership, international relations, military arts, and so on, all in the domain of the concept of *huitilozpochtli*, human will power. After emerging from intensive studies at the *calmecac*, graduates were required to deliver service to the *calpulli* and teach in the *cuicacalli* and other schools. Graduates are also compelled to take office on councils and lead the people in their areas of expertise. This sequence is illustrated in figure 4.1.

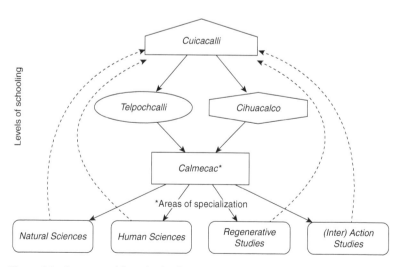

Figure 4.1   Sequence of formal schooling in pre-Cuauhtémoc central México.

Calpulli Tonalehqueh Efforts to Shape Semblances and Hearts

Moving into the present, I detail the formal and semiformal education palimpsest of Calpulli Tonalehqueh who boasts several learning
enterprises. In this text I have written about learning environments
built around the concept of *calpulli* and around the activities requiring
tequio, like the MNY ceremony. In the coming chapters, I discuss the
leadership activities, *ensayo*, public lectures, and the naming ceremony
as palimpsests. Here I focus on four sites organized for *tlacahuapahualiztli*, cultural transmission, and building capacity in members for
a more full participation in a modern Mexica life. First, a *calpulli* parent support group called In Ixtli In Yollotl is where members meet so
that their children can be socialized though contact with each other
and in ethnocentric activities. This group is also a venue for discussing
and exploring ways that *calpulli* children can be raised in a traditional
Mexica ways. Second, there has been organic farming and nutrition
initiative in the group. Calpulli Tonalehqueh members are partnering
with community organizations and learning how to grow their own
food, about traditional Mexica diets, and have been researching the
nexus between nutrition, ceremony, learning, and dance. Third, the
group has a special interest group that actively researches and discusses
Mexica philosophy, called *Consejo Quetzalcoatl* (Council of Precious
Knowledge). Connected to this arm of the *calpulli* are the frequent
and formal lectures organized for elders who arrive from México to
expound on various topics of Mexica life and culture. The *huehuetlatolli* are well attended (up to 80 participants), especially those delivered
by Ocelocoatl (see chapter 7). As stated previously, these are workshops by elders, with such topics as woodcarving, the myth of human
sacrifice, music, the Aztec calendar, the invasion of Anáhuac, traditional medicine, and nutrition. They take place at the cultural expositions and the MNY ceremonies organized by the *calpulli* and also at
various other times during the year. Fourth, the *calpulli* has instituted
a weekly music class to teach traditional songs and instruments. The
calpulli's *cuicapiqui* (musical leader) heads the class at a local community center. Here we have evidence of *calpulli* structure/roles leading to *tequio* toward education. The *calpulli* also holds several arts
and crafts workshops led by the core members on making ceremonial
attire, leather work, feather work, jewelry, beadwork, woodwork, and
whatever is needed to prepare the accouterments of ceremony. These
workshops are held as needed, usually when newer dancers seeking to

make their own attire for ceremonies gather enough momentum to ask for and populate the workshops. All together, Calpulli Tonalehqueh is demonstrating how community groups can provide its members a supplemental, comprehensive, organic, indigenous, and alternative education. I describe them in turn.

In Ixtli in Yollotl

There are many children in Calpulli Tonalehqueh. Dancers view their own nuclear family as a *calpulli* and the larger Calpulli Tonalehqueh as a larger alliance of families. Given that the culture of *Danza* is outside of the mainstream, dancers are often concerned with resisting the forces of mainstream US assimilation acting on their children. Peaking in the winter of 2008, a movement around child-rearing consolidated inside Calpulli Tonalehqueh. The activities had been growing, but members formalized an organization during that time. Nesaualcoyotl, Tleyollotl, and their son, Ollinteotl, instituted a group called In Ixtli In Yollotl designed to support *calpulli* parents in raising their children in a modern Mexica way. They led many activities including singing, crafts, fieldtrips, meals, gardening, calendar keeping, and dance, all centered on the children of the *calpulli*. A February 2008 memo from a dancer inviting members to the activities reads thus:

> Hola Calpulli,
>
> We encourage all parents to bring their children to the Family support group on Tuesdays @ Ollinteotl, Tletlyollot ihuan Nezahualcoyotl's (sic) home. They have so kindly opened up their home so we can work together to prepare our children for the future.
>
> Our current goal is to teach the children of our calpulli a song so they can present @ this year's Azteca Mexica New Year.
>
> Tlazo camati

Notable is the indication that parents in In Ixtli In Yollotl look to the future of *calpulli* children.[5] As with ancient Mexica *cuicacalli* (house of song), music is the starting point of education for *calpulli* children.

The collectively drafted goals of the In Ixtli In Yollotl group include:

- *huehuetlatolli: La base de la educación, conocimiento, y consejo* [the base of education, knowledge, and advise]
- *conocer nuestra identidad cósmica* [know our cosmic identity]

- *aprender a utilizar el* tonalmachiotl *en nuestras vidas a diario* [learn to use the *tonalmachiotl* in our daily lives]
- *respetar el ser padres como lo sagrado que es* [respect being parents and how sacred that is]
- *reconocer nuestros hijos como nuestro otro* tezcatlipoka *(espejo)* [recognize that our children are our other *Tezcatlipoca* (mirrors)]
- *conocernos como ser receptores y tramitadores de energía* [know ourselves as recipients and transmitters of energy]
- *vivir en harmonía con todos los seres cósmicos* [live in harmony with other cosmic beings]
- *hablar Náhuatl* [speak Náhuatl]
- *practicar Mantenimiento Agrícola* [practice agricultural maintenance]
- *ser merecedores de la Danza guerrera:* teopixtlalli [work to deserve *teopixtlalli*, the sacred dance]
- *mantener una vida y alimentación en balance* [maintain a balanced life and nutrition]
- *in xochitl in cuicatl: conocer la filosofía poética (la sabiduría del Anáhuac), viviendo en el camino de las flores y el canto* [live on the path wisdom, of flowers and song, getting to know Anáhuac's poetic philosophical tradition]
- *mantener la ceremonia en nuestras vidas a diario* [maintain ceremony in our daily life]
- *practicar el tequio, tomando responsabilidad por nuestros pasos y decisiones siempre pensando en los niños siete generaciones en adelante* [practice *tequio*, taking responsibility for our footprints and decisions, always thinking about children seven generations into the future]

The goals focus on family roles, *calpulli* life, Mexica traditions, health and nutrition, agriculture, language, and dance. We see this same focus in many of Calpulli Tonalehqueh activities, inherited from the *Mexicayotl* movement, and the ideals of ancient Mexica society.

The leaders of the In Ixtli In Yollotl group said that they referenced Websites like caminoflorido.com for information during discussions around the mission of their group. One quotation they highlighted refers to a Mexica life centered on children, resistant to the obstacles of modernity, and is cited as inspiration for the work of the parents in Calpulli Tonalehqueh:

> *El verdadero objetivo de esta vida rodea a los hijos. Lo importante en este mundo es aprender a dar nuestro amor, eso es todo; los enormes rascacielos, los veloces cuetes y los intentos por ir a la luna son insignificantes, tanto se podría lograr si cada uno solo diera de si, pero es difícil*

*convencerlos cuando se ha creado un mundo de concreto y un ritmo de
vida que nos impide pensar. (www.caminoflorido.com)*

[The true objective of this life surrounds children. The important thing
in this world is learning to give our love, that is it; the enormous sky-
scrapers, the swift rockets, and the attempts to reach the moon are
insignificant. All this would be possible if everyone only gave a part of
themselves, but it is difficult to convince them when a world of con-
crete has been created and the rhythm of life impedes our thinking. (my
translation)

Members of In Ixtli In Yollotl organized various activities where
calpulli children could interact, socialize, and be surrounded by Mexica
culture. For instance, in an effort to offer an alternative to Halloween
and the large amounts of candy that children might consume, In
Ixtli In Yollotl hosted an autumn equinox celebration at the home of
Nesaualcoyotl and Tleyollotl. In addition to weekly song/music gatherings, other monthly activities would follow. The group took *calpulli*
children on outings to see indigenous musical acts, birdwatching, nature
hikes, seed planting, and so forth. They held workshops and discussions on reusable diapers, beauty and health products, switching to the
Mexica calendar system, seeds, water, home schooling, and nutrition.

Also, Nesaualcoyotl and Tleyollotl secured a clean natural gas van
and offered it to the *calpulli* for carpooling to *ensayo* and other events.
Currently, the couple is converting their home into an eco-home (rain-
water collection, composting, solar power, etc.) and are looking to
partner with a local elementary school to make the house a demonstration area for environmentally friendly living and indigenous plants
and agriculture. Education is central to them. In a conversation around
my project, Tleyollotl conveyed that the couple was involved in many
types of activism but that education was primary.

We have been putting more effort in the educational part too, trying to
celebrate the seasons with other families, or *veintenas*, and if for whatever reason we have the weekend free, we take advantage and organize
something. There has been lately a lot of focus on education for us.
We feel that everything else we want to do falls underneath education,
so we just focus on education and everything else will come. (personal
communication)

Bridging ancient Mexica schooling models and the future steps of
their *semillas*, members of Calpulli Tonalehqueh established a palimpsestic organization centered on children and holistic family health. The

ancient ideal of In Ixtli In Yollotl is actualized in the group. On one of my visits to their home, Nesaualcoyotl explained:

> we can't lose focus, it's the children, because we can learn on our own but we're pretty much out-of-the-way; it's like we need to pass it down and be disciplined enough to help and not just know it, but know how to pass it down, learn how to teach and work with children, to work with their spirit. And not just curriculum, but learn to involve all different aspects of nature and life, and just follow their hearts instead of just being strict. The discipline that us as parents need to learn is how to work with children. (personal communication)

It is also important to note that In Ixtli In Yollotl was established through *tequio*. This couple and others offered their skills, their resources, their *tequio* to other members. As more than just a dance group, Calpulli Tonalehqueh's structure and ideology enables its members to develop groups that emerge out of individual and community-wide concerns.

Calpulli Agriculture

Next, many structured educational environments around agriculture were established in Calpulli Tonalehqueh. Nezaualkoyotl and Tleyollotl, along with Mitlalpilli, were again at the front of these efforts. Several *calpulli* initiatives around agricultural education were successful, including organic food distribution, home gardens, community gardens, workshops, and education.

Tleyollotl and Nesaualcoyotl established an organization called *Mantenimiento Agrícola Nacido en el Ombligo (de la familia)* [agricultural maintenance born from the navel (of the family)], which was a food distribution service, a community-supported agriculture initiative with Ledesma Family Farm/Splendid Salad that provided organic produce to Calpulli Tonalehqueh and the local community. The goal was to reduce family carbon footprints by supporting local farmers, in this case a Mexican-origin family farm, and to provide healthy, organic food to *calpulli* members. Connected to these efforts, Tleyollotl and Nezaualkoyotl developed two Websites: losantepasados.org and, later, chikomekoatl.org. These Websites, along with numerous presentations from the couple, were educational spaces for members of Calpulli Tonalehqueh. The couple maintained an informational booth at many MNY ceremonies to inform the public about Mexica nutrition, agriculture, and environmentally friendly health and beauty products.

In addition to these spaces, Calpulli Tonalehqueh partnered with a local organization called Green Table that provided many *calpulli* families with free raised plant beds for their backyards along with seeds and workshops on home gardening/agriculture. Calpulli Tonalehqueh families began growing traditional Mexica plants, herbs, fruits, and vegetables. Connected to this effort, *Temachtiani* Ocelocoatl gives lectures on the array of traditional Mexica foods.

Also, Calpulli Tonalehqueh secured land at the community garden at Emma Prusch Park in San José so that *calpulli* members can grow traditional Mexica foods. This effort saw less participation. Nonetheless, it demonstrates the desire of Calpulli Tonalehqueh leaders to return to agriculture, land-based activities, and indigenous nutrition and health.

All these efforts are palimpsests, where children and their parents create educational spaces about traditional Mexica agriculture and nutrition and then incorporate these practices into their lives. These lessons are then shared with the larger community. This focus carries over to the MNY ceremony booths, menu, and waste management.

Music Classes

Xochicuauhtli, along with other Calpulli Tonalehqueh leaders, instituted weekly music classes. Recognizing that music and songs were central in pre-Cuauhtémoc Mexica schooling and ceremonies, and that powerful cultural, visceral, and spiritual experiences are made available through music, Calpulli Tonalehqueh leaders organized *tequio* for these music classes. Many members of Calpulli Tonalehqueh are gifted multilingual singers, musicians, instrument makers, drummers, and teachers. Their skills are constantly leveraged for the good of the whole. Xochicuauhtli and his committee secured space, grants from the county department of health, and assistance from the larger network of Mexica musicians in California to produce a strong musical cadre for Calpulli Tonalehqueh. They play together weekly in sessions that are free and open to the community. They also constantly seek out veteran musicians like Xavier Quijas Yxayotl, Grupo Tribu, Martin Espino, Ernesto Hernández Olmos, Ocelocoatl, and many others for musical collaborations and lessons. Also, Calpulli Tonalehqueh members fundraised to purchase an sound amplification system for the *calpulli* musicians.

The singers and musicians dedicated play at each of the weekly *ensayos*, at the MNY ceremony, at other *calpulli* events, and during community performances. *Danzantes* recover Náhuatl as well as

Mexica poetry, lyrics, instruments, musical structures, and spirituality in a contemporary context.

Beyond child-rearing, agriculture, and music, Calpulli Tonalehqueh organizes many other formal and semiformal spaces for cultural education. There are workshops organized for sewing and crafting ceremonial attire, constructing drums and learning drum beats, loom building and beadwork, feather work, leather work, jewelry, and so on. The vast expertise of many veteran dancers and artists is exploited for the education of novice members in these areas.

In addition, members of Calpulli Tonalehqueh have established yet another educational branch called Consejo Quetzalcoatl (Council of Precious Knowledge). Led by Chimalkoyotl, it is a group that meets regularly to read, study, share, and debate Mexica history and philosophy. They also focus on learning Náhuatl. Members meet to study the ancient *amochtin* (books), colonial texts, and recent scholarship about Mexica topics. This group has also raised funds to secure space for storage and to hold their meetings.

On top of weekly meetings, the Consejo Quetzalcoatl coordinates the inviting and hosting of elders who come and give lectures to the group and the community. They oversee the scheduling, planning, hosting, publicity, and recording of these lectures. The lectures and workshops take place throughout the year but are concentrated at and around the MNY ceremony when many elders are in attendance.

An Alternative Education Palimpsest

Through my ethnography, I ascertained that many *calpulli* members feel responsible for supplementing mainstream US school curricula, which does not reflect the history, culture, or interests of native Americans, native Mexicans, or Mexicas. For this reason, a motif that characterizes this site of palimpsest in Calpulli Tonalehqueh is alternative education.

Dancers are concerned that even when information about native communities is included in school curriculum, the information is brief, misinformed, or otherwise problematic. Parents feel compelled to respond to miseducation, asserting themselves in the education of their children. Some *calpulli* parents go as far as to home-school their children. Calpulli Tonalehqueh provides several means to a modern

Mexica education, providing spaces for an alternative education. The different teaching and learning environments created by *calpulli* members successfully recover some of the key elements of pre-Cuauhtémoc Mexica schooling, including the ideology of In Ixtli In Yollotl.

Emerging out of modern San José, with its particular US, urban, linguistic, capitalist, neocolonial, educational, and historical contexts, Calpulli Tonalehqueh members reach back to the past and leverage their collective resources to construct an educational institution. Calpulli Tonalehqueh's organization is malleable enough and designed in a way that can empower its members to take the lead in implementing the mission and vision of the group. Not all the educational enterprises thrive or continue, but some of them do, and they have an impact on the lives of youth and all members. The collective resolve moves families forward.

The educational enterprises of Calpulli Tonalehqueh are not schooling, teaching and learning in the conventional sense, study that anticipates a test, or casual tips for raising a child. Instead, they are interdisciplinary and holistic environments where ages mix, spirituality develops, art and music connect to all other endeavors, and where physical, psychosocial, and community health are sustained.

The *tlacahuapahualiztli*, the formation of people, in Calpulli Tonalehqueh is a palimpsest. An examination of the total organization of education in the *calpulli* or any of the environments described in this chapter bears this out. The In Ixtli In Yollotl group's activities evoke the *cuicacacalmeh*[6] of yesteryear. The agricultural initiatives invite families to alter and adjust their nutritional habits, connections to the land, and care for Mother Earth in ways that are traditional. The music classes reconnect people with ancestral instruments, rhythms, and cultural productions while allowing them to compose new forms and songs. The workshops provide members with some of the original layers of the palimpsest, some of the early writings: history, imagery, language, cosmology, and philosophy. Dancers take these texts and use them to shape their group exploits, spirit practice, family activity, and their personal identities, which are the new entries in the *Danza* palimpsest. In Ixtli In Yollotl: people's hearts and identities are formed.

5

Cargos

Many twentieth- and twenty-first-century dance circles in the *Conchero* and *Tradición* veins have an organizational leadership structure that reflects colonial alterations to the classic Mexica *calpulli* governance models. Calpulli Tonalehqueh leadership is organized in ways recognizable to the student of *Conchero* or *Tradición* conventions, but as a modern iteration of a *calpulli* in the *Mexicayotl* tradition, it champions a recovery of the traditional *calpulli* leadership roles. Calpulli Tonalehqueh members remember and replicate the traditional system in their own group.

In the longer view of Mexica history, pre-Cuauhtémoc *calpulli* roles have been obscured by time and colonization. But with obscurity notwithstanding, Calpulli Tonalehqueh studies and makes interesting attempts to reinstitute the traditional leadership roles in a *calpulli*, called *cargos*. After a review of the erasure of historical *calpulli cargos*, this chapter details the process Calpulli Tonalehqueh undertakes to learn and relearn traditional Mexica governance at both the group and dance level. Next, the chapter relays the received categories of organizational leadership and discusses the dynamic concept of *palabra*, Spanish for one's word or the group's word. In the conclusion, I consider how the institutionalization of indigenous leadership roles is another site understood as a palimpsest.

I am including an examination of the *cargo* process and implementation for several reasons. One, it is an area that is important to the dancers. It is an area that receives much of attention and discussion. Second, a survey of other *Danza* circles in California and beyond reveals group leadership structures stemming from the *Conchero* tradition employed for their ceremonies. In other words, virtually no other groups in the United States are using pre-Cuauhtémoc *cargo* titles and associated principles, let alone intragroup administrative governance. Most groups have decision making and organizing centralized around an individual or a couple, who is supported by key members. Calpulli Tonalehqueh attempts to recover, revive, and compose traditional *cargos* and governance, adding to the historical palimpsest of *Danza* leadership roles. They may not satisfy all evaluators, the governance may not be as democratic or as collective as they aim it to be, and the leadership roles may be fluid, but the attempt is significant as it indicates that they are making that bridge to the past, recovering, reviving, and looking to *remember* that which others had tried to erase in order to move the community forward.

Cargos, Historically

Chapter 2 of this text outlined some historical features and general characteristics of *calpultin*. That chapter also referenced scholarly debates about the constitution of *calpultin*. Since this chapter centers on the elected roles recovered and reassembled by Calpulli Tonalehqueh, I briefly review the framework and roles of pre-Cuauhtémoc Mexica *calpultin*. Particularly, I summarize the findings of Eulalia Guzmán (1989) who reminds us that the nuclear family was conceived as a micro-calpulli in pre-Cuauhtémoc Anáhuac. The unit was led by a couple, a house. The basic *calpulli*, then, is an alliance of houses, of families who were tied to each other geographically or agriculturally, through marriages, through common occupations, and so on. At the *calpulli* level, ancient Mexica governance centered on an elected council of elders, consisting on prudent members of the *calpulli* identified as wise and experienced. It was in them that prime authority over *calpulli* matters resided. The council of elders and all the other elected officers had a physical meeting place, a building called the *calpulco*, built for *calpulli* storage and meetings.

The general governance council of the *calpulli* consisted of offices created according to the needs of the *calpulli* and charged to carry out the decisions of the council of elders. As a requirement, this council was led by two individuals with equal status but with slightly different roles. To reiterate, *calpulli* leadership in ancient Anáhuac never rested with one person; it was always a pair of persons—along with their cabinet—who executed the decisions of the council of elders. The leaders of the general council were the *tecuhtli*, something like the director, and the *calpulequeh*, the administrator or executive director (in modern terms). The first was the speaker, the figurehead, the voice, and the second was more hands-on, managing the work.

Assemblies elected the council of elders, the *tecuhtli/calpulehqueh*, and the other officers. There were two assemblies, the men's and the women's consisting of all the citizens of that *calpulli*. Each assembly met separately for business pertaining to their gender, and once a year they selected individuals to carry out the *cargos* (offices).

Depending on the size of the *calpulli*, professional guilds could be part of the structure. Quarry workers, fishermen, singers, artists, merchants, and other professional guilds were part of the *calpulli* and operated like a family, with an internal leadership structure also based on duality and local needs. The guilds could have representatives on the general council (pp. 41–47).

Other *calpulli cargos* on the general council developed organically as needed. *Calpultin* usually had judges, sheriffs, schoolmasters, musicians, accountants, historians, and so forth. Romerovargas Yturbide (1959) agrees with Guzmán and adds that *calpulli* structural variance depended substantially on its degree of rurality vs. urbanity (pp. 13–14).

According to Guzmán (1989), the city was a federation of *calpultin*. Each *calpulli* sent representatives to be on the city council, which was headed, again, by a pair of elected individuals (*tlahtoani* and *cihuacoatl*) who oversaw the work of an elected cabinet and executed the orders of the council. The city council was called the *Tlatohcan*, the place where one speaks (because it was comprised of representatives carrying the word of their home *calpulli*, along with other council officers in charge of larger guilds or operations). The *Tlahtocan* delivered decisions to the two primary public servants: the *tlahtoani*, or speaker of the council, and the *cihuacoatl*, the executor of the council. The *tlahtoani*, meaning the one who has the word (or the speaker of the people), was charged with interfacing with the larger public and other cities, expressing the desires of the council and inspiring the public to action. The *cihuacoatl*, meaning female serpent (executive counterpart), was charged with overseeing the mechanisms and labor required to carry out the council decisions. This pair of individuals— who could be of any gender—worked as a team. On the city council, there could be many representatives including elders, military generals, librarians, ambassadors, guild leaders, and any other leadership post represented in the city life. In 1517, there were 20 *calpultin* in México-Tenochtitlan (México City).

Larger regional confederations were possible. At the time of the invasion, México-Tenochtitlan was confederated with two neighboring polities, Tlacopan and Texcoco, each with their *tlahtoani, cihuacoatl*, and city council (pp. 47–71). This has been called the Triple Alliance by scholars. In the Triple Alliance, México-Tenochtitlan was the largest *altepetl* (city-state), thus it had a majority of the 30 representatives on the great council, called the *Huey Tlahtocan*. Because of its public leadership function, *huey tlahtoani*, first speaker, has been protagonist in world history. Names like Moctezuma and Cuauhtémoc have been made famous because they were executing their roles as *Huey Tlahtoani*, interfacing with or leading the resistance with invading Spanish forces. Behind them was always the *Huey Tlahtocan*.[1]

When the Spanish arrive in México, they had a difficult time understanding the structure and principles of the *calpulli* system and the *cargos* therein. They were familiar with European forms, including aristocracy, the Catholic church's structure, feudal-imperial states, and with ancient Roman political ideas, for example. They interpreted their encounters with the Mexica system through those lenses, and those interpretations have been utilized for centuries, giving way to myths of Aztec empire, emperors, expansionist warfare, and so on.[2]

Changes during the Colony

The *calpulli* system was systematically dismantled after the sixteenth-century colonization of México. It was an era of extreme erasure. Libraries were burned, sacred sites were destroyed, schools were closed, the native language was forbidden, and elders were killed, cutting new generations off from their ancestral heritage. Spanish colonizers imposed their government, judicial system, religion, language, and legislative bodies. This era gave rise to a system of land holding and labor that existed in Spain, called the *encomienda*. Vast tracts of land were usurped and given to Spaniards. This was devastating for a nation of indigenous people tied to communal land and agriculture and the *calpulli* system that stemmed from both.

Traditional holders of authority were demoted, communal decision making was supplanted, and civil and human rights were blithely disregarded. In many cases, the people themselves became property. Slavery was imported into Anáhuac. Moreover, the *encomienda* system was kin to enslavement. Thousands of "Indians" were "entrusted" to the new landholders for their education, conversion, and care. Economic benevolence and justice were scarce, and the only task that *encomendados* fiercely devoted themselves to was the labor exploitation of their charges. Indigenous people were baptized, given Christianized names, and were (figuratively) branded with the last name of their owner wholesale (see Florescano, 1987, 1996; Gibson, 1964; Gonzalbo Aizpuru, 1990; Lopes Don, 2010).

In these conditions, many aboriginal Mexicans lost access to personal and community capacity building. In their destitution, intragroup conflicts increased, assimilation accelerated the loss of memory, and *calpulli* life was stifled. The *encomienda* system ended in the beginning of the eighteenth century. In its place the *municipio* system was established, similar to municipal systems developed in Spain. States were divided into various municipalities with their own seats of power and were charged with public works and the distribution of funds. A council president headed the municipal council (at the state and federal level, México operated as a democratic republic since 1917). The *municipio* system of government survived several governmental regimes, the war of independence, the 1910–1917 Revolution, which produced a constitution that governs the municipal form of governance in México (below the state level) and the North American Free Trade Agreement (NAFTA). Throughout these centuries. the *calpulli* system survived, mostly in rural communities. The erasure of colonization has been proven incomplete.

Genesis of the *Tlahtocan*

The process pertaining to the organizational structure and the leadership roles, or *cargos* of Calpulli Tonalehqueh in 2007, was an occasion for recovery and reauthoring. Calpulli Tonalehqueh members underwent a process to learn about how *calpultin* operated in ancient Mexica society and made attempts to institute that governance structure within the group. As I have detailed in previous chapters, Calpulli Tonalehqueh has two main objectives: *Danza* and cultural diffusion. This chapter details the efforts this group made (and continues to make) to serve these goals through a return to traditional Mexica organizational structures and how that process can be understood through the conceptual framework.

A landmark activity in the group's functioning as a modern-day *calpulli* takes place in February 2007 in anticipation of the annual MNY ceremony. The leadership of the *calpulli*, along with Ocelocoatl, studies and discusses the administrative roles of a *calpulli* in order to establish them for the group. Ocelocoatl, familiar with numerous contemporary models in México City, suggested four types of councils for the *calpulli*: (1) an administrative and overarching one, called the *Tlahtocan*, meaning the place where one speaks; it would be the main decision-making body overseeing *calpulli* endeavors; (2) an important and traditional one constituted by the *Heuhuetque*, or elders who are the repositories of wisdom and leadership; (3) underneath the *Tlahtocan* would be a circle comprised of the leaders of the group's dance ceremonies called *Grupo de Guerra/Yaoxochitl*, or the group that goes to the flowery battles; and (4) a council comprised of traveling ambassadors who represent the *calpulli*, called *painales* (see figure 5.1).

In early 2007, *calpulli* members gathered at a local restaurant with Ocelocoatl who repeated his suggestions for the organizational structure of the *calpulli*. After this discussion, Calpulli Tonalehqueh members nominated and selected individuals to take roles on the councils,

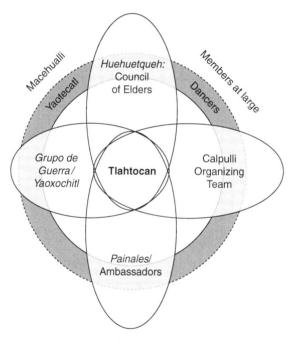

Figure 5.1   A visual representation of the leadership structure that Calpulli Tonalehqueh developed starting in 2007.

Note: It depicts the four councils installed to carry out different aspects of the *calpulli* work. The *Tlahtocan* was established as the overarching decision-making council. It draws from members of other councils. The figure's scale does not represent hierarchy, quantity, or space.

or *cargos*, effective immediately. I was present at this meeting as both an anthropologist and a dancer in the group. My field notes recorded the following general procedure:

First, the council of elders was easily chosen, for there were elders already established in the group from its inception. It was decided that the council of elders would remain flexible enough so that individuals who were beginning to get close to the group could be invited to be on the council at a later time.

Second, *painales* were designated as the members of the group who had moved away from the area but who still count themselves as members and could act as ambassadors for the group abroad. *Painales* would hopefully act as representatives and information conduits to other dance groups in the regions where they lived, including the United States and México. About three or four individuals were listed for this council.[3]

Third, the group discussed each of the *cargos* usually carried in Mexica dance ceremonies (see below). Usually, these *cargos* would go to the most experienced dancers in the *calpulli*, because they had been to many ceremonies, had observed the ceremonial protocols, and had skill sets and other material assets (ceremonial attire, feathers, accouterments, etc.) allowing them to lead other dancers and represent the group well. This council was to be called the *Grupo de Guerra*. Nominations ensued for members to fill these roles. The *Grupo de Guerra* was charged with maintaining harmony at the group's weekly dance ceremony (*ensayo*) and annual dance ceremonies (MNY, Día de los Muertos, Stanford University Powwow, etc.) In addition, they would represent the group at ceremonies and events hosted by other dance circles. The *Grupo de Guerra* is important largely because veteran dancers comprise it and are role models for newer dancers. They teach at the weekly practice and represent the group when invited to dance at community, regional, national, or international events. They would become the face of the group, literally and figuratively, for they will be photographed or recorded the most, will speak the most, and will leverage their relationships with other dance circles to advance the group's mission and vision. The *Grupo de Guerra* (literally: war party) would be the warriors who go on the (ceremonial, artistic) battles, and hence the name.

Below is a list of the roles and descriptions for ceremonial *cargos* upon which the *Grupo de Guerra* is based. In some cases there are modern interpretations of traditional roles. These are assembled from my notes at the meeting and though my years in *Danza*. These have also been published in Calpulli Tonalehqueh's handbook. I include them in this account because (1) they have bearing on this chapter as they are taken up by dancers; (2) they inform readers about the constitution of a *calpulli* (as in chapter 2) at a deeper level; and (3) the descriptions aid readers who encounter the roles in chapter 6, which focuses specifically on a dance ceremony and the roles effectuated therein. Below is the list of *cargos* for dance ceremonies:

- *Tlahtoani/Tlacatecatl*: The general or the captain of two or more groups, selected by the community to lead in dance, philosophy, language, artistry, etc.
- *Tlayacanqui*: The captain of the dance, who carries the first *palabra* of the group. S/he is directly responsible and in charge of the overall organization of the ceremony, including the time/place, the distribution of people, time, and space. S/he is in charge of the others with *cargos* and knows the strengths and weaknesses of her/his deputies.
- *Cihuacoatl*: S/he passes the dances and carries the second *palabra* of the *ceremony*. S/he watches over the dancers to make sure they dance or march with harmony and that all groups and honorable people have a chance to offer a prayer (dance).
- *Tequihua*: There should ideally be two *tequihua*s, one man and one woman. They have the third *palabra*. The term literally means workers. Their function is to fulfill the role of the *tlayacanqui* in his/her absence.
- *Tiaxcau*: S/he maintains discipline in the dance; orients others in the dance, conserving order, placing people in the circle, giving permission to leave/enter the circle, etc.; supports the work of the *tequihua* as needed.
- *Topilli*: S/he is the discipliner or security of the circle; has the ability to solve problems and issues in a smart, strong, and quick manner. They are the first one to receive visitors at the door of the circle.
- *Chicomecoatzin/Cihuapilli*: S/he is the incense/fire keeper. In ancient Anáhuac, this person could be man or woman. Today, it is usually a woman. Ceremonially, s/he is the counterpart of and works directly with the *tlayacanqui*. She watches over the purification rites and perfumes (with incense) all things that enter the circle, including people and their sacred instruments. Her role includes the management of the energy in the circle.
- *Atecocolehqueh* (sometimes *Atecozozonque*): They are the guardians of the conch, playing the conch to salute the four directions and greet dignitaries. There must be a minimum of one, but more is ideal. Within this group the *Teccistli*, or *Teccismama*, is the lead conch and coordinates the others.
- *Huehuetzozoque*: They are the guardians and in charge of the rhythm and percussion, including the *huehuetl* (drum), *teponaztle* (wooden slit drum), *tlapanhuehuetl* (large group drum), *mahuehuetl* (hand drum), *panhuehuetl* (large drum), and so forth. Within the group of *huehuetzozoque*, the *Huehuetqui* is the first *palabra*.

- *Cuicapiqui*: S/he is in charge of the wind instruments (human voice, *tlapitzalli* [flutes], ocarinas, whistles, *huijolas*, etc.). and accompanies the drums. *Cuicatl* is a song. A *cuicani* is a singer. *Cuicaltin* is a group of singers.
- *Tlahuizcatecatl*: The word derives from *tlahuilli* (luminosity or insignia), *tlahuilce* (dignity), and *tecatl* (person). They bear the insignia, the personality, and the identity of the group. They carry the banner depicting the name of the group/*calpulli*. There should be at least one, but can be two or four and should be strong and well-outfitted dancers. They show the group's identity and should be located either near the *tlayacanqui*, next to the drums, or opposite the door.
- *Tlatohtetl*: The word derives from *tlatoh* (word) and *tetl* (stone), meaning word of stone, or written in stone. They act as ambassadors, delivering group information, invitations, or documents in ceremonies. They may act as the first *palabra* of the *painales*.
- *Painal*: A messenger. S/he needs to stay close to the *Tlayacanqui* to receive instructions of various sorts. S/he is the only person allowed to leave the dance circle.
- *Tlameme*: The caretakers, transporters, special helpers. They protect the belongings of participants in the ceremony when they do not participate as dancers in the ceremony.
- *Yaotecatl*: Not a formal *cargo*. The warriors. They are the dancers at large.
- *Macehuales*: Not a formal *cargo*. The word derives from *macehui* (they who deserve). It is for them that the dance ceremonies are held and whom all *cargos* represent. They are group and community members.

The vast majority of *danzantes* in the United States and México do not use these specific terms. The duties that each of these roles executes are tacitly known, but even when they are labeled, they are called by other Spanishized or altered names. The lexicon of *cargos* has been distorted by the Spanish invasion and over centuries. As has been discussed, many dance groups still use European military terms to refer to their dance group's leadership structure (e.g., *capitán*, *sargento*, *teniente*, etc.); some use informal Mexican vernacular to refer to traditional roles or components in *danza* (e.g., *tamborero* instead of *huehuetzozoque*, *caracolero* instead of *atecozozonque*, *malinche* for *cihuapilli*, etc.). To this point, *danzantes* based their understanding of *cargos* (usually called *palabras*) on the *Conchero* or *Tradición* traditions. There the offices can be inherited or earned.

Instead of *calpultin*, *Conchero* and *Tradición* groups are organized as *Mesas* (large councils) made up of many associated groups. Each *Mesa* and each group has a set of founding documents, titles, obligations, oratory spaces, relics, territories, and ceremonies to host. There is a hierarchy of ranks that are simultaneously ceremonial and administrative. The titles of these ranks are based on Spanish military terms: *general, capitán, sargento, teniente, soldado, malinche, estandarte*, and so on (Cruz Rodríguez "Tlacuilo," 2004; González Torres, 2005; Hernández-Ávila, 2005; Luna, 2011; Rostas, 2009). These titles were superimposed on the earlier Mexica/Náhuatl roles and had been in effect in *Danza* for more than a century. But in recent times, *Mexicayotl* groups have called for a discontinuation of these terms and reclamation of the Mexica roles.

At the Calpulli Tonalehqueh meeting in February 2007, nominations for the *Grupo de Guerra* were given mostly to founding members and veteran dancers of the *calpulli* who were already fulfilling those roles to a great degree (previously and without these Náhuatl identifiers). The process of learning the names of the ceremonial *cargos* became an occasion for this *calpulli* to clarify the duties to be fulfilled and to define the lines of decision making and other nuances of conducting ceremony. As Ray McDermott put it when I explained the purpose of the *cargos* inside the *calpulli*, individuals were coconstructing "a structure of relations, nodes of a tree to be activated at certain times and for certain outcomes" (personal communication). Newly minted officers accepted their roles, queried Ocelocoatl further, and went on to execute their responsibilities at the New Year ceremony that same March and from that point forward.[4]

Members in attendance at that meeting nominated individuals for the three of the four councils Ocelocoatl suggested (elders, *painales, Grupo de Guerra*) with relative ease. The overarching *Tlahtocan* council would not be finalized at that meeting (see below).

In the discussion, Mitlalpilli proposed adding another council to the Calpulli Tonalehqueh—also under the *Tlahtocan* like the three that were just filled. The meeting had taken place in a time of frantic preparation for Calpulli Tonalehqueh's MNY ceremony. Many individuals had been involved in the planning and execution of the upcoming MNY ceremony, volunteering on committees to organize food, vendors, city permits, invitations, security, fundraising, art direction, and other components.

Because he felt that it would serve the logistical challenges of putting on ceremonies in modern times, Mitlalpilli, the *tlahtoani* of the *calpulli*, suggested adding a council that he terms the organizing team. This council would be composed of dancers or nondancers who are members of the *calpulli* and who participate actively in the cultural diffusion efforts of the group. These individuals were already taking leadership of committees to organize the large *calpulli* ceremonies. This would be a council of the *calpulli* organizers, who have experience and contacts in the community that could be mined in service of the *calpulli* mission. No one opposed the institution of this council and it was established.

This organizing team is notable as a modern innovation allowed by the mutability of Mexica cultural institutions. I discuss this further in the concluding section.

At this point, Calpulli Tonalehqueh established four councils, yet the matter of the overarching leadership council, the *Tlahtocan*, was still at hand. Years before with Calpulli Huitzilopochtli, Ocelocoatl had described the traditional positions of the *Tlahtocan*, and the list was printed for distribution. That *calpulli* never put them into effect. The attempt to institutionalize a *Tlatohcan* emerged once more, now in Calpulli Tonalehqueh. The reemergence was motivated, in part, because the leaders of the group often had difficulties coming to consensus on large decisions and wished to avoid frequent clashes of wills with more clearly defined roles and auspices.

Many days after the initial February 2007 meeting/elections, another meeting was held to clarify the chain of command and the functioning of each of the *Tlahtocan* roles. Members were asked to nominate individuals to the *cargos* or to think about taking office themselves. Within two weeks, Mitlalpilli called a meeting to nominate/install the members of the *Tlahtocan*, inviting the most active members of the group.

The following is a list of the roles that emerged as a point of departure for the construction of Calpulli Tonalehqueh's *Tlahtocan*. Members were reminded that a traditional *Tlahtocan* had a general framework adapted to respond to local needs.[5]

- *Tlatoani*: The word derives from *tlatolli* (the word) and *ni* (her/him), meaning s/he who speaks, or the one who speaks with the words of others. S/he delivers the decisions of the *Tlahtocan*.
- *Tecuhtli*, or *Cihuatecutli* (if woman): The word derives from *tequitl* (work) and *utli* (revered person), meaning the person who works or works the most. S/he is the executor, the one who carries out the decisions and actions of the *Tlahtocan* based on his/her interpretation of the will of the *calpulli*. S/he can be the same person as the *Tlatoani*.
- *Cihuacoatl*: The word derives from *cihuatl* (woman) and *coatl* (serpent or knowledge), meaning the woman of knowledge. She is the administrator and would start the meetings by presenting the issues or topics on

the agenda. She is in charge of passing the *palabra* in the *Tlahtocan* and facilitating order in the meeting.

- *Calpixque*: S/he has a role similar to a treasurer and is in charge of the finances, resources, and recourses of the *calpulli*. S/he manages the *calpulli* inventory and property in terms of gifts, supplies, feathers, flags, instruments, and so forth. It is her/his job to report to the *calpulli* on a regular basis in the *Tlahtocan*.
- *Painal*: A messenger who delivers word of *calpulli* actions to other *calpultin*. These messages include invitations, advisories, information, flyers, responses, etc. S/he acts as a representative or liaison between their *calpulli* and external *calpultin*.
- *Topilli*: Literally means revered child. One of the discipliners who keeps order, respect, and harmony in the circle. S/he has the ability to solve problems in a smart, strong, and quick manner. As a group, *topilli* are the eyes, ears, and hands of the *calpulli*, watching out at all times for the security and harmony of the *calpulli*.
- *Tlacuilo*: S/he is the scribe in charge of official *calpulli* writing/graphics, including the *Tlahtocan* notes, official letters, testimonies, official documents, etc.
- *Paleoani*: S/he is the helper or secretary, one who takes notes of important information. S/he also helps take notes at the meeting in terms of who said what at what time.

The meeting to ratify those individuals who would take each *cargo* in the *Tlahtocan* was far more contentious and politicized than the one for the other councils. If legitimized, the *Tlahtocan* would serve as the overarching decision-making body for this group. Up until that time, no one had been part of any Mexica dance group where this type of structure was put into effect. As I stated before, *Danza* groups in the United States and elsewhere usually have authority centralized in one person. The weight of the council's impending authority coupled with individual desires to be selected provides context for lobbying and back-channel communication in anticipation of the meeting, either to promote or prevent certain people from office. The most active members of the group gather at a dancer's house. After hours of deliberation, most of the offices are filled. At this meeting, I was elected *Tlacuilo* (artist/scribe), in part due to my graphic design competencies and my role as researcher/anthropologist at a university.

Cargo Dynamics

In my time with the *calpulli* since the spring of 2007 initiation, I have been able to witness some of the evolution of *cargo* dynamics. Of all the councils established that spring, the most initially coherent was the *Grupo de Guerra*. Members of this council were more easily identified and their duties were more easily listed. Because *ensayos* and community performances were so frequent, this group was constantly needed. The *Grupo de Guerra* organized a weekly advanced dance class where they established the official dances of the group and their respective sequence of steps. In addition, they developed a mentoring system to build capacity in novice dancers. Each ceremonial *cargo* took at least one apprentice. Furthermore, the ceremonial *cargos* alternated their *cargos* at *ensayo* in what turned out to be a successful cross-training. Also, the *chicomecoatzin* of the group successfully recruited other women to take the *cargo* and train together. Instead of having one *chicomecoatzin* for the group, at least five women took the *cargo* successfully.

The council of elders continues to be involved, but in a way that is slightly different than traditional Mexica society. Calpulli Tonalehqueh is still primarily a youth-driven organization. The veteran dancers—still young—set the agenda. Elders are crucial to the work of Calpulli Tonalehqueh but serve in advising, consulting, teaching, and other leadership capacities. One of the major contributions of the council of elders is their community network. Elders of Calpulli Tonalehqueh help connect the group to other nations, ceremonies, community organizations, and resources. Their personal and community contacts are essential to the *tequio* of the group.

The Organizing Team is identified with more difficulty. This council is not as consolidated as the others. There is significant crossover from other councils that the lines of the councils blur. In other words, members of the *Grupo de Guerra*, the *Tlahtocan*, and the Council of Elders are also organizers, and few organizers are not dancers or part of other councils. As a result, people do not carry an Organizing Team identity, and the portfolio of *calpulli* work gets organized in collective, not centrally in that council. It was never officially dissolved; it just never consolidated. Nonetheless, there are many *calpulli* volunteers who lead and support the great number of *calpulli* activities, events, workshops, etc.

The *painales* are only loosely organized. Members abroad are consulted and contacted for news as friends, but few carry an identity as a *painal*. They usually carry an identity as *danzantes*, as former members of Calpulli Tonalehqueh, or as current members who are living far away. Moreover, their role is effectively fulfilled by the networking, invitations, communication, or general exchange that happen over e-mail/Websites and through the frequent travels of core members of Calpulli Tonalehqueh to other ceremonies, or core members from other groups who visit Calpulli Tonalehqueh and bring news.

The *Tlahtocan* is another council with fluid membership. One of the challenges that all the *Tlahtocan* members had is that it largely drew its membership from other councils. As big as Calpulli Tonalehqueh is compared to other dance groups, it still became difficult to populate this council, especially given the blurred lines between identity in council memberships. Furthermore, the *Tlahtocan*'s stability is challenged by the attrition of some core members and influx of new dancers willing to take leadership roles, but with less awareness of the development of the councils. The *Tlahtocan* did operate with some degree of formality for a time, but after a period, decision making reverted to less formal customs. Open business meetings are still called often, e-mail discussions still circulate, consensus-gathering conversations still take place, dancers come and go with varying degrees of commitment. As important and central as the *calpulli* is in the lives of members, it still competes with other parts of people's lives (e.g., family, work, school, community involvements) that require time. Calpulli Tonalehqueh members are not full-time dancers. Membership is voluntary, fluid, and free of charge. As a result, it is difficult for the councils to demand certain kinds of commitment from members.

Both the ceremonial and administrative *cargos* of the *calpulli* are revisited with an annual regularity. Shifts in formal appointments (not elections) do occur. Though a precise fit of traditional *cargos* with contemporary *calpulli* tasks is impossible and the fluidity of membership, among other things, challenges the *cargo* system of Calpulli Tonalehqueh, the exercise of recovering the ancient structures and innovating upon them is noteworthy.

In the end, the ceremonial cargos consolidate more easily because they are better defined in the *Danza* universe and because dancing is so central to *calpulli* life. Administrative tasks are more polemical, more contentious, and less appealing on different levels, and although there is a significant amount of *tequio* that members deliver to the group, individuals are less willing and/or able to lock into the responsibilities of *cargos* in that area. Administratively, Mitlalpilli carries the group. He is a hub for information, logistics, decisions, initiatives, and agendas. He wears the *tlahtoani*, the *tecuhtli*, and many other hats. He and the *calpulli* mission/vision are supported by the entire group, but largely without the structure of a formal *Tlahtocan*.

Palabra: Its Fluidity and Use

Palabra is a crucial word in the *Danza* universe. It is a term that has at least four meanings, referring to: (1) an individual's words, (2) the word of a group, (3) a person who holds a rank/*cargo*, or (4) an actual time/space to offer words.

First, individuals are acquired by a Mexica culture that values rhetoric, poetry, and songs. There are frequent occasions where individuals are invited to speak their mind, speak their heart. It could be at the end of an ensayo, inside a temascal, at a *Tlatohcan* meeting, or after a performance. It is customary for all *calpulli* activities to end with an open session where people can express their thoughts or prayers. When they do so, they are giving their *palabra*, words that represent them as an individual. People will say, "I offer my *palabra*," or "that was a powerful *palabra*" referring to individual comments.

Second, in larger activities and ceremonies where many dance circles get together, there is a session programmed for the representatives of each attending group to speak. The *tlahtoani*, or speaker, of each group offers a message that represents their whole group. At that moment, that individual is carrying the collective *palabra* of the *calpulli*. People will say, "we need all the *palabras* to come receive instructions," or "at this time, each group will give its *palabra*." One message will represent the whole dance group. In common parlance, the *primera palabra* or principal leader of any particular group is the one who would speak on behalf of the group. In that person's absence, the next *cargo* in the chain of command would be the representative, and so forth.

Third, *palabra* is a term used in the mainstream *Danza* universe to identify a person in an official leadership position in a particular group or within a particular ceremony. In other words, it is used to mean *cargo*, referring to a person who has a leadership role in a dance circle or ceremony. Usually, there is a designated ranking of the *cargos*, or *palabras*, in a group. A group, for example, will have a *primera palabra* (first word), *segunda palabra* (second word), and so on. People will say, "Our *primera palabra* is not here so I (the *segunda palabra*) am taking the *palabra*" or "do you have *palabra* in your group?"

Inside a formal ceremony, the *cargos* elected to execute that particular ceremony are often called at *palabras*. These can be held by anyone in attendance. For example, at a ceremony where lots of groups get together, the group hosting the ceremony customarily invites leaders from other groups to run the ceremony. They will ask members of various groups to pass the dances, take care of placing people, and so on. Those *cargos* are called *palabras* (*primera, segunda, tercera*, etc.) for that ceremony. People will say, "who is the *segunda palabra* of this ceremony?" or "can you please do us the honor of taking the *palabra de las mujeres?* (the one who places women on the circle and gives them permission to leave/enter)," referring to ceremonial *cargos* in a ceremony.

As I have outlined, a hierarchical chain of command in the *Conchero* tradition echoes Spanish military ranks. The idea of a ranking of *palabras* matches this tradition. Calpulli Tonalehqueh negotiates this idea and attempts to reinstitute traditional *cargo* terminology, renaming them *tlayacanqui, cihuacoatl, tiaxcau*, etc.

The fourth usage of the term *palabra* refers to time and space. The *palabra* is a designated time after any activity where people involved are allowed to speak. The *palabra* time can occur after any *calpulli* activity. It can happen after a road trip, after a performance, after an *ensayo*, or after any *tequio*. A *palabra* is a time to offer gratitude, offer apologies, air grievances, make invitations or announcements, pray, etc. People will say, for example, "gather around, we are going to do a *palabra*," "you should mention that at the *palabra*," or "she invited us to her ceremony at the *palabra*," referring to the time for speaking.

It is clear that there is fluidity about the meaning of the word *palabra* and the people who take it.

Remembering: The Palimpsest of Leadership

The theme that emerges after a consideration of the palimpsest of *cargos* in Calpulli Tonalehqueh is remembering. The construct of palimpsest requires remembering. The process that Calpulli Tonalehqueh underwent to reinstitute the councils and define and elect the leadership roles in the group is part of the whole palimpsest of the group. This palimpsest is characterized by remembering because although *Danza* groups operate successfully under a system that has evolved over time, members of this *calpulli* are intentional about remembering the structures and roles that were developed through the ancient *calpulli* system.

Calpulli Tonalehqueh had existed for years, operating well by most dance group standards, and yet it took the opportunity to organize itself along new lines. Why is this compelling to the present text? For one, the institutionalization of a new order moves the group into alignment with a more endemic social structure. Any clarity achieved in the process aides the group's efficacy and alignment with indigenous traditions. Moreover, the reorganization makes available new categories for individual identity formation and collective imaginings. Individuals can locate themselves on the organizational structure. Roles are more clearly defined and allow role-takers to work at them. Efficiency is aided by structure. Individuals often note a psychosocial stability achieved through the defined roles and an eagerness to learn more about the *cargos*. When they go to other ceremonies and are asked to carry out the *cargos*, their anxiety level is greatly diminished. The roles become meaningful, the councils legitimized. Third, the *calpulli*—now conceptualized as a collective—serves as a powerful nexus of resources and learning sites. This includes the opportunity to become a model for other dance groups. In December 2008, for example, Calpulli Tonalehqueh is invited to provide a workshop on the *calpulli* roles at a gathering of the Aztec dance groups of the Southern California region. At all times, *calpulli* making is a case of palimpsest, a time when individuals or groups trace their lineage and make traditional practice real.

The process of defining and constructing a *calpulli* is not static. Two years later in late April 2009, core members of the *calpulli* met to revisit the mission, goals, and operation of the *calpulli*. The *Tlatohcan* called the meeting in hopes of evaluating the current state of the group. There Mitlalpilli recounted some of the original purposes the founders had when forming Calpulli Tonalehqueh, saying they wanted "support for cultural and political events, a positive place to socialize and learn culture, ceremony" (personal communication). He then fielded emerging concerns, such as the unsustainable growth of the group, the increasingly inefficient capitalization of talent, high turnover in the councils, and ignorance about or sense of disconnection from the original vision of the *calpulli* felt by new members. The attendees of the meeting provided advice that would inform the continuing endeavors of the *calpulli*.

As I outlined in an earlier chapter, members hoped for permanent base of operations (physical location), increased grant writing/fundraising, secured land for a community garden, more regular craft workshops, a focus on physical health, as well as scaled back *calpulli* growth through an increased focus on the core of the group, on children, and on long-standing community alliances. This meeting illustrates how the structure of a *Tlahtocan* allows the *calpulli* to regenerate *cargos* dynamically. Over time and through more growth, recalibrating, and remembering, the *cargos* and traditional *calpulli* structure take hold in this circle and is an available model for other groups in the *Danza* universe.

The process itself is an educational environment. It includes an opportunity to study, receive, and discuss the ancient form of sociopolitical governance, learn the Náhuatl terminology, and compare that system with the current organizational forms in other *Danza* groups and with the larger political system of the United States or México.

By "remembering" through the building of capacity, mentoring, or carving out meetings to evaluate the structure/mission of the group, Calpulli Tonalehqueh helps ensure its permanency and renewal. The *cargos* enable ceremony, *tequio* on large and small scales, and helps move the group forward. The process facilitates entries into the larger palimpsest of the group and invites other groups to consider their structure. Building leadership capacity is a strategy for the sustainability of the palimpsest project.

6

Macehualiztli (The Art of Deserving)

Dance was a central facet of human life in pre-Cuauhtémoc Anáhuac, as it was around the world. There are no surviving pre-Cuauhtémoc narratives of dance ceremonies, though there are archeological records and an oral tradition that give insight to the ubiquity of dance in ancient times. Scholars often look to the written records of early colonial writers to characterize the nature and execution of Mexica dance ceremonies. Other scholars examine current indigenous Mexican dance traditions as echoes of ceremonies past and as rich sites for contemporary socialization and cultural production.

This chapter repeats the above exercises, contemplating *Danza* as another site of recovery, remembering, and reauthoring. I present various colonial accounts of *Danza* and then turn to examine the dance ceremony Calpulli Tonalehqueh builds every week. This chapter focuses on the educational space created through dance, called *macehualiztli*, in Calpulli Tonalehqueh. For this purpose, I examine one dance ceremony carefully. I trace the movement of several individuals carrying different *cargos* through the space arranged for the *macehualiztli*, commenting on the considerations they manage and the elements of the ceremony they undertake. At the end of the chapter, I discuss the palimpsest features of this embodied learning environment.

General Definition, Forms, and Components of Ancient *Danza*

The record is not entirely clear on the names given to the various types of dance practiced in pre-Cuauhtémoc Náhuatl-speaking

México. Durán (1581/1995) wrote that there were a thousand variations of dance and games done by children and adults alike. Sahagún
(1577/1992) wrote that he witnessed an incredible diversity of dances.
Many of the colonial writers described Mexica dancing as *areyto*,
areito, *danza*, or *baile*. Some writers began writing *mitote*, a Spanish-
language conversion of *mitotiliztli* or *netotiliztli*, two words for dance
in Náhuatl. There are several words for various kinds of dance in
Náhuatl, though researchers disagree about terminology. The word
I chose here to refer to *Danza* is *macehualiztli*, which is usually recognized as a more solemn, spiritual, ceremonial dance (as opposed to
dancing for pleasure).

Macehualiztli means the art of deserving and generally speaks
to a worldview embedded in *Danza* (in ancient times and now).
Macehualiztli is about more than bodies in motion; there is a focus on
fostering humility through dance. The word reference signifies humankind's position in the world. In anthropocentric cultures, humans are
given dominion over nature, or humans are the measure of all things.
On the other hand, some cultures, like that of indigenous Mexica,
held a worldview where humans are integrated with or connected
to all living beings. The ancient Mexica acknowledged that without
all the elements of the universe, including the sun, rain, plants, and
animals, one could not live. The ancient Mexica worldview equated
human life to a gift from Creation, a debt that must be paid through
human productions. Two requirements are central to this worldview:
gratitude and reciprocity. *Danza* was a vehicle to offer gratitude and
gifts in return for precious gifts received. If people received energy
and sustenance from the universe, what precious things could they
give in return? The answer was total effort, prayer, and energy (in the
form of dance), and in the most beautiful things that people could
gather or create—things like poetry, works of art, flowers, incense,
jewels, food, and so on.

María Sten (1990) authored one of the most extensive works on
dance in pre-Cuauhtémoc and early contact Mexica society. She
pointed out that dance was a total societal endeavor involving each
and every citizen. Unlike some other spheres of life, everyone participated in dance. At times, Mexica dances were executed exclusively by
either men, women, or elders, but overall, dance ceremonies included
mixed age and gender groups (pp. 29, 137). In any case, elders were
always present to guide the ceremonies whether in formal institutions
like school or in the community (pp. 137–141). Sahagún (1577/1992)

pointed out that elected community leaders were always in charge of organizing the ceremonies and led the fabrication of attire and jewelry, employment of music, hosting of guests, and giving gifts, especially to visitors from other nations. Mendieta (1596/1980) also mentioned the international character of the large ceremonies where thousands attend. At many ceremonies, representatives from other nations would be present and were often invited to present their native dances (pp. 140–143).

Vetancourt (1698/1982) explained that ceremonies had eight to ten concentric circles of 1,000 dancers, each engaged in synchronous singing and dancing. Mendieta (1596/1980) is among those who confirmed these figures. Clavijero (1780/1987) agreed with those who remarked on the festive nature of all dance ceremonies, where not only dancers but actors, acrobats, merchants, athletes, and artists showcase their craft. In other words, surrounding dance ceremonies were ball games, games of chance, festival games, markets, athletic competitions, and theatrical productions. The entire community attended dance ceremonies.[1]

In terms of dance spaces, colonial authors relayed that ceremonies took place in schools, next to *tzacualtin or teocaltin* (large sacred buildings) marking sacred sites, in urban courtyards, and around fires and trees in natural settings. Sahagún (1577/1992) confirmed that dance was taught at the *cuicacalli*, school for young children, and that each night, older students gathered at their schools to dance. In both places, dancers were taught by special educators and by professional singers and dancers trained at the *mixcoacalli* academies. Dance was obligatory in school and was heavily disciplined. Sometimes dance was divided around gender, but at other times, cross-gender interaction and courting were allowed under the watchful eyes of elders (the *teyecanqueh* and *cihuatequizqueh*) to whom parents entrusted their adolescents (pp. 43, 466–468, 471, 474–475). María Sten (1990) affirmed that through the use of ritual any common space could be converted into sacred space (p. 55).

Beyond dance that occurred every day in school settings, large formal ceremonies took place at important civic, agricultural, astronomical, social, and political junctures. Indeed, weddings, elections, commemorations, and other celebrations included dance. They also held a large ceremony each of the 18 months of the Mexica year.[2] The events of that calendar were tied to agricultural cycles, and the dances and elements included in each *veintena* ceremony were different. The

Mexica also had dance ceremonies to mark important dates on the *tonalpohualli*, a 260-day ceremonial cycle.[3] Mexica dance ceremonies were cyclical and perpetual.

Eliade (1967) offered an interesting commentary on the sacredness of time for the Mexica, irrespective of the specific century to which they belong. She explained that dancers who reenact ceremonies make time sacred through repetition of ceremonies and mimic the cycles of nature. Ceremonies recall an ancient mythical time, which is relieved for generations in perpetuity. She added that in this way dancers live (paradoxically) in two experiences of time, one cyclical, reversible, and repeatable indefinitely and the other linear, chronological, and cycling forward (pp. 63–64).

In terms of length of time, colonial authors described the lengths of dance ceremonies from four hours to several days and also describe extensive rehearsals by the professional and common dancers before large ceremonies (de Mendieta, 1980; Durán, 1995).[4]

Colonial authors including Mendieta, Clavijero, Durán, Sahagún, Motolinía, and Vetancourt made several observations about structures, attire, instrumentation, and offerings. For one, these authors confirmed various formations for dances. Usually groups danced in concentric circles, especially at the large ceremonies. They executed dances in rows, in pairs, or in snaking processions.[5] All the colonial authors were astonished at the beauty and high caliber of dancers, singers, and musicians in ceremony. Mendieta (1596/1980), who arrived in México in 1554 and soon witnessed a dance ceremony, stated:

> *toda aquella multitud traen los pies tan concertados como unos muy diestros danzadores de España; y lo que más es, que todo el cuerpo, ansí la cabeza como los brazos y manos van tan concertados, medido y ordenado, que no discrepa ni sale uno de otro medio compás, más lo que uno hace con el pie derecho y también con el izquierdo, lo mesmo hacen todos y en un mesmo tiempo y compás; cuando uno abaja el brazo izquierdo y levanta el derecho, lo mesmo y al mesmo tiempo hacen todos. De manera que los atabales y el canto de los bailadores todos llevan su compás concertado: todos son conformes, que no discrepa uno de otro una jota, de lo cual los buenos danzadores de España que lo ven se espantan, y tienen en mucho las danzas de estos naturales, y el gran acuerdo y sentimiento que en ellas tienen y guardan…no sólo llamaban e honrabna e alababan a sus dioses con cantares de la boca, más también con el corazón y con los sentidos del cuerpo, para lo cual bien hacer, tenían e usaban de muchas memorativas, ansí los meneos de*

la cabeza, de los brazos y de los pies con todo el cuerpo trabajaban de llamar y servir a los dioses.

[all that multitude has their feet in concert like some very skilled Spanish dancers; and what is more, that the whole body, the head like the arms and hands move in such concert, measure, and order, that it does not differ nor falter one from the other even a half beat, and what one does with their right foot and also their left, likewise all the others and at the same time, on the same beat; when one lowers their left arm and raises their right, so do they all and at the same time. So that the drums and the songs and the dancers are all on the same beat: they all conform, none differ one from the other one bit, in a way that the good dancers from Spain that witness it are astonished and regard the high level of the dances of these naturals, and the great accord and feeling that in them they have and hold…not only do they call and honor and praise their gods with the songs from the mouth, but also with the heart and the feelings of the body, for which they well had and used many commemoratives, like the swaying of the head, of the arms and feet as with the whole body worked to call and serve the gods.] (cited in Sevilla, 1990, pp. 245–246, my translation)

Dancers committed their entire mind, body, and spirit to enormous dance ceremonies and executed dances with thousands in synchronization, signaling deep devotion to and practice in the art. All the colonial chroniclers commented on the variety of drums, wind, and percussive instruments elaborated by musicians. They observed that dancers carried some of their own instruments and also carried flower bundles, garlands, feather bundles, shields, fans, headdresses, flags, and formal regalia during their dance offerings. In addition to face paint, dancers all wore elaborate jewelry (for ears, nose, labret, neck, wrists) made of precious stones and metals. Additionally, dancers erected altars with flowers, food, incense, precious stones, shells, feathers, embroidered cloth, aromatic wood, rubber, chocolate, paper, and so on.

All together, the participants, places, times, and accouterments of *macehualiztli* in pre-Cuauhtémoc and early contact Mexica society connected to the community's entire way of life. Mexica worldviews and society can be understood through dance. Concerns about the ideologies embedded in dance practices caused colonial authorities to outlaw ceremonies and countless other cultural practices—the partial erasure in the *Danza* palimpsest. Those cultural practices they did allow in the colonial era—and beyond after independence—were significantly altered by the new world order. *Danzantes* throughout the centuries created new writings in the *Danza* palimpsest. For instance, the *Conchero* and *Mexicayotl* traditions are products of centuries of adaptation in *Danza* to changing contexts. Dance has been so intractable from the fabric of indigenous communities that it has persisted despite impressive counterforces.

One *Ensayo*: Structure and Dynamics

Dance is the starting point for every component of Calpulli Tonalehqueh. At its core, Calpulli Tonalehqueh is a dance group. Beyond its many other enterprises, dance is the most indispensible component of Calpulli Tonalehqueh, because it is the element that draws most members, activity on which most time is spent, and fundamental teaching/learning space, making it a requisite site of educational analysis.

   This section is concerned with using one dance session to convey the modus operandi of cultural practice in Calpulli Tonalehqueh. Being aware of the basic structure and enterprises of the historical *calpultin* and their schools and dance ceremonies, Calpulli Tonalehqueh organizes an altogether sophisticated educational institution around *Danza*. Educational endeavors of this dance circle are sometimes directed at the perceived need to learn the dances and artistry for community performances. At other times they prepare dancers for participation in large formal ceremonies. At all times, they create spaces for remembering and reviving indigenous Mexican culture/identity.

   The *calprulli* organizes three weekly classes centered on dance: beginners, general *ensayo*, and advanced. Newcomers and children who receive parceled and explicit instructions populate the beginner's class. Dancers in the *Grupo de Guerra* lead the beginner's class. The participants and dynamics of this class fall outside of the focus of this chapter.

   The other class organized by the leaders of Calpulli Tonalehqueh is the advanced class. In those sessions, experienced dancers (those in the *Grupo de Guerra*) synchronize their steps seeking to elevate their mastery of the artistic elements of dance in order to better instruct others and perform in the community. This class is lead by the *calpulli cihuacoatl* (dance leader). A discussion on this class lies outside of the focus of this chapter.

   The third and most important class—if it can be called a class—is Calpulli Tonalehqueh's general, open practice. Colloquially this activity is often called *ensayo*, Spanish for practice/rehearsal. It is a typical

dance ceremony done weekly but stripped down in terms of formal
pomp and pageantry such as ceremonial attire that would be present
at "official" ceremonies. That is why it is called *ensayo*; it is rehearsal
for the "real" ceremony. In some *Danza* groups, *ensayo* is for all
intents and purposes a rehearsal; it is the time to learn dance steps
and go through the procedures of ceremony. For many in Calpulli
Tonalehqueh, the line between practice and ceremony is blurred at
ensayo. While incidentally providing conditions to practice dances,
cargos, and music so that these are executed with greater fluency at
the formal ceremonies, many dancers see no reason why the weekly
ensayos cannot be ceremonial, spiritual, occasions to offer prayers in
the form of dance, songs, and oration. They reference ancient times
when *Danza* was so intrinsic to people's lives that it was at all times
prayerful and ceremonial.

The *ensayo* ceremony is the main point of entry for *calpulli* members. At the *ensayo*, group leaders execute their official ceremonial
roles (*cargos*), organizing dancers in concentric circles, alternating
leadership of the dances, playing instruments, arranging the central
altar, maintaining discipline, proclaiming prayers, and directing other
dancers.

At the end of each ceremony, time is allotted so that every participant can speak their mind/heart, a session called *palabra*, Spanish for
"the word." The rhetorical and ritual protocols of both the ceremony
and *palabra* are learned through immersion into all of these roles/
components.

In nearly 20 years with various groups, I had attended hundreds of
ensayos. Each group executes its *ensayo* differently. Most of the other
groups in which I participated have been quite fluid with their *ensayos*,
especially in terms of protocols, spirituality, and *cargos*. Through my
participation with Calpulli Tonalehqueh, I had to relearn how to carry
out the structure of leadership and execution.

This chapter is an account of my findings, detailed through the
description of one *ensayo*. I chose one video record and analyzed
ensayo to serve as a representative for all. I focused primarily on the
analysis of a video segment of 1 minute 37 seconds from the heart of
the session to unpack the ceremonial structures, leadership roles, and
educational features of the dance. For a detailed summary of the entire
ensayo ceremony, see appendix D.

The *ensayo* featured in this chapter took place in January 2008 in
the cafeteria/multipurpose room of a San José high school that allowed
Calpulli Tonalehqueh to use it on Wednesday evenings. Dancers began

Figure 6.1 Images of *momoztli* typical of those prepared for a large ceremony (top) and one arranged for the center of an *ensayo* (bottom).

Notes: Construction was led by the *chicomecoameh* of Calpulli Tonalehqueh who were assisted by other dancers attending the ceremonies.

arriving shortly before 7.00 p.m. to clear the tables and chairs and prepare the space for ceremony.

For each *ensayo*, a *chicomecoatzin* of Calpulli Tonalehqueh erects an altar in the middle of the room that serves as an axis for the entire ceremony. It is her charge to arrive before anyone else, erect the altar, and light the fire and coals that will be used to burn the incense during the ceremony. The altar is called the *momoztli* (see figure 6.1) and it represents a naval, the center around which the energy of the dance will move. The art of arranging the *momoztli* is transmitted between the women. Each *momoztli* is ephemeral; it is arranged differently every time. Sometimes it is called an *ofrenda*, Spanish for offering, because the woman who arranges it is offering her time, essence, art, prayers, and sacred elements to the spirit of the ancestors and to the present company. At a minimum, the *momoztli* requires some representation of the four elements that create life: earth, wind, fire, and water. Also, the *momoztli* must mark the four cardinal directions. Beyond this, the women should place items on the altar they deem will make it as beautiful as it can be. Generally the *chicomecoatzin* places colored cloth, candles, fruits, flowers, herbs, ceramic statues, feathers, images, and any other ceremonial item to create the *momoztli*. The *momoztli* will be the repository of the *popoxcomitl*, the incense burner that the *chicomecoatzin* uses to manage the energy of the circle. The *popoxcomitl* represents the four elements as well. It represents earth because it is made of clay. It holds burning coals representing fire. These coals burn *copal* incense in small pieces. The saliva placed on the copal in the biting sizzles represents water. The incense rises as smoke, making wind visible.

Around 7:30 p.m., drummers arrange their *huehuetl*, or drums, along a semicircular line facing east behind the *momoztli* as the dancers who arrived early join Mitlalpilli in an impromptu review of a dance called Tezcatlipoca with veteran dancers in front of newcomers. Meanwhile, more dancers arrive and get ready.

There are several *armas*, ceremonial "weapons," that the dancers must carry at the *ensayo*. Dancers of Calpulli Tonalehqueh use a headband called an *ixcuaimecatl*. It represents the duality of the individual as it divides one's face (outward personality) from the top of their head (inner thoughts). The *ixcuaimecatl* also signals the moment of birth, as the crown of one's head is the first thing to come to light when one is born. The next item that all dancers use is the *ayacaxtli*, the hand rattle. It is used to keep the rhythm, to create harmony. Some say that it represents the rattles of a serpent, the symbol of mathematics and wisdom. Next, dancers use a *faja*, or broad woven sash, around their midsection. It has symbolic and practical purposes. Symbolically, it

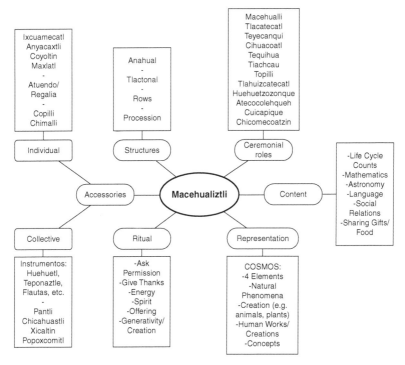

Figure 6.2   A concept map of the components and products of modern *macehualiztli* in Calpulli Tonalehqueh, many of which echo components of ancient Mexica dance.

Note: The figure is a visual representation of the elements discussed in this chapter.

represents protection for one's naval and solar plexus, the place where one's energy resides in life. On the practical side, the *faja* will help prevent injuries to the lower back, abdominal tissue, and ovaries that might occur with the strenuous movements of the ceremony. The last of the essential *armas* are the *chachayotes*, sometimes called *ayoyotes* or *coyoltin*. These are the sets of hardseed shells tied to dancer's ankles that keep rhythm as they mark their paces. In addition to these basic elements, some dancers carry items such as feather shields (symbolizing being a culture warrior) or feather fans (traditional status symbol).

At 7:40 p.m., the ceremony opens. The drums roll, dancers form circles, and the individuals who are in charge of incense and the conch shells join Mitlalpilli, the *tlayacanqui*, who will lead the invocation. Mitlalpilli paces the circle, stopping at each cardinal point (east, west, north, south) to ask for permission from various elements to offer up dance, and then in the middle greeting the sun and the earth. Incense, conch shell sounds, music, salutations, and *ayacaxtli* combine to greet each direction.[6] In the eastern section of the circle, two people are in charge of holding an invisible door through which dancers enter and exit the circle. The east is chosen because it is the place where the sun rises, the first direction.

The dance begins at 7:50 p.m. with Tekolpoktli, who has been chosen to take the *cargo* of *cihuacoatl* of this *ensayo*, meaning he will be in charge of those who, in turns, lead the rest of the dancers in prayer/dance. About 37 dancers from various groups form the initial set of circles. It is not uncommon for members of other dance groups to visit the Calpulli Tonalehqueh practices. Several other community members come and observe from outside the circle. Tekolpoktli begins with a brief dance called the *nahui ollin* (four movements), sometimes called the *permiso* (permission), *cruz* (cross), or *firma* (signature). This is a dance required just before any other dance can be offered. Each dancer, before they select a dance to lead, must first "ask permission" to do the dance. The basic structure of the *nahui ollin* is well known, but each dancer places ornamental movements and variations on top of that framework. This is partially why it is called the *firma* (signature), because each dancer will have their own unique offering of the *nahui ollin* in the same way each of us has a different signature. Some dancers say that the Creator knows the identity of each dancer who is about to offer a dance based on their *permiso*. It is like one's fingerprint; no two are exactly alike. The dance represents multiple concepts including the activation and acknowledgment of the entire universe through the marking of the four cardinal directions and the act of the sowing of seeds by hand and foot. In the *nahui ollin*, dancers simulate planting seeds in the ancestral fashion by dropping seeds into a hole made with a staff and covering the seeds with dirt moved with one's foot. Tekolpoktli offers a *permiso* that everyone follows to open the ceremony and then selects another dancer to offer a dance.

By 8:19 p.m., dancers from visiting groups offer five different dances. More than 50 dancers are now in the *ensayo* in three concentric circles. In keeping with traditional custom, Calpulli Tonalehqueh offers turns for the dances of the evening, first to *danzantes* who come from other groups followed by members of their own group.

The following is an account of the analysis of a video segment of 1 minute 37 seconds of the *ensayo* that started at 8:19 p.m. Figure 6.3 depicts a special representation of the *ensayo*. I trace the movements of the dancers who have *cargos* in this *ensayo*, followed by a commentary that unpacks the structure and dynamics of the *ensayo*. I present the account in this format because even a fraction of the *ensayo* contains elements that point to the whole event and, in turn, to all *ensayos* throughout the year. A description of the activity in this 1 minute 37 seconds prompts further discussion of the *cargos* and features of the *ensayo*. Appendix D provides context for what happens in the *ensayo* before and after the 1 minute 37 seconds.

Following an account of the video clip, I conclude the chapter with a discussion of the *ensayo* as an embodied learning site, examining the structural features that support teaching and learning.

Video link: The video clip analyzed in this chapter can be found at the following link: http://www.youtube.com/watch?v=g74GikJCdlc. I recommend viewing the video after every timed description below (see Tables 6.1–6.5) with a focus on the person being described (see Figures 6.3–6.11).

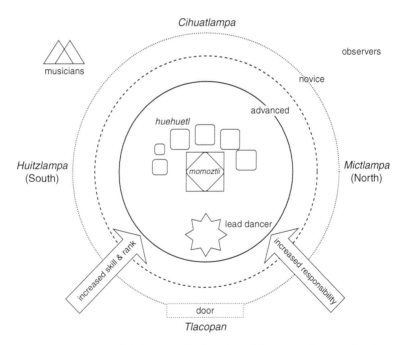

Figure 6.3 Depiction of the layout and orientation of the *ensayo*, featuring the place-ment of the *momoztli*, door, drums (*heuhuetl*), musicians, lead dancer, and the circles of dancers.

Note: With advanced skill and rank, dancers are placed closer to the center, increasing their respon-sibility to be models for more novice dancers and their opportunities to take *cargos*.

Figure 6.4 Visual identification of the *cargos* that execute a weekly dance ceremony.

Note: Depiction of concentric circles of dancers arranged around the *momoztli* (1). Also pictured are the *tlayacanqui*, Mitlalpilli (2); the *chicomecoatzin*, Nauhxayacatl (3); the *tiaxcau*, Atlaua (4); the *cihuacoatl*, Tekolpoktli (5); the dance leader for this turn, Melissa (6); the *heuhuetqueh*, Xochitecpatl (7); Yeucatizini, who is holding the door for dancers who come in (8); some beginners: dancers/drummers (9); and the *cuicapiqui*, Xochicuauhtli and Temaquizcuini (10).

Figure 6.5 Tracing the *cargo* of the *tlayacanqui*

Table 6.1   Mitlalpilli: Executing the *cargo* of *tlayacanqui* of the *ensayo* ceremony

min:sec	
0:01	Mitlalpilli points to Nico, a guest dancer from the Xipe Totec group, so that he moves over to fill in a gap in the middle of three concentric circles. He traces with his hand the imaginary circle he wants Nico to dance in.
0:10	Mitlalpilli looks over the entire circle while others dance. He stands and surveys per the requirements of this *cargo*.
0:13	Mitlalpilli resumes his dancing from a position near the eastern quadrant of the circle, near the door. He follows Melissa, a visiting dancer, who is offering her *nahui ollin* dance.
0:30	Mitlalpilli turns toward the door and stops Cuauhxayacatl, a dancer who has just entered and was moving clockwise around the circle to a position Atlaua had previously indicated. Mitlalpilli stops her and points her in the opposite direction, walking her over. After a few steps, he engages dancers on the outside circle telling them to dance arm lengths apart.
0:45	Mitlalpilli moves dancers who have skewed the symmetry of the circle. Down the northern arc of the circle, he shows them to dance arms lengths apart to keep even spacing. Cuauhxayacatl follows several paces behind.
1:00	When he reaches the southern quadrant of the circle, Mitlalpilli raises his arm and turns, looking for Atlaua who is placing dancers on the opposite side of the circle. He raises his arm as if to ask Atlaua a question about locating her on the circle. Mitlalpilli places Cuauhxayacatl in a gap he has found on the outside circle. He gives her an arm shake, releasing her to that spot.
1:19	Mitlalpilli takes a position in the southeast part of the middle circle. He immediately joins in a dance in progress.

Mitlalpilli's movements and actions in the circle can be understood through his *cargo* as *tlayacanqui*. This *cargo* is sometimes called the *primera palabra*, the first word, because ultimately the responsibility for the ceremony rests with him. Earlier he was teaching dancers in the group he leads, polishing the steps of veteran dancers who simultaneously serve as models for newcomers. Later he opened the ceremony with the invocations. He had spent time drumming, and here he can be seen surveying the ceremony and supporting the work of the *tiaxcau* who is placing people who enter the ceremony into one of the dance circles.

Both in and out of ceremony, Mitlalpilli is the lead organizer for the group, its spokesperson and primary representative. In this part of the *ensayo*, he worries about the spacing and balance of the circles and walks Cuauhxayacatl counterclockwise around the circle to a position on the outside circle. The reason she was going the "wrong" way may be attributed to the fact that some groups make their primary movements in ceremony in that direction. Calpulli Tonalehqueh has adopted all movements in the counterclockwise direction because they subscribe to the idea that *Danza* has its roots in agricultural and astronomical representations. Many dancers relay that *Danza* on earth is supposed to be a mirror of the universe. In the middle, the *momoztli* has elements that include fire, which represents the sun at the center of the solar system. Around that sun, dancers are arranged in circles like the planets: bodies in orbit. Putting aside the technicality that the universe is infinite and any direction is a relative term in three-dimensional space, Calpulli Tonalehqueh claims that the earth has a counterclockwise rotation both around its own axis and in its path around the sun. And so Mitlalpilli and Atlaua ask Cuauhxayacatl to honor that group norm.

Mitlalpilli is allowed to come off of his dancing spot because of his *cargo*. Other dancers are placed in the circle and generally occupy that same space during the whole ceremony. Protocol requires one to ask

Figure 6.6   Tracing the *cargo* of the *chicomecoatzin*

Table 6.2 Nauhxayacatl: the *chicomecoatzin* (*cihuapilli/saumadora*), in charge of the fire, incense, and altar

min:sec	
0:01	Kneeling at the *momoztli* she has arranged with other women, Nauhxayacatl places *copal* resin in her *popoxcomitl* and blows to stoke the coals and produce billowing incense.
0:04	She stands and walks toward the door, continuing to blow into the *popoxcomitl*. She cuts across two circles of dancers to arrive at the door where Cuauhxayacatl awaits.
0:17	Nauhxayacatl proceeds to "smudge" or purify with incense. Starting with Cuauhxayacatl navel, Nauhxayacatl blows incense. She blows incense onto her feet, then her face. Cuauhxayacatl then turns 90 degrees to her right as Nauhxayacatl moves behind her to blow two more stream of incense. Nauhxayacatl traces a circle and a cross in the air behind Cuauhxayacatl's back.
0:22	Nauhxayacatl nods her head and makes eye contact with Cuauhxayacatl who hugs her and walks off.
0:25	Belen, a dancer from the Ehecatl Quetzalcoatl group who was waiting at the door, steps up. She gets incense blown from Nauhxayacatl to the face, navel, and then feet. She also gets a hug before being passed off to Atlaua.
0:32	Jorge, another dancer, steps up. He gets "smudged" on his face, navel, and feet. Nauhxayacatl gives him a hug and passes him off to Atlaua who has been waiting for him with Belen nearby.
0:44	Nauhxayacatl walks back in the direction of the momoztli when something catches her attention (someone must have called out her name). She looks back, points to someone off screen at the door, and nods as if asking if they wish to come in to the ceremony. She walks back to the door and cleanses someone off camera with a big smile. (I presume it was a child because of how low she had to go and the fact that the person manages to be off camera while others have their upper torso visible as they enter.)
0:56	Nauhxayacatl moves back to the center of the circle.
1:03	She kneels, places her *popoxcomitl* on the altar, rearranges a few items, and picks up a fan made of feathers and her rattle.
1:17	She walks behind the drums, around to the southeast side of the second circle and joins the ongoing dance.

for permission to leave, move, or reenter. Dancers are also encouraged to finish any dance they started and not to start a dance if they arrived late. Mitlalpilli is allowed to break the norms because his responsibilities supersede. He is charged with supporting all the other *cargos*. He helps Atlaua place people and space the dancers out at a moment when Atlaua needs to attend to other dancers entering the circle. This is why he raises his hand and looks to Atlaua for acknowledgment of the chosen location for Cuauhxayacatl.

Later in the ceremony, Mitlalpilli is the one who decides when to pause the ceremony for one dancer's *palabra* (Texcallini) and when to end the ceremony. He is the celebrant of a gift give-away to some of the members of the *Grupo de Guerra* and the overseer of the *palabra* session at the end. From start to finish he is the overall responsibility for the ceremony as the *tlayacanqui*, the one who works.

If one examines the surviving pre-Cuauhtémoc *amochtin* (books) such as the ones commonly known as the Bodley Codex, Selden Codex, or Nuttall Codex, there are many scenes of male figures offering fire, *copal*, and *ocote* wood at *teocalli*s and using the *popoxcomitl* or its cousin the *tlemaitl*, incense burner. In fact, a slight majority of the figures in the ancient texts that handle incense are men. I am not sure and have not been able to ascertain when or why this changed, but the role of *chicomecoatzin* (sometimes called *malinche*, *saumadora*, or *cuahuapilli*) is almost exclusively a female *cargo* in modern-day *Danza*. Indeed, many would find it quite disconcerting for a man to take this charge in modern-day *Danza* ceremonies although you do see some male elders wield the *popoxcomitl* in other purification ceremonies. Men rarely help in arranging the *momoztli*.[7]

In a similar way, drumming has become an almost exclusively male *cargo*, though the possibilities are increasing for women to drum; female drummers are increasingly present in *Danza*. One of Calpulli Tonalehqueh's best drummers is a woman. That said, Nauhxayacatl has been the lead *chicomecoatzin* in Calpulli Tonalehqueh since its inception. She is an important role model and a teacher.

In this *ensayo*, her movement is free like the *tlayacanqui*. She can dance but is not required to do so. Her *cargo* is to tend to the *momoztli*, keep the fire (in the form of hot coals and sometimes candles) burning at all times, and, with these, manage the energy of the circle. It is often said that while dancers deliver energy externally in the circle, most of the work of the *chicomecoatl* involves the internal management of the spiritual energy. This fits with the important ideology of duality in all Mexica traditions. While the other *cargos* do extroverted management of the dancers, she does introverted work. She is the caretaker of the altar, the center to which all the energy and prayers of the dancers are directed. Also, since one of the overall goals of *Danza* ceremonies is to create harmony (between dancers, between dancers and the universe, etc.), the *chicomecoatzin*'s *cargo* is to purify the energy of the dancers with fire and incense. Dancers are received at the door, partly to identify them in order to place them in the appropriate space (see Atlaua's analysis in this chapter), but also to cleanse them and so the hosts can assure that people bring positive elements into the dance circle. Dancers at Calpulli Tonalehqueh *ensayos* cannot enter the ceremony without first engaging the *chicomecoatzin*. Part of her task is to gauge the state of the incoming dancers, cleanse them with incense, and receive and clean any gifts they may have brought for the *momoztli*. She has the authority, in consultation with the *tlayacanqui* and *topilli*, to eject any dancer who brings negative elements to the ceremony.

Some of the advanced crafts of the *chicomecoatzin* seem esoteric. Some told me they could read the smoke coming out of their *popoxcomitl*, or read the palms, faces, and/or auras of the incoming dancers to gauge their energy state (Miquiztli, personal communication). There have been instances where people sneak items into the ceremony and

Figure 6.7   Tracing the *cargo* of the *chicomecoatzin*

Table 6.3 Atlaua: The *tiaxcau*, in charge of placing people in the circles of the *ensayo*

min:sec	
0:06	Atlaua appears at the door, seeing that dancers are making ready to enter. The dance ceremony is ongoing behind him with Melissa offering her *permiso*. He looks back behind him six times, appraising the gaps that exist in the circle.
0:25	He greets Cuauhxayacatl. Both of them turn to face the center of the circle, and Atlaua traces a path around the circle with his finger, a path of about 340 degrees counterclockwise for her to end up at a location near the door, which he points to. Cuauhxayacatl begins walking in a clockwise path toward the indicated point when Mitlalpilli intercepts her. Atlaua signals a second and third time for her to go all the way around the circle.
0:35	Cuauhxayacatl follows Mitlalpilli as Atlaua moves back to greet Belen, a dancer from another group. He looks to see where he can place her (presumably) as they stand by the door. They wait as Nauhxayacatl smudges Jorge at the door.
0:43	Atlaua greets Jorge and walks between the inner and second circles, in front of the two dancers. Atlaua arrives in the northwestern part of the inner circle and asks Tonalcoatzin and Tonalmitotiani (who had been dancing there since the ceremony's opening) to slide over and make room between them for both Jorge and Belen. Jorge and Belen shake hands with Tonalmitotiani and Tonalcoatzin and immediately start dancing as Melissa starts her dance. Atlaua misses Mitlalpilli who is trying to get his attention for the placement of Cuauhxayacatl.
1:09	Atlaua walks over and places himself in the second circle, in the due south portion of the circle. This is a new location for him. He looks on to Melissa to gather what dance she is doing and after a moment joins her and the other dancers in collective movement.

place items on the *momoztli* to harm others and the spiritual harmony being generated. I had heard of people bringing black magic items, tarot cards, and other symbols to attempt spiritual harm to others. The *chicomecoatzin* is charged with monitoring these aspects of the ceremony.

More than most *cargos*, being a *chicomecoatzin* in Calpulli Tonalehqueh requires a commitment to that way of participating in the ceremony. Two elder advisors of Calpulli Tonalehqueh, Miquiztli (personal communication) and Ocelocoatl (personal communication), had told me that choosing to be a *chicomecoatzin* is a weighty decision because it is a lifetime commitment, a commitment that requires deep sacrifice and vulnerability. They explain that the *chicomecoatzin* should arrive before everyone, should have secured the elements for the momoztli and fire/incense, should prepare herself spiritually so that she does not contaminate the harmony of the ceremony, should be deeply focused throughout the entire ceremony, and should leave last. There are no breaks for the *chicomecoatzin*. Because of this recognition, the current set of *chicomecoatzin* in Calpulli Tonalehqueh has instituted a series of trainings for others who have chosen to prepare for this *cargo*. With the combined experience of Miquiztli, Ocelocoatl, Nauhxayacatl, Zihuayaocuicatl, and others, this training has been designed. Three dancers, Cihuachimalli, Atezcazolli, and Cuauhxihuitl, recently completed their training and serve as *chicomecoatzin* in the group.

Next, I examine the *cargo* that oversees the placement of dancers on the circle.

Atlaua has been selected the *tiaxcau* of this *ensayo*. His charge is to place people in the ceremony in a way that serves goals of learning, balance, and respect for status. Ideally, Atlaua receives each person at the door and walks them to their spot, but in this video clip he is forced to signal a position to Cuauhxayacatl because he has other people waiting for him at the door. Mitlalpilli moves in to support him when he sees that Cuauhxayacatl is going the opposite of the indicated direction.

At some point in time after this *ensayo*, Calpulli Tonalehqueh recognizes that having two people at the cargos of *tiaxcau* and *cihuacoatl* would be ideal for several reasons:

- It is customary to have pairs at these *cargos* at many *Danza* ceremonies, so replicating this would align the *ensayo* ceremony with those
- Having two people at those *cargos*—ideally a woman and a man—would fall in line with the Mexica emphasis on duality
- Two people executing these *cargos* would support efficiency by eliminating the "backup" that sometimes occurs at the door. With this, more people would get to offer a dance
- Having more people mentored and trained at each *cargo* serves the group well in future *ensayos*, ceremonies, and the human capacity pipeline

Soon after this *ensayo*, the members of the *Grupo de Guerra* take on mentees at each of the *cargos* during *ensayo*, and in their absence, understudies move up to take care of the responsibilities (see chapter 5). Taken a step further, the mentors and mentees are often given other *cargos*. The idea is to cross-train so that *calpulli* members could be able to execute any *cargo* at any time, or, at the very least, grow in empathy and understanding for the other *cargos*.

Early in the video clip, Atlaua is seen looking back several times as he takes into consideration several variables. His is the art of placing dancers. Depending on the size of the space and the number of dancers, the *tiaxcau* decides how many circles there will be. Calpulli Tonalehqueh *ensayos* average 50 dancers, so there are frequently two or three circles. On this date, there are three by his decision. As the *tiaxcau*, Atlaua has learned that at least one representative from each of the visiting groups must be placed in the inner circle, closest to the *momoztli* and in front of others. The inner circle in some ceremonies is reserved for the elders, children, or both. At Calpulli Tonalehqueh *ensayos*, the inner circle is designated for leaders or emissaries of other groups. In this video clip, we see dancers visiting from at least seven other groups beside Calpulli Tonalehqueh. In addition to visiting leaders, the *tiaxcau* has the option of placing strong veteran dancers in the inner circle. Other dancers, especially beginners, are placed in the outer circle. The reason for this is that if beginners have strong dancers in front and beside them, they will have many

Tekolpoktli

Figure 6.8   Tracing the *cargo* of the *cihuacoatl*

Table 6.4 Tekolpoktli: The *cihuacoatl* of the *ensayo*, in charge of "passing the dances"

min:sec	
0:01	Tekolpoktli is running in from behind the drums in the west end of the circle toward the door as he signals to Melissa to come and dance. She had already been told she was next. Xochinecuhtli has just finished her dance and the drums are playing the rhythm that accompanies the *nahui ollin*, or *permiso* dance.
0:04	Melissa runs up from her position in the east end of the circle to a space in front of the drums on the inner circle. Tekolpoktli turns and dances to Melissa's left as Xochinecuhtli takes a position on her right. Xochinecuhtli occupies a position for the outgoing dancer, a transition space.
0:07	Tekolpoktli sidesteps Nauhxayacatl who is coming in from the *momoztli* as someone off camera (in the northeast) yells his name. He looks back and nods but continues dancing. As he does so, he picks up debris from the floor. He adjusts his *faja*.
0:28	After Melissa's *nahui ollin*, Tekolpoktli walks behind her to go and thank Xochinecuhtli with an arm shake. Xochinecuhtli has completed her offering. She shakes Melissa's hand and returns to her spot on the second circle in front of the door where Atlaua waits with Belen.
0:38	Tekolpoktli walks slowly around the circle and surveys the circle from a position next to Iztacoatl. He turns to her as she tells him that she feels cold.
0:46	Tekolpoktli walks around the circle slowly (I estimate he is contemplating who he shall invite to offer the next dance). He comes all the way around to his starting point behind Iztacoatl and to Nico's right (360 degrees). Tekolpoktli is between the second and outermost circles.
1:17	Tekolpoktli taps Nico on the shoulder and points to the middle of the circle. Nico asks him something and Tekolpoktli points to the middle once more repeating that he is next to offer a dance. Nico nods affirmatively.
1:20	Tekolpoktli walks around counterclockwise and slowly between the middle and outer circles. He takes a position between the second and outer circles on the north side of the space and dances behind Tezcacoatl and the other dancers who have been following Melissa.

teachers, many models upon which to draw. In this *ensayo*, a circle between the inner and outermost is needed to avoid collisions and overcrowding. It is Atlaua's decision to create this third circle, in consultation with the *tlayacanqui* (Mitlalpilli). A person can be moved at any time according to the needs of the balance of the circle as assessed by the *tiaxcau*.

Politically, the *tiaxcau* works in service of good relations with visiting groups. Spiritually, the *tiaxcau* is responsible for placing people in the circle so that there is equilibrium. Educationally, the *tiaxcau* is mindful of placing beginners where they can be successful learners. Toward these ends, the *tiaxcau* considers gender by making attempts to balance men and women throughout the circle. Furthermore, the *tiaxcau* needs to identify the providence of each dancer at the door, or ascertain that through questioning, so that the individual can be placed in the appropriate circle. There is a certain status that many visiting dancers expect to be given. Location has meaning. Some visitors are more patient than others when placed in a location that they deem does not match their status. Also, the *tiaxcau* considers age and experience, attempting to distribute adept dancers in between beginners. There are also space and sightline appraisals (many dancers do not like to be behind the drums because it is difficult to see and that the movements are harder to follow, or because one has to move counterintuitively sometimes when following the lead dancer), so the *tiaxcau* places people accordingly.

The work of the *tiaxcau* supports all the other *cargos*. For example, the *tiaxcau* cooperates with the *chicomecoatzin* and door holders to funnel people into the ceremony efficiently, and if she or he places dancers in the inner circle according to the norms, then the *cihuacoatl* has easier time giving out turns for dances. If the *tiaxcau* does their job well, then the good relations are more easily maintained between groups and the *tlayacanqui* is supported. If the beginners are supported, they will return, learn, and grow in the *Danza* and in the *calpulli*. The spirit of *tequio* and *calpulli* is present in the work of every *cargo*.

As outlined in chapter 5, the *cihuacoatl* is the main dance leader in the group or of a given ceremony. In this *ensayo*, Tekolpoktli is selected as the *cihuacoatl* largely because of his vast experience—he has traveled extensively picking up dances, and he mentors others frequently at the beginning and advanced levels. As the *cihuacoatl* of the *ensayo* this evening, he leads a brief warm-up and then selects individuals to lead the ceremony in dance.

There is an art to passing the dances. Being invited to come up and lead everyone in a dance is one of the many symbols of respect and honor bestowed upon an individual during the ceremony. Tekolpoktli has several considerations to weigh for his sequence of selection. Early on, he is compelled by protocol to give dances to visitors, starting with the most veteran and/or accomplished leaders from other groups. Also, he must pass dances to visitors who have come from far away. On top of that, he must recognize visitors who have not visited in a long time. After those considerations, Tekolpoktli will give dances to other strong dancers and, where possible, to dancers from within Calpulli Tonalehqueh.

Within the above parameters, the Tekolpoktli attempts to build the energy of the *ensayo*. In other words, the *cihuacoatl* usually gives preference to veteran or knowledgeable dancers who will build upon the energy of the ceremony. The *cihuacoatl* has to estimate how many dances will fit into a given timeline and gauge the number of candidates who attended the ceremony for offering dances. If time and attendance permits, novice dancers will also get an opportunity to offer their dance and gain experience from leading the group.

Another layer to the art of passing the dances is gender consideration. It is preferable for the dances to be passed in a man-woman-man-woman sequence. This is ideal but not easily attained given that (1) most of the principal heads of dance groups are men, (b) the majority of dancers are women, and (c) there is great variability in the number of outside visitors who will attend the ceremony. In this *ensayo*, about 70 percent of the dancers are women. Negotiating all the competing variables, Tekolpoktli invites five men and six women to lead dances on this night (the sequence is M, M, F, M, F, F, M, F, F, M, F for the entire *ensayo*). The ideal of male/female equity is more easily obtained when the *cargo* of *cihuacoatl* is shared by a male/female pair in an *ensayo* or given ceremony. In that case, the two *cihuacoatl cargos* alternate the role of inviting individuals up to dance, with the male *cihuacoatl* inviting female dancers to lead while the female *cihuacoatl* inviting male dancers (in as much as possible).

There are other elements of the ceremony that the *cihuacoatl* dictates in consultation with the *tlayacanqui*. The *cihuacoatl*, for example, decides if two or more individuals will come up to offer a dance as a group. This is a recourse the *cihuacoatl* will sometimes use when there are more candidates than time. Also, the *cihuacoatl* decides if an individual who is called up is allowed to bring others (usually members of their own group) up with them. Another element dictated by the hosting group and the *cihuacoatl* is the amount of *nahui ollin* (*permiso/cruz/firma*) dances done prior to each dance. Many groups and ceremonies have two or three *nahui ollin*s between each dance. If, for example, a *cihuacoatl* does a *nahui ollin*, then selects a dancer to come up to dance and that person does a *permiso* before their dance, then there would be two. Some dancers who are called up prefer executing a *permiso* before and after their dance. If the selected dancer does a *permiso* before and after their dance, then there could potentially be three *permiso* dances done (one by the preceding dancer, one by the *cihuacoatl* who then goes out to signal an incoming dancer who then does their own *permiso*). In order to streamline this process, Calpulli Tonalehqueh has elected what the video illustrates: The *cihuacoatl* tells the person they will be up next during an ongoing dance. That person then comes up and does their *permiso* simultaneously with the outgoing dancer. Therefore, only one *permiso* is offered between dances. In this case, Melissa comes up and offers her *permiso* next to Xochinecuhtli who has just finished her dance and Tekolpoktli who accompanies each dancer at the start. When the *permiso* is over, Melissa calls for her dance and Xochinecuhtli is done. Tekolpoktli then searches for and selects Nico to follow Melissa (while Melissa is dancing). When it is Nico's turn, he goes up and offers his *permiso* with Tekolpoktli and Melissa flanking him. The *cihuacoatl* in Calpulli Tonalehqueh will not do a *permiso* dance alone, save for the opening and closing of the entire ensayo. This protocol eliminates up to 20 *nahui ollin* dances in the *ensayo* in question, leaving more time for dancers to be invited up.

Another aspect of the *cargo* of the *cihuacoatl* evident in the video clip is that she or he must thank the person who has just offered their dance. In the clip, right after Melissa finishes her *nahui ollin* dance, Tekolpoktli moves to thank Xochinecuhtli (she follows this by greeting Melissa).

Melissa is called up to offer the sixth dance of the *ensayo* because she is a visitor from another group. She comes up to a position on the inner circle, always reserved for the lead dancer. She immediately

Figure 6.9   A dancer takes her turn leading the ceremony

Table 6.5   Melissa: A dancer (*macehualli*) invited to lead

min:sec	
0:01	Melissa runs up to the position of the inner circle directly in front of the drums and *momoztli* from where she will lead the ceremony. Facing west and with Tekolpoktli and Xochinecuhtli on either side of her, she immediately goes into her *nahui ollin* (*permiso*) dance, which the drums had already been drumming.
0:32	The drums stop after the *nahui ollin*. Melissa does an arm shake with Xochinecuhtli. Melissa looks down at the floor as she does a slow 360-degree turn (I presume she is thinking of what dance to call for). She signals the beat of the dance she wants with her *ayacaxtli*.
0:44	The drummers are talking among themselves and do not see or hear her at first, but soon they lean in to listen to her. Xochitecpatl, the lead drummer, catches on to her beat and starts to drum.
1:01	After four counts of the dance, Melissa bows to her right and then starts her dance. Some call the dance she chooses "Ehecatl" (wind). In the video clip we see her execute two ornamental steps (*flores*), four times each, with a two-part base in between.

goes into her unique interpretation of the *firma* (*nahui ollin*). She then calls out a dance with her *ayacaxtli*. There are times when a dancer will verbally request a dance. The difficulty with this is the great variability in the naming of dances. For instance, there are sometimes different dances that are known by the same name in different groups. At other times, there is one dance known by multiple names. Sometimes, dancers have learned the Náhuatl name for a dance, but others call by its Spanish name, and so on. Therefore, rather than playing a guessing game with the name of the dance, many dancers will signal the beat they want with their rattle. The drummers listen in, and once they recognize it, they will begin to drum. (I discuss the role of the drummers in further detail the next section.)

All of the dancers in the circle are obliged to follow the lead dancer. In some ways, Melissa and her energy, placed at the center of the circle, becomes heliocentric and the dancers around her orbit. She is placed in front of the *momoztli* because she is making her offering, her prayer. She dictates the speed of the dance, its pace. She dictates the length of the dance. Once the drummers begin drumming the beat of the dance, the lead dancer decides the moment at which they actually start dancing. It is customary for the dancer to wait four cycles of the central beat of the dance to allow other dancers to catch on or remember the dance and prepare to start in sync with the lead.

Another crucial aspect that all dancers learn is the logic of the patterns of the dances. Dances have repeating patterns and a logic that will allow anyone to follow a dance even if they had never seen it before. It is analogous to a writer who uses an alphabet (a set of letters) to form words, and words to form sentences. *Danza* has a movement set and syntax. The English alphabet has 26 letters (and a set of punctuation marks) with which one can spell all the words of the language. For the sake of explanation, let us say that there are 50 "moves" in *Danza*. A move could be something like a 360° turn, a squat, a forward-facing waist-high kick, a tap of the floor with the ball of one's foot, etc. If a dancer acquires the complete set of moves and uses the pattern logic of dances, then they are equipped to perform any dance in the *Danza* universe. It is said that there are more than 365 dances, at least one for every day of the year. Dances represent creatures (coyote, rabbit, frog, eagle), natural phenomena (rain, wind, sun, fire), or other concepts (human memory, wisdom, willpower, children's laughter) (see

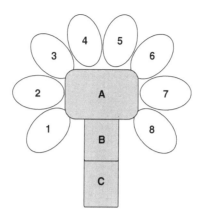

Figure 6.10   A conceptual representation of a typical dance.

Note: The *bases* of a dance are often described as a stem, while the *flores* are like petals, each connected to the stalk.

figure 6.2). Each dance is a unique combination and pattern of subset of the total available "moves."

Usually, moves are executed within two, four, or eight beats (drum beats, counts) and are repeated at least once, if not four or eight times. The vast majority of dances have a base move repeated throughout the dance, with ornamental steps inserted alternately. Moves can serve as either a base or an ornamental move, depending on the dance. In Calpulli Tonalehqueh, the base move is called a *base*, Spanish for base, and the ornamental steps are called *flores*, Spanish for flowers (see figure 6.10). Some dancers use *cambio* (Spanish for change) in place of *flores*. *Flores* and *bases* are always repeated in dances. For the sake of illustrating patterns, I use letters to represent base moves and numbers to represent *flores*. A dance can begin with either a *flor* or a *base*, though they tend to start with *flores*. The most common sequence for dances is

1 A 1 A 2 A 2 A 3 A 3 A 4 A 4 A...

where each *base* and *flor* is composed of a move repeated four times.

The dance Melissa offers at this *ensayo* has *flores* interwoven between two *bases* in the following sequence

1 A B 1 A B 2 A B 2 A B 3 A B 3 A B 4 A B 4 A B

Here also, each *base* and *flor* is composed of a move repeated four times.

Melissa decides to end her dance after the insertion of four *flores*. In dances with more complex patterns, *bases* and *flores* both change throughout the dance in sequences such as

A 1 A 1 B 2 B 2 C 3 C 3 D 4 D 4...

or

1 A B 1 A B 2 C B 2 C B 3 D B 3 D B...

or

A B C D E 1 A B C D E 2 A B C D E 3 A B C D E 4

Dances generally have 4, 8, 13, or 20 *flores* that go along with a *base* or two. Dancers rarely learn more than eight *flores* per dance. Some dancers theorize that many of the dances had many more *flores* that have disappeared over time. Dances range in duration from about two minutes on the low end to twenty minutes on the high end. Most dances last about four or five minutes.

Dances and movements generally start to the left. This is because the left is the side on which one's heart lies. Each move, whether in a *flor* or *base*, will always start to the left; followers know that the first step, turn, stomp, or kick in a series will initiate on one's left hand side. This helps dancers follow the leader. The patterns of *Danza* serve the ideal of harmony. Dancers can more easily dance in sync, stay on beat, flow in the same direction, start and stop, because there are

Xochitecpatl

Figure 6.11 Tracing the work of the *huehuetqueh*

Table 6.6   Xochitecpatl: The *huehuetqueh cargo*, leading the drums

min:sec	
0:01	When the video opens, Xochitecpatl is drumming the *nahui ollin* as Melissa runs up and takes her position in front of him and the *momoztli*. Zihuayaocuicatl is on his right and Chuy is on his left. There are three drums on the semicircle with no drummers. A boy, about three years old named Techimalli, drums on a children's drum. Xochitectpatl embellishes his drumbeat with ornaments.
0:33	After the *nahui ollin*, Xochitecpatl turns to Zihuayaocuicatl to show her callouses (or blisters) on his hands. She also shows him her hands.
0:44	Xochitecpatl looks up to listen in on the beat that Melissa makes with her *ayacaxtli*. He identifies it and starts to drum. He drums the complete dance, including the *flores* and the *bases* of Melissa's dance all the way through to her finish.

known patterns, norms, and defaults. So even if a dancer, who has had a different teacher or knows a different sequence for a dance, offers a dance you do not know, the patterns of *Danza* will give each dancer a framework for successful leading, following, teaching, and acquisition.

The role of the *huehuetzotzoqueh* (drummers) is to follow the dancer who is leading the prayer/dance. This is the opposite of most European musical art forms, where the dancers follow the music. Here, if the dancer speeds up or slows down, the drummers must adjust. The players must drum the dance in the fashion that the lead dancer requests. The drummers are led by the *huehuetqueh*, the lead drummer whom they are all obligated to follow. It is important that the drummers play in concert. It is quite jarring when there is dissonant or syncopated drumming.

Much like the *chicomecoatzin*, drummers have a particular identity in *Danza*. Dancers choose to join the ranks of the drummers and musicians. They learn to drum through immersion like the young Techimalli in the video clip, or come to the drum after some dancing. Drummers help each other learn how to make drums, take care of them in storage and transport, skin their drums with hides, fabricate drumsticks, and so forth. The name for the drum is *huehuetl*, meaning venerable old one. It is called so because drums are carved out of a single tree trunk, often hundreds of years old. Nowadays, access to materials can be costly and drums have been fabricated from metal barrels, wooden planks, and other cheap materials. Drums in different sizes, heights, and tones each have a specific name (e.g., *tlapanhuehuetl, mahuehuetl, panhuehuetl*). In pre-Cuauhtémoc Anáhuac, drums were played exclusively with the hands, but through the years, drummers began using sticks. The drum is supposed to represent the heartbeat of Mother Earth and the heartbeat of the ceremony. The first and most basic drumbeat simulates the beating of a heart.

It is often said it is ideal for a drummer to be a dancer first. This experience gives the drummer sympathy for and knowledge of what a dancer requires. Drummers play in service of the dancers. They are charged with continually adding dance beats to their repertoire so that they are able to drum any dance evoked by a dancer. In the case that a drummer is not familiar with a dance the lead dancer asks for, the drummer must first make an attempt to learn the dance beat quickly in the ceremony. The drummer will use the same knowledge of the patterns of dances to learn the drumbeat (repetition, counts of two, four, eight, etc.). Some dances have the same beat repeated throughout the entire dance, irrespective of the *bases* and *flores*. Most of the time, the entire sets of base and ornamental moves will have their respective beat. In other words, most dances have two beats, one for *base* moves and one for *flores*. As would be expected, there are dances that have more complex beats. As a player gains fluency on the *huehuetl* (drum), there are opportunities to embellish the drumming. A drummer can embellish their drumming, for example, by adding ornamental notes within measures and counts or in transitions within the dance sequence.

In addition to the drummers, Calpulli Tonalehqueh has other musicians. This *ensayo* features two *cuicapiqui*, or singers/musicians, Xochicuauhtli and Temaquizcuini. At this *ensayo*, they play several *tlapitzalli*, or flutes, and wind instruments that they fabricated through participation in Calpulli Tonalehqueh workshops. They stand outside the circle and near the sound amplification equipment. Traditionally, other musicians play right beside the drums. The switch from hands to sticks for playing the drums would dramatically increase the decibel level of the drums at the expense of other instruments. Also, a vast majority of the songs that accompany dance and musical pieces have disappeared over time.

There are two additional aspects of this *ensayo* that merit analysis as important sites of education within the *ensayo* construct. The first is the time set aside in this particular *ensayo* for a dancer, Texcallini, to offer her public commitment to *Danza*, a process commonly known as "testing." The second is the time set aside at the end of *ensayo* for *palabra*. I discuss my observations of these two aspects of Calpulli Tonalehqueh in turn.

Grupo de Guerra Benchmarks and Commitments

Throughout 2007, Calpulli Tonalehqueh's leadership encountered a steady increase in the number of invitations to community and performance events as well as the continual obligation to attend ceremonies hosted by *Danza* groups regionally and beyond, while at the same time having a core of veteran dancers (the *Grupo de Guerra*) who are progressively less able to meet those obligations. At this time, many of the founding members of Calpulli Tonalehqueh had important family, school, work, and personal commitments that required attention; the *Grupo de Guerra* was less and less able to attend the numerous ceremonies to which the group was invited, accept the cultural diffusion performance invitations, or attend the weekly *ensayo* and ceremony-organizing endeavors of the *calpulli*. The need to grow the membership of the *Grupo de Guerra* and create a pipeline of members who are able to take *cargos* at *ensayo* or represent the group in ceremony and in the community was the subject of many meetings. The group was developing a handbook outlining the precepts, norms, roles, and expectations the group would operationalize. The *calpulli* was in its formative years, looking to formalize its structure and sustain its efforts.

In these conversations, at least two ideas took hold. One was that the members of *Grupo de Guerra* taking *cargos* at *ensayos* would do so with an apprentice of sorts, an interested novice dancer who would be mentored in the fundamentals of the role. The apprenticeships would be rotated with some frequency so that people would have experience at several roles. This practice was successful. A new cadre of dancers was soon able to execute the *cargos* at the *ensayos* in the absence of *Grupo de Guerra* members. Furthermore, these newer dancers were more often the ones who would attend the ceremonies hosted by other groups and would represent Calpulli Tonalehqueh. A reward system was instituted, where a dancer would receive feathers for learning new dances and for attending a set number of ceremonies.

They also concluded during the 2007 meetings that the *Grupo de Guerra* needed to grow its membership. As I discuss in chapter 5, veteran dancers who founded Calpulli Tonalehqueh and others who arrived early on with enough experience to perform the duties originally constitute the *Grupo de Guerra*. New efforts to identify candidates to join the *Grupo de Guerra* emerged. Calpulli Tonalehqueh leaders made a list of individuals who were making independent progress and who would be asked to join the *Grupo de Guerra*. A meeting was held where invitees were presented with a newly developed framework of norms and expectations for members of this cadre. I outline some norms below:

Grupo de Guerra Florida

(1) Purpose:
    (a) Actualizes the *calpulli* objectives through the tradition of *in xochitl in cuicatl* (the flower and the song), sharing ceremonial dance, native theatre, spoken word, and aboriginal music
(2) Qualifications:
    (a) 1 year active with Calpulli Tonalehqueh
    (b) Have the ability to lead at least four dances by themselves
    (c) Have a complete *traje* as defined by the *calpulli*
(3) Process for entrance into the group:
    (a) Talk with the *Grupo de Guerra Florida*
    (b) Lead four different dances in front of the group for four consecutive weeks (one each week)
    (c) Express your commitment in front of the whole group during *palabra*
    (d) Finally, we will do a Temascalli ceremony
(4) Expectations:
    (a) (Be prepared to) take on a *cargo* within dance and be versed in the other *cargos*
    (b) 1 year commitment
    (c) Be early to all activities
    (d) Be an example at all activities
    (e) Be a leader at all activities
    (f) Attend 85 percent of practices per year
    (g) Attend 2–5 of major *calpulli* events
    (h) Attend 13 out of 25+ ceremonies per year

      (i) Attend 50 percent of presentations throughout the year (average is 15–20 per year)

      (j) Support the Mission of Calpulli Tonalehqueh and represent the *calpulli* with dignity and respect

(5) Attire/*Traje*

      (a) *Traje* (*Manta, Luces, Piel, o Chaquira*)

      (b) *Cahctli* (*Guaraches* or Mocassins)

      (c) *Rodilleras*

      (d) *Maztla*

      (e) *Faja*

      (f) *Pectoral/Chaleco/Queshquemitl* (optional)

      (g) *Cozcatl* (necklace of precious stone [selected according to your Tonalamatl])

      (h) *Pulseras* (bracelets)

      (i) *Chimalli* (shield)

      (j) Other *armas*: fan, axe, *Macuahuitl*, bow/arrow, etc.

(6) *Calpulli* dances

      (a) *Fuego, Guerrero, Tezcatlipoca, Huilotl*

Many dancers declined the invitation, but the first five dancers who did undergo the process of initiation were Texcallini, Tonalcoatzin, Cihuachimalli, Cuauhxihuitl, and Atezcazolli. These women spent months making attire, learning and rehearsing numerous dances, attending ceremonies, mentoring at *ensayos*, and presenting their public intentions to join the *Grupo de Guerra*.

At the *ensayo* featured in this chapter, the ceremony is paused after eight dances, and Mitlalpilli announces that Texcallini will offer her dances and her *palabra*, her public commitment to the process. She is purified with incense, received with calls from conch shells, and given the floor. She offers words of gratitude to the people who have given her space, energy, friendship, tutoring, and support. After her words, she offers two of the Calpulli Tonalehqueh dances (Yaotecatl and Tezcatlipoca). Subsequently, she is given a set of feathers, hugs, and cheers. The *ensayo* then proceeds as normal.

Over time, the initiation ("testing") process for the *Grupo de Guerra* faded. Few others submit themselves to the process henceforth. In interviews with a few women, they identified important criticisms of the process. Some were uncomfortable with the fact that none of the original members of the *Grupo de Guerra* were "tested" in the same way. They made the rules for the process and then were "grandfathered" in. The new initiates were required to be proficient in the "official" dances of the *calpulli* even when current members of the *Grupo de Guerra* did not always have proficiency. Also, the original members of *Grupo de Guerra* did not meet the expectations of time-lines, attendance to ceremonies, performances, and *ensayos*. In this vein, many *calpulli* members told me they felt the expectations out-lined in the handbook were unrealistic, causing many to shy away from coursing the process.

Other negative critiques were that initiates did not feel well sup-ported, that the process was too Western, inorganic, or too close to the kinds of tests seen in schools, causing anxiety and stress, and detracting from the general experience of membership. They held that if *Danza* was voluntary, noncompulsory, and meant to be enjoy-able, dancers should have the freedom to move to deeper membership without having rules or the threat of negative consequences for not meeting arbitrary benchmarks and rigid formats. Outside the formal initiation process, many members advanced quickly in their skill and depth of participation, and the number of dancers able to handle *car-gos* at *ensayos* and represent the group in the community increased. Their critique was that institution of the "testing" system for entry into *Grupo de Guerra* was more an assessment-driven process than a *calpulli*-building process.

The Palabra

The second aspect of the *ensayo* that is not seen in the video clip but worthy of mention is the ending, a session called *palabra*. As discussed in chapter 5, the *palabra* in this case is a session where dancers are allowed to voice their thoughts. The *ensayo* is a ceremony in and of itself, but in the larger context, the *ensayo* is a rehearsal for the formal ceremonies that take place throughout the year. All formal ceremonies end with a *palabra*. Calpulli Tonalehqueh replicates this in the same way most groups do at their *ensayos*. On this particular night, the *palabra* begins at 9:17 p.m., and 34 people stay in the circle for the session. Nine people listen on from outside the circle. The remaining dancers must pack up and go, as it is always an optional session and many need to leave for various reasons.

The *tlayacanqui* of the host group initiates the *palabra*, and each person can have a turn in a counterclockwise direction. Each person begins their comments with the greeting/proclamation, "*Ometeotl*."[8] Each dancer in the circle of *palabra* must at least use the *Ometeotl*. The rest of the dancers will answer the greeting with their own *Ometeotl*. In large ceremonies, *palabra* is given customarily to one representative from each group. In this *ensayo*, each dancer is given the opportunity to speak.

During *palabra*, veteran dancers model the rhetoric, register, and discourses common during these sessions. The typical framework for a *palabra* is to begin with words of gratitude to all of creations, then to elements such as the sun, the earth, the ancestors, and to those in attendance. Afterward, dancers usually thank the host group for hosting the ceremony and having their doors open. Then, dancers usually acknowledge particular foci in the *ensayo*, which can be anything from a visiting elder or a dancer like Texcallini who underwent a special initiation. Next, the dancer delivers any personal message, makes announcements, or gives invitations. The *palabra* time is also available as a space to air grievances or offer apologies. If someone is displeased or feels offended, they are invited to share their criticism at the *palabra* so that the issues can be resolved. On the other side, dancers will offer apologies for any transgressions they have committed. At other times, dancers will offer ceremonial songs during *palabra*. It is also customary for children from Calpulli Tonalehqueh to take the food, drink, flowers, and herbs placed on the *momoztli* during the *ensayo* and distribute them to the visitors and dancers while *palabra* is ongoing. This rhetorical sequence is customary, and though there may be slight variations, this structure of *palabra* is known and repeated in *Danza* circles throughout the world. Again, after my participation at over 100 *ensayos* with Calpulli Tonalehqueh and elsewhere, I can affirm this pattern as a constant.

Palabra has a multilingual nature. Dancers offer their words in Náhuatl, Spanish, English, and a variety of other indigenous languages. At this *ensayo*, for example, 16 of the 34 participants offer words. Of the 16 who speak, seven do so in Spanish with an infusion of Náhuatl. Eight speak in English, and one in an aboriginal language I could not recognize.

The comments delivered by the participants at this *ensayo* revolve around themes of gratitude for gifts, traditions, energy, and ceremony. Other dancers announce a newly formed group and invite Calpulli Tonalehqueh to visit. Many dancers congratulate Texcallini for being such an exemplary member of the *calpulli* and giving her commitment. Finally, Mitlalpilli ends with encouraging dancers to see themselves as part of a large network of dance circles throughout the continent.

Dancing to Deserve?

At the beginning of the chapter, I reviewed literature on the various reasons ancient Mexicas had for participation in *Danza*. Participation in *Danza*, in *macehualiztli*, materializes through various motivations in the present as well. For ancient Mexicas, *Danza* was a site of physical prayer directed at ancestor worship, cosmic energy, gratitude and deserving, recreation, and social relations. Variety in the motivations for participation in *Danza* in Calpulli Tonalehqueh is no different. Conversations with dancers reveal several different responses to questions about what dancers identify as motivations for dancing and the art of deserving. The following quotations exemplify the patterns I identified with some illustrative quotations:

- Danza *for a connection family and culture*:
  - I'm interested in a positive representation of my people and my culture. I've always wanted to dance—since I was a child. My parents would take us to Chicano Park every year for the annual *Danza* ceremony that happens there. It's been ingrained that it was a valuable activity by my parents. (Alvarado, personal communication)
  - I dance because it makes me feel good, connects me to my culture and creates a sense of purpose and reason in life. It's also a good means to be part of a caring group of friends and family who share the same mission and values. It's an excellent way to express my creativity and dedication to serving others. (Colon, personal communication)
- Danza *for family, community, and prayer*:
  - I first started dancing to bring culture into the lives of my children. I supported them by dancing with them and learned it was more then just dancing. I continued on my own, but my daughters and family members followed and felt what I felt. The drums woke us up and we knew we belonged where we were. So, I participate because it's the foundation of what I believe in. It's the original way of our people of how we pray and is an important part of how we pray. I do this because of the blessings and healings it brings for all of us. I cannot dance anymore, but I participate in all the other ways. (Trinidad, personal communication)

- Danza *to connect to heritage*:
  - *Danza* is part of who we are as *Mexicanos*. It is the perhaps a part of our ancestry that I value the most. (Hernández, personal communication)
- Danza *as embodied passion*:
  - Porque me gusta. Para mí la *danza* es mí pasión. Lo llevo en la sangre y cuando escucho el sonido del *huehuetl* mi cuerpo, mi corazón, comienzan a sentir la fuerza y la energía que se genera cuando la gente danza y comparte en armonía. [Because I like it. For me, Danza is a passion. It runs in my blood and when I hear the *huehuetl* my body, my heart feel the force the energy generated when people dance and create harmony.] (Fernández, personal communication)
- Danza *for healing and spiritual health*:
  - To clean the spirit. Gain energy. As ritual. To learn about my culture. (Pedrizco, personal communication)
  - *La Danza* feeds my spirit. (Salcedo, personal communication)
  - To feed my spirit. (Nieves, personal communication)
  - I dance to center myself spiritually. I like the space that *Danza* circles provide. I also like the people who are involved in *Danza*, they're great people and for the most part appreciate the type of community space that dance provides. (De Unamuno, personal communication)
  - It started out as a form of physical and creative expression. It's now one of many ways I connect to my inner strength and power. (Chavira, personal communication)
  - I *Danza* to be in touch with the earth. Not often do we feel the earth with our bare feet. *Danza* allows me to do so and be connected to her. *Danza* helps me remember the work that our ancestors did in the past. In the ceremonial aspect it helps me keep the earth in balance by being in constant prayer so that we're connected to the earth and the spirits. (Romo López, personal communication)
- Danza *for all of the above*:
  - I like the community, relationships, and feeling of dancing with others in the circle. I like the feeling of exhilaration as well as calming effects of *Danza* on me. I dance because it's the most visible experience in learning about and maintaining indigenous traditions of my heritage. I enjoy the physical, spiritual, and mental challenges and rewards from dancing. (Gamboa, personal communication)

Calpulli Tonalehqueh dancers arrive to *Danza* mainly for family, community, spiritual, and cultural reasons. *Danza* is foundation from which the work of Calpulli Tonalehqueh emanates. In the same way ancient *macehualiztli* involved multiple motivations;

modern iterations involve numerous hopes for personal, family, and community concerns.

Embodied Learning: Dance Ceremony as a Palimpsest

The theme of embodied learning characterizes the palimpsest of the *ensayo*. In this chapter, I presented information on ancient Mexica *Danza* and the erasure and changes it underwent. I traced the dynamics, *cargos*, *armas*, elements, sequence, and arrangement of the *ensayo* dance ceremony in Calpulli Tonalehqueh. In this conclusion, I discuss how the concept of palimpsest applied to the *ensayo* reveals it is rooted in the history and takes place in a multilayered physical space, but also in and through the body.

The *ensayo* is a location of palimpsest, which involves a complex assembly of groups, *cargos*, ages, styles, ideologies, art, *nahui ollin*s, prayer and performance, exercise, spirit and energy, sights, and sounds. In addition, the *ensayo* is a palimpsest as a modern reiteration of ancient tradition. Recreating the *ensayo* puts Calpulli Tonalehqueh on a centuries-old cycle of creating sacred time and space through dance ceremony. The weekly nighttime *ensayo* recreates nights at the ancient Mexica schools where youth and their teachers danced. The *ensayos* also invoke the ancient *mixcoacalli*, the schools of professional singers/dancers/musicians, and their rehearsals for big ceremonies.

Ancient Mexica schooling was founded on dance. The experience built through the *ensayo* is holistic and involves a curriculum of mind, body, and spirit. Through prayer, vigorous dance, symbols, music, *cargos*, and *palabra*, dancers receive a comprehensive *Danza* education. Through participation in dance ceremonies like *ensayo*, dancers inductively acquire mathematics and patterns, multiple languages, physiology, music, leadership and interpersonal relations, hospitality, art, astronomy, and spirituality.

Although an extensive comparison of the educational environments of mainstream US schools and the *calpulli* is outside the focus of this book, some comments about distinctions can be made. Some of the best practices of ancient *calpulli* schooling have been reinstituted through dance in Calpulli Tonalehqueh. For one, learning in Calpulli Tonalehqueh takes place mostly through apprenticeship and structured immersion. The explicit rehearsal of steps that took place at the beginning of this *ensayo* is an exception to the norm. Usually, learning the dances, drum beats, *momoztli* construction, etc., happens through these pedagogies. The concentric circles aid in the acquisition of the dances. More experienced dancers in front of beginners in the outside circle and all those to the right or left of a dancer become resources and models for dance.

Alternating leadership is a second feature of the educational environment constructed in *ensayo*. Dancers alternate leading and following, being mentors and novices. As the dances get "passed" among the dancers in attendance, new dances are learned, new capacities built. Dancers are simultaneously teacher and learner.

Third, there is cross-training and mentoring of the *cargos* of the *ensayo*. Leaders of Calpulli Tonalehqueh alternate the *cargos* they take over different *ensayos*, experiencing the varying considerations of the door, placing people, the *momoztli* building/fire keeping, drumming, passing the dances, etc. Apprenticeship is a classic educational arrangement. Learning is resourced through mentoring in Calpulli Tonalehqueh.

Fourth, both failure and competition are deemphasized in the dance ceremony. As a result, affective filters, or learning noise, are reduced, allowing for a more positive experience and an easier acquisition of the dance. Dancers are allowed to learn at their own pace. There was some attention paid to helping dancers advance and instituting "testing" (although that effort faded). But unlike some educational environments, extensive records are not kept about who knows what, where people rank, who is failing, who is better than others, who won, who lost, who is in what percentile, who is learning-disabled, etc. There is competition, and some markers of success and failure are manipulated in the group, but they are not as brutal or consequential as those managed in mainstream schools.

Fifth, the educational environment produced by the *ensayo* engages the whole person. With flowers, incense, music, drum beats, spins, bare feet, handshakes, elevated heart rates, food sharing, proclamations, etc., a dancer's five senses are engaged. The activity is multimodal. The learning that takes place through the dance is also embodied, visceral. It involves the presence and generation of spirits and energy as well as the embodiment of ancient memory. Lessons are imprinted in the muscles as well as the mind.

Lastly, the educational environment of the ensayo is embedded in family and community. It leverages family and community funds of knowledge. The *ensayo* is a space for young and old, children, parents, and elders. Whole families come together for cultural practice and diffusion. Everyone is adopted into the *calpulli* sense of family. The dance ceremonies are also in relationship with the community. *Danza* leverages community spaces, organizations, and resources for learning materials. Through a certain kind of reciprocity, the dance ceremony responds to community needs.

7

Decolonial Pedagogy

From March through July 2010, the J. Paul Getty Villa museum[1] in Los Angeles opened an exhibit of antiquities from the Aztec world of the fifteenth and sixteenth centuries. Museum director Michael Brand commented that he wanted to expand the scope of the museum's offerings and that the idea of an exhibit on the Aztecs developed after a conversation with Harvard professor Thomas B. F. Cummins about the similarities between the Aztec state and the Greco-Roman empire, including their "innumerable gods," monuments, and state politics (Pohl and Lyons, 2010, p. x). Staff at the Getty curated the exhibit in collaboration with UCLA adjunct Art History professor John Pohl and with support of numerous individuals from Mexican, Italian, and US museums (e.g., CONACULTA, INAH, National Anthropology Museum, Museum of the Templo Mayor from México; Biblioteca Medicea Laurenziana from Italy).

The exhibit would certainly reach wide audiences, because the Getty possesses formidable financial, organizational, and cultural resources. For the first time in more than 400 years, the famed Florentine Codex returned to Anáhuac. The Villa also displayed significant sculptures from the most important museums in México City, including the head of *Coyolxauhqui* (the Mexica representation of the moon) and the seated *Xochipilli* (the Mexica representation of art, poetry, and music), as well as several centuries-old texts and images from European authors intended for European consumption of Mexica life and societal organization. The exhibit foregrounded the idea of comparing the world of Athens and Rome at their apices with that of the Mexica.

To its credit, the museum made attempts to provide programming, courses, performances, symposia, family activities, and publications to supplement the exhibit. The assembly of this collection's works, from both sides of the Atlantic, was remarkable. The title of the exhibit, *The Aztec Pantheon and the Art of Empire*, signaled a conventional treatment of the subject matter. For example, a wall of images taken from the *amochtin* (Mexican painted books; codices) was described as the pantheon of Aztec gods. The exhibit relied heavily on colonial and Western archeology for the captions to all the pieces. Sacred items and the symbolism of others were represented exclusively through a Eurocentric frame; many of the references in the exhibit centered on Western and Greco-Roman concepts and interpretations of Mexica concepts and art.

I called the director of antiquities at the museum, explaining my research for this book and to ask her for some background on the exhibit's development and in case she had tracked any feedback or attendance for the exhibit. She exclaimed the exhibit broke all attendance records for the museum. She informed that the attendees were younger than ever before, more international, first-time visitors, and heavily Mexican American. She was gracious in the interview and commented that the focus was to juxtapose Western frames onto Mexica cultural productions because this was what occurred with European arrival in México. She conceded that there are many interpretations and reinterpretations available for the exhibit.

I describe this exhibit because it helps explain part of the approach I am taking in this book. There is no question that a majority of readers, as the curators and visitors of the Getty museum, will be much more familiar with a Eurocentric or colonial view of the Mexica. Students from middle school to college are compelled to learn about history, philosophy, art, politics, and figures of the ancient Greek and Roman worlds of antiquity. Familiarity for contemporary mainstream US audiences also comes indirectly, because so many of the ideological, linguistic, sporting, governmental, artistic, and educational conventions of the United States trace back to Greece and Rome. The European missionary scholars of early colonial México held a similar lens as they struggled to understand what they are encountering in the sixteenth century. They were trained in the "classics" and had just emerged from a 700-year battle with Arabic nations. Their perspectives were skewed further by their colonial mission. Their writings have become the basis for a substantial amount of the mainstream understandings about Mexica life and have deeply informed museum exhibits, such as the one hosted by the Getty.

Members of Calpulli Tonalehqueh would be able to engage that exhibit and criticize the precepts of the title and the captions that surround many of the ancient pieces of art. They would be interested in erasing some of the mainstream conventions and providing a deco-lonial reauthoring of the information. The reason they would be able to do this is that some to the spaces carved out in Calpulli Tonalehqueh for decolonial pedagogy. As part of the cultural diffusion mission of Calpulli Tonalehqueh, scholars and elders are frequently invited to give workshops and lectures on topics of interest to the group. Many of the presenters provide counternarratives to many accepted notions about the Mexica. They hope to provide materials with which to restore cultural pride, resist hegemonic narratives, and construct their *calpulli*. They aim a critical eye toward the *Aztec Pantheon and the Art of Empire* exhibits of the world.

These lectures support the palimpsest work of Calpulli Tonalehqueh. The elders who visit Calpulli Tonalehqueh inform almost every aspect and activity of the *calpulli*, with their conversations and formal lec-tures. From *calpulli* structure, ceremonial organization, and language to identity, dance, and social relations, these lectures provide erasing tools and writing materials for *calpulli* palimpsests.

There were more than ten of these formal lectures given every cal-endar year during the most active era of Calpulli Tonalehqueh. They are attended by an average of 40 people, and thousands would view them when uploaded to the Internet. The lectures are often recorded and disseminated by *calpulli* members online. Ocelocoatl has given the largest number of lectures to the community. I have noted his influence over the definitions utilized by members of Calpulli Tonalehqueh as well as his guidance of the organization and practice of the group in all of the previous chapters. Below I focus on a formal occasion for his pedagogy.

I attended more than 30 of these formal lectures, some of which I videorecorded in preparation for this book. Additionally, I reviewed several others posted at video-sharing Websites (e.g., YouTube). In this chapter, I present one of the lectures delivered by Ocelocoatl (from December 2007). To understand the tradition of lecturing in Calpulli Tonalehqueh as a palimpsest, I first present the historical Mexica tra-dition of *huehuetlatolli*, or words of the elders. I demonstrate how Calpulli Tonalehqueh recovers the practice of *huehuetlatolli* by creat-ing spaces for elders and others to lecture and then use the information to create all of the aspects described in this study, such as the *calpulli*, the concept of *tequio*, the MNY ceremony, the *cargos*, the naming ceremony, and so on. I also discuss the features that make Ocelocoatl an effective pedagogue, reviewing conversations I had had about how members of Calpulli Tonalehqueh review his lectures. His pedagogy is decolonial and greatly enables palimpsestic *calpulli* practice.

Huehuetlatolli: The Venerable Teachings

Skill in the art of rhetoric was highly valued in ancient Mexica (Anderson and Talamantez, 1986). Elected leaders, especially the *Tlahtoani*, were selected because of and celebrated for capacities in this area. Formal rhetoric, or *tecpillatolli*, meaning the noble, careful language, was taught in the *calmécac* by scholars in the arts of discourse called masters of the words, or *tlatolmatinime* (León Portilla, 1980, pp. 199–200). We know of the accomplishments of professional song composers, poets, and school teachers. Nezahualcóyotl, the *Huey Tlatoani* of the Texcoco region, has been recognized for his timeless poetry and songs for more than 500 years.

The Náhuatl language itself is highly figurative and metaphorical and is a language that lends itself to flowery discourse and compound words that can take on multiple simultaneous meanings. Náhuatl ideas often come as diphrases (see, e.g., *in ixtli, in yollotl*, or *in tlilli*, and *in tlapalli*). I offer that these language features signal an ideology of blending and multilayered meaning. Early colonial authors such as Torquemada, Olmos, Sahagún, and Acosta all mention the beauty of Náhuatl and the graceful way that all Nahua peoples speak. Both in form and function, graceful rhetorical devices are central to Mexica socialization, formal education, and civic life. When someone delivers a moving oration, counsels people well, and makes herself or himself well understood, people say, *Ontetepeoac, chachayoac*, meaning there was a sowing, there was a scattering (of jades). This idea signals a wider meaning captured in Sahagún's Florentine Codex: "the people have been informed, they have been enriched, they have become wealthy. There was a sowing, there has been a great scattering of jades." (Book VI, p. 205v, cited in Sullivan and Knab, 1994, p. 110)

An oral tradition among modern-day Mexicas is strong, and though time has lost many books, songs, poems, and stories, some important works remain, among them the *huehuetlatolli*. From *huehue*, meaning "venerable, old, ancient," and *tlatolli*, meaning "words, discourses, speeches," the *huehuetlatolli* are the venerable teachings handed down by community elders. They have been referred to as "rhetorical orations" (Sullivan, 1974), "compendia of wisdom" (Echeverría, 2011), and "monologues…from community leaders" (Díaz Cíntora, 1995; Mignolo, 1992). Mignolo (1992) explains that these discourses were some of the main tools for socialization in public and formal education in Mexica society. They were a formal discursive genre used for knowledge transmission and education (p. 330). The ancient *huehuetlatolli* were "paradigmatic examples of the authority of the elders in a society in which oral transmission is more important than written communication, and wisdom is deposited in the living body" (Mignolo, 1992). Thelma Sullivan, a student of Angel María Garibay, one of the foremost authorities on *huehuetlatolli* (Sullivan and Knab, 1994), had arguably the best description. For her, the *huehuetlatolli* were

> the words of the mothers, the fathers, the rulers, the elders, the wise men, and the ancients. They embodied the wisdom passed down by tradition through the ages…The knowledge the wise men of tradition left behind was precious. These words were jewels: precious jades, turquoises, and quetzal feathers…The *huehuetlatolli* were formal rhetorical orations. They were known to the elders, the trained orators…Formal rhetorical orations were a part of many events in life, for they imparted the wisdom of the ancestors in such situations…These words were not always kind: They warned, they admonished, and they cautioned. Such words of wisdom were part of an ancient tradition that kept the fabric of society together…These precious words guided people. They taught them and were woven into their very being: their throats, their entrails. These words were the wisdom of generations of ancestors; they embodied the precepts by which the people were expected to live. (pp. 109–111)

Miguel León Portilla (1963) adds that the *huehuetlatolli* were included in

> several documents of different derivation, whose contents are of pre-Hispanic origin. They are the didactic talks or exhortations addressed to the boys of the *Calmécac* or the *Telpochcalli*, and also to adults upon such occasions as marriage and funeral rites, for the purpose of inculcating moral ideas and principals. (pp. 192–193)

About 180 ancient *huehuetlatolli* survive today in early colonial texts from Fray Andrés de Olmos, Fray Juan Baptista, and Fray Bernardino de Sahagún, collected from native informants (Echeverría, 2011; León Portilla, 1963). Their topics include speeches to and from community leaders on public affairs and civic government, speeches to youth regarding their duty to the community, gender-specific advice from parents to their children, and various prayers, songs, idioms, and metaphors (Mignolo, 1992).

When Bernardino de Sahagún asked his sixteenth-century informants about the origin and composition of the *huehuetlatolli*, they responded

> at a time, in a place, which no one now can reckon, which no one now can recall, by those who sowed the seeds of the ancestral grandfathers, of the ancestral grandmothers; those who came first, those who arrived first, who came sweeping the way…were wise men. (Florentine Codex, Book X, p. 190r, cited in Sullivan and Knab, 1994, p. 109)

The wisdom of elders and the oral tradition have become crucial in modern Mexica education, particularly given the loss of the libraries of books and the generations who have shifted their traditions and language. Therefore, I cannot adequately account for the organization of teaching and learning in Calpulli Tonalehqueh without discussing formal cultural diffusion workshops. I had decided to examine a modern *huehuetlatolli* session, a lecture given by a Mexica elder, Ocelocoatl Ramírez Muñoz. It is emblematic of the types of dynamic educational spaces that are generated within groups like Calpulli Tonalehqueh.

Ocelocoatl appears throughout this book in different roles. This chapter analyzes the achievements of his pedagogy within Calpulli Tonalehqueh. A brief biography with relevant information on his genesis as a scholar and dancer in the ZT is followed by a close examination of one of his presentations. I review biographical information to provide background on his areas of expertise, development of lectures in the *Mexicayotl* movement, and formation in the *Danza* universe. His workshops and experience in the *Mexicayotl* movement in México City inform Calpulli Tonalehqueh and other allied groups.

Ocelocoatl: On Human Sacrifice

Biography of a Tlamatinime

Ocelocoatl was born in 1958 in México City. His parents, both city workers, decided that they wanted his formation to be based in a more rural environment, closer to the family language, stories, and traditions. As an infant, Ocelocoatl was sent to live with his grandparents in Huactzinco, Tlaxcala, separated from México City by 120 kilometers and the peaks of the Iztaccíhuatl and Popocatépetl volcanoes. In a conversation, he recalled that as a toddler he noticed all the livestock—pigs, sheep, cows, goats—having offspring; they all grew up together. He recalled working on the fields with his family, the teachings of his elders, and how his grandmother could forecast the weather. His upbringing was in Náhuatl. He received many *huehuetlatolli* from his grandparents.

At 14 years of age, Ocelocoatl went back with his parents to pursue more formal education in México City. In school, he was frequently teased for his accent and his rural sensibilities. As a student, Ocelocoatl joined the council of the *Zemanauak Tlamachtiloyan*. He was deeply interested in the study of México's indigenous foundations and offered the ZT his skills in drawing, graphic design, redaction and editing, and language interpretation. He also got involved in *Danza* in México City. In 1980, during a dance ceremony, Ocelocoatl was given the rank of *Capitán*. At 22 years of age, Ocelocoatl's ascendency to this rank was highly unusual. He said jokingly, "I was a captain of no one" (personal communication) because he was not a part of any particular dance group and had not led any dancers before. He was given the title in recognition of his scholarly accomplishments, his closeness to Felipe Aranda (a high-ranking dance elder in the city), and his work at the ZT.

In 1982, Ocelocoatl helped coordinate the taking of México City's *Zócalo* by *danzantes*. At that time and for several years since its inception, the ZT had relied upon Felipe Aranda's dance group to lead dance ceremonies, but some friction in that arrangement and the increase in invitations for the ZT compelled Ocelocoatl to suggest to the ZT governing council that it establish a circle of dancers (the year was 1983). The council agreed, and as is often the case, the person who submits an idea is asked to carry out the endeavor. Ocelocoatl saw himself as a scholar first and foremost; his primary identity was not that of a dancer at this time. Ocelocoatl agreed to take the lead in the dance efforts of the ZT if given two years to prepare. He proposed to study, interview, observe, and participate on an individual tour of ceremonies, dance circles, and rituals throughout México City and its surroundings. The council denied his request, saying the most he could have was six months to prepare. After some negotiation, both sides settled on a year, and Ocelocoatl left school, his job, and his post at the ZT for a yearlong immersion into the world of *Danza*. He recalled how difficult it was to leave his job and many comforts to go on this immersion quest. On the other hand, he received much in the countless *ensayos* and talks with *generales*, where he learned dances, songs, and took note of how ceremonies were executed. He gathered invaluable advice from *generales* and elders. Though he did not have a penny in his pocket, Ocelocoatl never worried for food, a place to stay, or willing interlocutors. Such is the tradition of hospitality and reciprocity among dancers. It is partly why Aguilar (2009) calls *Danza* the "rituals of kindness."

In 1984, Ocelocoatl returned to the ZT and considered himself much more ready to help grow the dance circle. The ZT had no operating budget and suggested Ocelocoatl charge a fee for the dance classes in order to fundraise to buy a drum and other *armas*. He opposed doing so and committed himself to finding a way to do it free of charge. The ZT was headquartered at the *Club de Periodistas* (national press building) in México City where Kuauhkoatl and others had membership. So with a five-gallon plastic bucket, he went to the rooftop of the historic building and began to play the "drum," inviting anyone who would come up for a smoke or lunch to come and dance. He invited people who attended the language and culture classes to come up and dance on Saturdays. Few people came, but even with a handful of dancers, Ocelocoatl continued. Soon, club members complained about the noise and the shaking roof of the 400-year-old building, so Ocelocoatl was forced out to the plaza next door in front of the national congress.

Because practice was usually on Saturdays, practicing in front of the senate chambers was not usually a problem, but one day, the senate was in a special session and Emilio Sánchez, the senate leader, came out and complained of too much noise. Sánchez suggested they move to the Plaza Tolsá in front the National Art Museum a block away. Once there, the art museum called the police to remove the dancers for assembling without a permit and interrupting classical music recitals in the museum. Ocelocoatl marched over to the senate chambers, interrupted the debate session, and requested Emilio Sánchez to assist. The director of the National Art Museum happened to be a friend of Sánchez and so he brokered a deal where the dancers can dance at Plaza Tolsá every Saturday but would hold off drumming for the one hour that the musical recitals took place. Ocelocoatl agreed, and the ZT dancers have been there for decades and to the day. During the breaks in the *ensayo*, Ocelocoatl delivered workshops on Mexica and *Danza* history and culture, language, and philosophy. These were the beginnings of the workshops Ocelocoatl would develop and deliver worldwide. His grassroots pedagogy was honed through immersion and participant observation and through a tenacity and determination he still holds. Ocelocoatl is tireless.

Within eight months at the *plaza*, Ocelocoatl had 60 regular dancers every week—to the amazement of many, including the council of the ZT. The name of his circle was (and is) *Tetzahuitl Tezcatlipoca*. The dance circle continued to grow throughout the 1980s, and invitations to participate in ceremonies and presentations around the world poured in. For this purpose, Ocelocoatl developed a *Grupo de Guerra* and called them the *Mazatl* (deer) dancers. Ocelocoatl took the group to neighboring states and abroad to Canada, Spain, France, Portugal, Panama, Guatemala, Argentina, and the United States. Ocelocoatl remembers that, apart from touring and dancing at Plaza Tolsá, the dancers performed in front of the Iraqi embassy in México to protest their invasion of Kuwait, in front of the Canadian embassy to protest a golf course that was built on Mohawk burial grounds, in front of the Italian embassy to clamor for the return of sacred Mexican treasures stored in the Vatican, and so forth. This practice fell in line with larger *Mexicayotl* movement traditions. His *Mazatl* dancers took the lead in hosting the runners from the Peace and Dignity Journeys in 1992. When Ocelocoatl went abroad, he left a cadre of 32 *palabras*, leaders who shared the responsibility of running the *Tetzahuitl Tezcatlipoca* group. Though he learned from many *danzantes de Tradición*, Ocelocoatl was never a Catholic. He identifies with and in fact shaped the *Mexicayotl* movement.

Ocelocoatl helped establish groups in Tijuana (Baja California), Oaxaca (Oaxaca), Acapulco (Guerrero), Silao, Saltillo, Camargo, and Lerdo (each in Guanajuato), and México City. In the United States, he helped establish groups in Houston, Chicago, Iowa, New York, and San José. He recently told me that his goal was to help all *Mexicayotl* dance groups communicate and collaborate. He knew it is a lofty goal, but he dreams of the *Huey Tlahtocan Nechicoliztli*, *La Gran Confederación de Anáhuac*, the Great Anáhuac Confederation.

What does his biography reveal with regard to the concerns of this study? Over the years, Ocelocoatl mined his personal experience in support of *calpultin* and *danzantes*. He had a deep commitment to scholarship and a strong base in dance, having done years of ethnography and participant observation with numerous dance circles in Central México and around the United States. Furthermore, Ocelocoatl is a primary source on the *Mexicayotl* movement. His participation there and his adherence to its ideals helped shape the *calpultin* he advises. In Calpulli Tonalehqueh, for example, facets such as the *calpulli* and *tequio*, the elements of the MNY and *ensayo*, the *cargos* and the *Grupo de Guerra*, the names dancers carry, and so on, are directly influenced by his interpretation of the vision of the *Mexicayotl* movement. His biography reveals a committed activist and community organizer, with a lifelong and selfless commitment to helping indigenous communities and *danzantes*.

I turn to examine the fruit of his decades of participatory research and scholarship.

Decolonial Pedagogy

Ocelocoatl has given hundreds of formal and informal lectures. His pedagogy is widely lauded by the *Mexicayotl* community. To many he is an inspiring, brilliant, pivotal, and transformational teacher. I attended more than 30 of his lectures and became his personal interpreter for a time with Calpulli Tonalehqueh. Also, I am the translator on one of his self-published works. I danced with him in ceremonies in both California and México City, sat with him in *temazcal* (sweat lodge ceremony), gone through *In Toca In Tocaitl* (naming ceremony), and had numerous conversations with him during the preparation for this text.

Several of his lectures are available on YouTube. His online *huehuetlatolli* (lectures) have been viewed hundreds of thousands of times. The commentaries on the videos by viewers are generally positive and expressive of gratitude. He had developed lectures on indigenous medicine, the native resistance to invasion, Mexica education, indigenous Mexican flora and fauna, the codices, indigenous architecture, understanding calendar cycles, the Mexica sun stone, the Mexica flag, the founding of México-Tenochtitlan, Aztlan, Cuauhtémoc, Tezcatilipoca, Quetzalcoatl, Huitzilopochtli, the concept of duality, the concept of death, on serpents, mathematics, the Catholic inquisition in México, the concept of *calpulli*, on *Danza*, and numerous other topics. I selected one, *El Mito del Sacrificio Humano*, the Myth of Human Sacrifice, to typify them all and as a focus of my analysis of his pedagogy. Through an account of his content and style, as well as with the information gathered from his audiences, I outline the features that made him an effective and palimpsestic pedagogue.

I acknowledge many scholars' and members' hotly debate on the information he delivers in many of his workshops. He is unquestionably imperfect. He has been wrong. He sometimes contradicts himself or errs in other ways. Ocelocoatl has plenty of detractors. But I am not as concerned with evaluating the merits of his arguments as I am with examining him as a locus of education, as a beacon, as a fountain of knowledge for the Calpulli Tonalehqueh palimpsest. I argue that despite his faults, he delivers vital information to audiences.[2]

El Mito del Sacrificio Humano was delivered as a formal lecture on one evening in December 2007 at the Center for Training and Careers in San José. A *calpulli* member and local television personality, Cihuapilli Rose Amador, was the executive director of the community center at the time. There were about 50 people in attendance, and the talk was videorecorded with permission by three individuals, including me for this analysis. The *huehuetlatolli* itself lasts just under two hours and consists of a video and lecture attached to 61 digital projections.

The full sequence, slides, timing, and content summary of the talk can be found in appendix E.

Ocelocoatl's objective for the lecture was to provide evidence and argue that human sacrifice did not exist among the Mexica. He contended that, at best, claims of human sacrifice were a gross misreading of Mexica imagery and, at worst, part of a propaganda campaign by zealous evangelists to justify the genocide and ethnocide that occurred in México in the sixteenth century. The friars, the inquisition torchbearers, and colonizers were compelled to sell the idea about the indigenous people as demonic barbarians in desperate need of baptism, the true faith, and European order and cultural refinement. Massacre, pillaging, enslavement, torture, and imposition of every kind by the Spanish in México were well documented and not easily refuted by history (c.f. Casas, 1981). Furthermore, a European public well-versed in wars of empire, religious crusades, and centuries-long occupations was a readily consuming audience for the tales of distant lands (Keen, 1990). How better to justify the atrocities than to paint the natives in as poor a light as possible?

Throughout written history, many scholars posited variations of the maxim that the bigger the lie, the more likely people are to believe it, or if a lie is repeated enough times, people will come to believe it. This is a fundamental premise for all scholars seeking to challenge Mexica human sacrifice. Human sacrifice is one of the activities most closely associated with the Mexica. Virtually all major works on the Mexica take human sacrifice for granted (see, e.g.,Carrasco, 1999; Coe, 1977; Guerrera Estrella, 2010; Hicks, 1979; Miller and Taube, 1993; Soustelle, 1970; Townsend, 2000; Vaillant, 1941).

Harner (1977) and Harris (1977) add to the feverish debate with arguments that the Mexica sacrificed humans because of a lack of protein in their diet and that they were a cannibalistic empire. Several critiques of these arguments emerge including ones from Price (1978) and Ortiz de Montellano (1983). Unfortunately, though these scholars critique the Harner-Harris arguments, they continue to take for granted that human sacrifice indeed existed, often on large scales.[3]

Particularly disappointing to scholars in the *Mexicayotl* tradition is the work of Mexican scholars like Yólotl González Torres's (1985) *Human Sacrifice among the Mexica*, in which the author reviewed and gave credence to a wide variety of studies on the purposes of Mexica human sacrifice. Critics worry about her synthesis of archeological and textual evidence. Torres is a scholar with many close relationships with *danzantes*. She had done embedded research with *Danza* circles and has published extensively. At one point, Ocelocoatl and other scholars from the *Mexicayotl* tradition implored her to retract her statements and publish a countertext after giving her all the proofs of the myth of human sacrifice. She did not heed to it, and the book that made her career had second and third editions printed in 1994 and 2006, respectively. The work of Leonardo López Luján (López Luján and Olivier, 2010) is also disappointing to some scholars. He along with Guilhem Olivier led 28 scholars in an enormous compilation of research arguing the existence of human sacrifice, slavery, infanticide, ritual decapitation, human flaying, etc., across indigenous nations in México. Many Mexican scholars sustain claims of human sacrifice in their scholarship. In these works, the Mexica are generally characterized as ruthless, war-making, stratified, empire builders who sacrificed victims to provide their pantheon of Gods with human hearts and blood.

Perhaps, responding to Fernández Gatica's (1991) call to all university professors, high school teachers, historians, researchers, and speakers to cease their negligence and inertia by realizing that mechanical repetition of lies—such as the one about human sacrifice among the Mexica—is based on profoundly biased sources and lenses of interpretation that have caused a tremendous national and community trauma (pp. 5–8), Ocelocoatl provides at least 16 proposals that cast serious doubt on human sacrifice among the Mexica or their neighbors. The following is a report of his lecture:

First, Ocelocoatl opens his lecture with a seven-minute video of an open-heart surgery. Cuauhtlequetzqui, a clinical perfusionist and a member of Calpulli Tonalehqueh involved in dozens of heart surgeries, received permission to record the surgery. With the patient sedated, it takes five cuts with a laser scalpel to get through the skin and connective tissue, several passes with an electric high-speed rotary saw to cut through the sternum, the opening of the ribs with a separator, and insertion of a plastic bypass tube for the major artery to the artificial heart machine. This initial process takes seven minutes for the doctors to get to the heart. The video shows how protected the heart is in the human body and how difficult, if not impossible, it would be to open a person's chest with a stone blade or pull out a beating heart.

Next, Ocelocoatl argues that the idea of human sacrifice belongs to the Judeo-Christian worldview, not the Mesoamerican, and therefore was already part of the schema with which chronicles understood Mexica cultural productions. Ocelocoatl references the Old Testament where God tells Abraham to kill his own son to prove his faith. He would have done it if not for divine intervention. Also part of this worldview, from the Western and Middle Eastern, is the tradition of sacrificing lambs to ask God for things. The crucifixion of Jesus of Nazareth—at the core of Christianity—testifies to the tradition of putting people to death for punishment, or of Jesus "giving himself up," sacrificing himself for the good of others. Each week at Catholic mass, the priest quotes Jesus' Last Supper invitation to drink his blood and eat his flesh. Catholic doctrine holds that, through transfiguration and a priestly blessing, the bread and wine are *actually* converted into the body and blood of Jesus. With this, Ocelocoatl asks the audience, "So, who is sacrificing? Who eats flesh and drinks blood?" Early chroniclers could only ideate human sacrifice if it already existed in their worldview.

Third, Ocelocoatl refutes the position that the Mexica lived in constant fear of the sun not rising if not supplied with ample and constant amounts of human blood and hearts. Ocelocoatl argues that the Mexica had scientific and agricultural concerns with the sun, rather than colonial author styling and personifications. The sun marks time. Its movement along the horizon creates the seasons and tells an agricultural society when to plant, when to expect rains, and when to harvest. All ancient Anahuacan cities are aligned with heavenly bodies, and all had structures to mark the equinoxes and solstices. The main *teocalli* complex in México City marks the spring equinox. Ocelocoatl explains that there is archeological evidence that nations across the hemisphere and in México built astronomical observatories thousands of years before Europe and could predict not only solstices and equinoxes, but also comets and eclipses, solar flares, the orbits of the planets, knew about the Milky Way, and many other astronomical phenomena. Because the Mexica had such a deep astronomical knowledge of the solar system, they would not be concerned with the sun not rising.

Fourth, Ocelocoatl claims that colonial scholars read Mexica symbols erroneously. Many stone carvings and the few pre-Cuauhtémoc books that survive include images of blood, hearts, serpents, and so forth. Without exception, friars read these images with ethnocentric lenses. For example, when discussing an image from the Laud Codex that has a tree made of smoke, flanking a humanoid figure with no eye, a mirror on its neck, smoke rising from its head, sitting on a pool of running blood with three images of human hearts and a human head, Ocelocoatl explains that the absence of an eye means that the figure is looking inward, the smoke represents thinking, and the mirror, human memory. He continues thus:

> Observe! There are hearts, blood, and a head. *Simple* [sarcastically]. The anthropologists say those are hearts from sacrifice, and blood offered, and the head of a decapitated victim...This image *actually* speaks about one's inner essence, what is in one's heart. Blood represents life. Face represents identity. *In Ixtli, in Yollotl*. The face, identity, and to have feelings, senses, an essence. It is a metaphor. When we say, "with our heart in our hand," we didn't literally take it out of our body and hold it in our hand! (my translation.)

The statues and stone carvings of serpent heads and necklaces of human hands and hearts, the images of flowing blood, the craniums, the images of body parts are not seen as Mexica symbols of wisdom, duality, mathematics, labor, essence, life, time, and action. Rather, Westerners understand them as icons of death, gore, sin, and demonic activity. Wide audiences are reading the images and books used as proof of anthropophagi and human sacrifice incorrectly.

Linguistic ignorance, Ocelocoatl's fifth proof, contributes to misinformation about the Mexica worldview and consequently about the nonexistence of human sacrifice. He uses an image of the concept of *Tlaloc* from the Laud Codex to explain.

> It means "earth's drink" or "earth's liquor." That is why it is important to know the language. Because people will say, "it's the God of Rain." First of all, rain is *quiahuitl*. [all rhetorical questions] How do you say "god" in Náhuatl? The answer is "god." How do you say "elephant"? Answer is "elephant." How do you say "giraffe"? Exactly. The words do not exist because the Mexica never knew an elephant, a giraffe, or any god. The word for god does not exist. Consequently the idea of gods did not exist. [Pointing to the image] This is *tlaloc*, personified. It shows the days of rain, ground water, a lightning rod, in the form of a white

serpent. Look at the [image's] style, color. Look at the [artist's] capacity for synthesis. (my translation)

Near the end of his lecture, Ocelocoatl provides linguistic evidence.

From a linguistic standpoint, the verb to sacrifice does not exist. The word for priest did not exist. If the word does not exist, the idea does not exist. And if the verb does not exist, then the place [the sacrificial altar] designated for the verb does not exist and if the verb does not exist, then a perpetrator of the verb cannot exist or a victim of the verb cannot exist. The verb *nezahualli* means "to fast." There were no priests. The word for the high scholars, the elders they called priests is *tlamacazque*, meaning the person who knows, the wise person. (my translation)

These two examples also allude to Ocelocoatl's sixth and seventh points of evidence. The sixth has to do with the fact that a culture's language is intimately connected to the culture.[4] Thus, if the word for God did not exist, then it was not possible for the Mexica to have a God of war, of corn, of music, of the sun, of fire, of the rain, or any other concept. The Mexica personified concepts and wrote/drew them as humanoid figures, but did not believe them to be literally Gods. Ocelocoatl's seventh proof—illustrated in the quote and throughout his lecture—is that if polytheism is now shattered, and if the Mexica did not conceive of God as a capricious blood-thirsty being, then there would be no reason for sacrifices to the Gods.

Throughout the *huehuetlatolli*, Ocelocoatl provides an eighth proof: the fundamental distortion of impetuous colonial reauthoring. He also provides a ninth: the religious bias embedded in new texts. He says one of the most lamentable aspects of the events of the invasion was the loss of books and knowledge holders. The death, silencing, or killing of most of the Mexica elder scholars coupled with massive book-burning campaigns left a knowledge chasm unparalleled in the world (c.f. Lopes Don, 2010). Hundreds of thousands of volumes were burned. Less than ten pre-Cuauhtémoc Anáhuac books survived. Several decades after the book burnings, Spaniards like Sahagún began redrawing books on Mexica life ways, ceremonies, calendars, symbols, flora and fauna, attire, concepts, and so forth. In addition, friars and others began writing grammars, histories, observations, dictionaries, and other gatherings in narrative form.[5] All of these texts included distortions, some of which were grave. Ocelocoatl guides the audience in the comparison of pre-Cuauhtémoc imagery and the hastily composed, slanted, and falsified postinvasion texts produced in the colony. There is a clear distinction in style, in representation.

The tenth proof is that all of the imagery and descriptions of human sacrifice scenes and barbarism come from postinvasion texts, written either by Spanish friars or native-born Mexicans who were in various ways compelled or conditioned to repeat the information (c.f. Velazco, 2003). These are the texts cited by modern scholars contending that there existed human sacrifice. The drawings and texts were ripe with religious judgmentalism of native structures and the erection of new-world orders.

The next area that Ocelocoatl offers as evidence for the absence of human sacrifice is poor research then and now. Though early colonial texts may be primary sources for some historians and archeologists, they are altogether problematic. For example, Sahagún had a small group of informants from Tlaxcalla report on Mexica culture decades after the invasion. Some colonial writers who began exclaiming the beauty and sophistication and wonders they witnessed from Mexica life ways quickly remembered their sponsors and audience and turned to admonishment and disparagement in the same text (Keen, 1990). Many scholars agree about the deep disdain that writers like Sahagún, Durán, and Motolinía had for the Mexica; yet today, scholars base most if not all of their conclusions and assertions about Mexica life and culture on these authors without more than cursory acknowledgments of their deep flaws as source material. The research cannot be sound if native sources, oral traditions, and different lenses are not included in the analysis of things, such as the existence of human sacrifice.

Ocelocoatl develops a twelfth proof in his *huehuetlatolli*. It holds that poor literary sources and analysis leads to poor modern archeological conclusions. Conclusions about the archeological record should dispute evidence of human sacrifice. Ocelocoatl cites, for instance, the recent archeological digging that was documented at México City's Templo Mayor. There large clay pots were uncovered with human remains inside.

Sarcastically, Ocelocoatl discusses an image of the dig led by the renowned director of the museum there, Eduardo Matos Moctezuma, and a clay pot with human remains found on site:

> The dig at the *Templo Mayor*...Of course, it is common sense! A clay pot is for food. Human bones equals food. Here they had *pozole* made with a baby!...Yesterday we had the winter solstice. Lets see, who wants to give their child so we can all have communion?...This [clay

pot] is used as proof of human sacrifice, but it was a burial…We call the Earth, *tonantzin*, "our precious mother." We have the entire periodic table of elements inside our bodies…We are "born" from Earth. That is why we call it our mother. So when we die, we are bundled in cloth, in a fetal position and are put in the ground, sometimes in clay jars. It means that we are returning to Mother Nature. The body here is fully intact. If we were cannibals, then the pieces would be chopped up and divided. (my translation)

Soon after, Ocelocoatl discusses the origin of the word cannibal as linked to the misunderstanding of native burial practices. Ocelocoatl projects on screen an image of cannibalism from a postinvasion text and admits he is speechless. He points out the clay pot over a fire with a head sticking out and people feasting on body parts. He points out the curly hair on the subjects, who look like actors in Greek myths. One is eating a human leg, hip to heel. Ocelocoatl points out that the representation of fire is much different than in the ancient Mexica books.

He asks the audience if they know the origin of the word "cannibal" and explains that it originated from Christopher Columbus, who had came to the islands, what is now called the Caribbean, and perpetrated massacres. On the beach, he found clay pot burials. He asked the people what they called it. They said *Carib(es)*. Columbus takes the story of the human remains in clay pots back to Europe, calling it *Caníbales*. The term was coined, the myth perpetuated: cannibals and cannibalism. Columbus, Matos Moctezuma, and many other proponents of Mexica sacrifice failed to understand the Mexica worldview. Ocelocoatl explains that we are born from the earth and to the earth we return, sometimes in a large pot, representing the uterus that carried us as a fetus.

Next to a misinterpretation of the artifacts, Ocelocoatl argues that eating humans is irrational, given universal human values (thirteenth point of evidence). Human sacrifice and anthropophagia are globally taboo for a reason. Indeed, they are extreme and almost unthinkable for any human culture. It is less of a stretch to believe that the Spaniards invented a lie that human sacrifice and anthropophagic practices existed for a highly sophisticated and humanistic culture to actually carry it through, especially on the purported scale and the almost universal nonexistence in human cultures. Some authors (c.f. Harner, 1977) contend that anthropophagia was practiced by the Mexica because of the lack of protein in their diet. This is absolutely false. The Western hemisphere, and México itself, had the most diverse and nutritious flora and fauna in the world. With corn, chia, avocado, tomato, amaranth, chili, spirulina, fish, turkey, cactus, fruits, and countless other food staples, the Mexica did not need human muscle for protein, nor did they have any dietary deficiencies.

Ocelocoatl's fourteenth proposal in the lecture is that human sacrifice was not attributed to other indigenous nations that shared very similar worldviews, intellectual genealogies, and culture areas. Evidence of the commonalities between nations can be seen in shared iconography, language, architecture, etc. The list of parallel cultural traits is long. If human sacrifice did not exist in those nations, this casts a serious doubt on its existence in Mexica practice.

Ocelocoatl challenges popular understandings of war, explaining that wars were mainly exercises of capture (not homicide), physical trials for theyouth, and existed nowhere near the scales reported in chronicles. Many scholars contend that Mexica human sacrifice was tied to a large political and religious complex of conquest, war, manipulative priests and rulers, and slavery. Ocelocoatl also challenges the idea that priests or slavery existed. He explains how people often paid their debt or crimes with labor and that colonial authors misinterpreted this idea.

The last proof of the myth of human sacrifice among the Mexica that Ocelocoatl offers is the set of Mexica ethical, moral, and spiritual tenets. We may find this through a study of Mexica poetry and the *huehuetlatolli*. For example, Ocelocoatl relays that there are pre-Cuauhtémoc poems that survived and reveal a humanistic Mexica worldview. Ocelocoatl quotes one from Nezahualcoyotl printed on the 100 peso bill ofMéxico:

"*Nehua nictlazohta in tzentzontototl in cuicauh / Nehua nictlazohta in chalchihuitl itlapaliz / Nehua nictlazohta in yolaxtli xochicuepolli / Ma nehua in tlazohta in tlahca noniuctzin*"

Tradicción, "Amo el canto del tzentzontle ave de 400 voces / Amo el color del jade / Y el enervante perfume de las flores / Pero amo más a mi hermano el hombre." ¿Cómo es posible que se lleve ese pensamiento y se sacrifice al HOMBRE, su hermano? Y luego está la otra máxima. Tehuatl Tinehuatl, Nehuatl Titehuatl. Tú eres yo y yo soy tú. Si me dañas, te dañas, y si te daño, me daño.

[Translation, "I love the mocking bird, bird of 400 voices/I love the color of jade/I love the enervating perfume of flowers/But I have more love for man, my brother"

How is it possible to sacrifice man, one's brother, under that kind of ideology? And then there is the other axiom: *Tehuatl tinehuatl, nehuatl itehuatl*: You are me. I am you. If you hurt me, you hurt yourself. If I hurt you, I hurt myself.] (my translation)

Ocelocoatl argues that one can look to the surviving pre-Cuauh-témoc literature, poems, and sayings to understand the Mexica ethos and moral tenets, including the appreciation of beauty, regard for nature and universe, the deep philosophical meditations on mortality, the demand for honorable and just leadership, and the humanistic love transmitted throughout. These philosophical tenets are found in aboriginal people's worldviews all over the world and do not square with the inhuman portrayals of the Mexica, nor with people who supposedly perpetrated large-scale human sacrifice and cannibalism.

Ocelocoatl ends his talk about human sacrifice within the Mexica thus: "It is an absolute lie."

Pencils and Erasers: Tools for a Palimpsest

In this section, I discuss Ocelocoatl's decolonial pedagogy. Through his teaching and his position as an elder, he provides *danzantes* in Calpulli Tonalehqueh with metaphorical pencils and erasers for their palimpsest. He hopes individuals erase colonial accounts about Mexica life as well as detrimental foreign cultural impositions and, in reconsideration of their history rewrite their *calpulli* practice in a way that respects the positive Mexica achievements.

Ocelocoatl is a fountain of cultural resources for Calpulli Tonalehqueh. The *calpulli* fundraises to fly him to California for several weeks, sometimes multiple times a year. They house and feed him, organize numerous *huehuetlatolli*, music, and dance workshops, and other cultural diffusion work. Ocelocoatl visits other dance circles in the area and attends to local television appearances and newspaper interviews. He leads theMNY, In Toca In Tocaitl, and *temascalli* ceremonies. There are many elders who are respected and do similar work, but the personal attributes Ocelocoatl marshals helped outlay the elements that made him effective. Ocelocoatl's celebrity is earned.

Supported by interviews, observations, and my field experience, my first conclusion is that Ocelocoatl is effective because audiences are hungry for his teachings. There is a notable scarcity of human repositories, human resources like him in the United States. *Danza* context. US *danzantes* are sometimes far from the ceremonial centers, museums, publications, cultural programming, ceremonies, indigenous languages, established dance lineages, elders, and so on, of México, and even there, *Mexicayotl* elders can be hard to find. *Danzantes* in the United States are authoring *calpulli* life with different sets of materials.

Ocelocoatl is valuable for his command of a variety of topics, each tremendously relevant to modern-day US-based *danzantes*.

Second, Ocelocoatl is effective because he endeavors to support "personal and community empowerment through identity development." Mexican-origin communities seek organic paths toward community building and are looking for alternatives to mainstream self-empowerment proposals and models of successful engagement in US life. People are in quest of alternatives to individualistic capitalism, Catholic religiosity, sexism, school failure, gang participation, and other social challenges. Ocelocoatl provides a vision for possible alternatives in all those areas, envisioned and carried out through autochthonous Mexica traditions. Furthermore, many students of Ocelocoatl are attracted to the "myth debunking" central to his pedagogy. Ocelocoatl sets out to restore pride and dignity in an indigenous identity and to celebrate the achievements of indigenous peoples in the Anáhuac. He is not shy about hounding the "sacred cows" in the field of Mexica studies. He complicates popular and scholarly misconceptions that circulate about human sacrifice, slavery, colonial imposition, ethnocide, history, and so forth. This is perhaps why authors like Howard Zinn (*A People's History…*) and James Loewen (*Lies My Teacher Told Me*) are popular.

Third, Ocelocoatl is a gifted orator. His use of humor, histrionic talent, irony, tone, and story are skillful. One *calpulli* member noticed:

> The topics and substance always first attracted me because it is not really easy or accessible to learn about *tezcatlipoca* or *quetzalcoatl* or the meaning of dance from someone who has studied it by books as well as with elders, teachers and families who maintain oral tradition. Also he [Ocelocoatl] is an interesting teacher who is skilled in speaking, teaching and humorous which makes him effective to deliver his presentation. (Yapaltecatl, personal communication),

This chapter's narrative of his style and skill are inadequate to fully capture his pedagogy. His passion, use of multiple languages (Náhuatl, Spanish, English, Latin, etc.), impersonations, laughter, and physical movement make him an extremely engaging presenter.

Ocelocoatl consistently invites his audiences to critical thinking. He questions the audience often and encourages them to be skeptical of any source—including him—stating that it is important for individuals to investigate topics themselves. Nonetheless, audiences value Ocelocoatl's research. When asked about Ocelocoatl's *huehuetlatolli* talks, Atlaua said he was attracted to "the fact that he presented an alternative perspective in the philosophy and history of the Mexica. Many of the past elders from this have the same ideology, same teachers, and same tradition, that hearing something 'new' is refreshing" (personal communication). Atlaua has attended more than ten of Ocelocoatl's workshops, and so too Itexcatlayohualli, who evaluated Ocelocoatl and said:

> *Ocelocoatl es una persona muy instruida que ha recorrido varios lugares del mundo. Siento que es una persona que nació en un ambiente humilde y poco a poco debido las circunstancias se vio forzado a estudiar y analizar mas acerca de sus ancestros y de conocer mas de sus abuelos. Para mí es una persona de respeto, sincera y eso le da más credibilidad a todo lo que dice. La forma en que da sus pláticas es muy amena y siempre nos invita a indagar más acerca de todo lo que nos dice para comprobar todo por nosotros mismos.* (personal communication)

> [Ocelocoatl is a very learned individual who has traveled various parts of the world. I feel he is a person who comes from humble beginnings and, given those circumstances, has slowly found himself needing to study and analyze more about his ancestors and know them better. To me he is a respectful, sincere person and this gives him and all he says more credibility. The way that he delivers his talks is pleasing and he always invites us to investigate more about all that he tells us to verify it all for ourselves.] (my translation)

In all his workshops, Ocelocoatl presents more than information; he presents arguments. He uses logic to support his claims and helps guide students through the reasoning.

Fifth, the fact that he presents so many pieces of evidence virtually guarantees that there will be something for everyone to connect with. Two *calpulli* members praise him to be adroit in this area. One (Mozahuani) told me, "he is accessible and approachable. He is not dogmatic and he is not trying to sell you a bill of goods. He is invested in our learning and not in his ego" (personal communication). One of the founders of Calpulli Tonalehqueh, Cuauhcihuatl, calls him the *Maestro*. She has been to dozens of his talks over the years and connected with his message despite a language barrier. She said:

> The information he talks about makes so much sense. He knows how to explain everything in a way, which keeps your attention. His energy and personality are a great part of his *tlahtocameh* [talks]. I cannot speak Spanish, but I have learned so much from him. I appreciate his teachings and hope to learn more. (personal communication)

Next, Ocelocoatl's mastery of his content areas is impressive. He uses no notes and has given weekend workshops all from memory. He recites biblical passages, papal decrees, fifteenth-century Náhuatl poetry, chronologies, and countless refrains with ease. His lectures are always interdisciplinary, mixing science, astronomy, history, literary criticism, psychology, comedy, cultural anthropology, ethnology, and art. And he gets better with time. I argue this after a review of several of his lecture notes and videos of his talks. He is constantly building his knowledge base. One dancer (Omicuauhtli) appreciates Ocelocoatl's "knowledge of the sacred books and language, and also that he is one of the leading experts in our tradition, and his collaboration with other nations" (personal communication).

In addition, Ocelocoatl embraces new technology. In earlier years he gave conventional oral lectures. Occasionally he used chalkboards or poster paper to draw images or write a few terms. Now, he uses PowerPoint. Most of this work has been done by *calpulli* members. I had helped him gather images, scan ancient texts, and arrange the presentations as well. Ocelocoatl now travels with a laptop, USB drives, and an external hard drive. He often jokes about using "the white man's magic" to present information. He also embraces the diffusion of his lectures through YouTube. His talks are widely available, and he knows that the visual media are now necessary tools in the work he aims to do.

Ocelocoatl's approach to education is holistic. His breadth of activities and his versatility brings him more opportunities to teach, gives him valuable experiences on which to speak, and also garners him more respect among *danzantes*. He is not just a scholar. He sings and teaches song. He plays numerous instruments and teaches music and instrument making. He concocts homeopathic remedies and teaches others. He studies ancient texts and teaches people how to use them. He is an accomplished graphic artist. He runs dance, fire, sunrise, inter-tribal, and purification ceremonies. He teaches dances and joins in. Ocelocoatl is a generative individual who lives a full modern Mexica life and leverages all of his experiences to teach. Calling him a human repository of wisdom is appropriate.

In this vein, Ocelocoatl has dedicated his whole life to the cause, having spent the last 34 years completely devoted to dancers and ceremony, scholarship, and diffusion. He lives *Danza* and the *Mexicayotl* in a way few people ever can. And then he passes what he has learned to others selflessly. Any remuneration Ocelocoatl receives goes to his travel expenses and into buying materials for his work or for his art and dance circles in México. Ocelocoatl has lived a variation of a monastic lifestyle, with very few possessions, from the time he was sent in the early 1980s to learn from other *Danza* circles. Zihuayaocuicatl summed it up well: "Ocelotlcoatl's *tlatokans* are oral traditional knowledge that has been given to him to pass to the people" (personal communication). Ocelocoatl told me, "*esto [el conocimiento de la cultura] no es mío. Los abuelos nos lo dejaron. Es de todos, por todos, para todos.*" [This (cultural information) is not mine. Our ancestors have left it for us. It belongs to everyone, through everyone, and for everyone.] (my translation)

In part, this chapter submits that Ocelocoatl delivers a contemporary *huehuetlatolli*. His pedagogy supports the palimpsest construction of Calpulli Tonalehqueh. Ocelocoatl achieves a caliber of discourse and rhetorical skill that would make the *tlatolmatinime* of yesteryears proud. His strategies are those of a cultural palimpsest: strategic survival, appropriation, and resistance to erasure. He helps shape the cultural paradigms of *danzantes*. The *huehuetlatolli* Ocelocoatl gives are formal and semiformal spaces where he can transmit materials and experiences gathered from his own elders and the multitude of elders he encountered in ceremonies across the continent, most to whom *calpulli* members may have no access. He supplements the oral tradition with decades of scholarship. His talks are interdisciplinary, multilingual, and include various genres. Moreover, In Ixtli in Yollotl is activated when he helps *danzantes* conduct themselves more consciously in *Danza* and supports community esteem and personal empowerment; he provides materials (pencils and erasers) for individuals to develop their identity (face) and heart. Through the clarity provided by his lessons, arguments, and models, people become informed, they become wealthy. There is a scattering of jades, a sowing of precious jades.

Ocelocoatl's *huehuetlatolli* can be understood through the lens of palimpsest. His sessions are more than just recitals of fifteenth-century words or monologues. His sessions are public, multilayered, interactive, and are "rewritten" onto videos, Websites, and in the minds of audiences. He comes from the oral tradition, having grown up in it, but he adds his scholarship and editorializes. Ocelocoatl helps modern audiences understand the "rewrites" of the Mexica and *Danza* traditions through the invasion, the colony, the independence and revolution, through the *Conchero* tradition, after transfer to the US context and in Calpulli Tonalehqueh's iteration. Ultimately, he gives dancers materials with which to author their *calpulli*, their *tequio*, their

Figure 7.1   Ocelocoatl delivers lectures at *calpulli* events.

ceremonies, their identities, their understandings. His pedagogy allows dancers to critically engage exhibits like the one at the Getty. His pedagogy is decolonial.

The *Maestro*'s teaching engages every aspect of *calpulli* participation. He helps shape dance and music. He guides ceremony and *cargo* training. Ocelocoatl leads cultural diffusion, transnational, and intertribal efforts. He assists with conflict resolution and leadership development. He models a *Mexicayotl* lifestyle. And he helps individuals reinscribe themselves through their names, their *tonalamatl* studies, and their total participation in *Danza*, the subject of the next chapter.

8

Reinscribing the Self

Calpulli members author a personal palimpsest when they select a new name according to the Mexica day count system and gain an understanding of the symbols and elements that correspond to them because of the time of their birth; the generation of a new name and a new identity is a palimpsest of the self, written over a preexisting personal identity. This chapter examines the process by which *calpulli* members acquire a Náhuatl name, acquiring a new set of materials with which to construct the self. It is both a private and public ritual, involving deeply personal decisions, performed in the public sphere. The naming process is part of a contemporary revival of Mexica naming conventions and divination led by Calpulli Tonalehqueh in California and beyond. This chapter reviews the history of ancient Mexica naming practices, discusses the components of the ritual, which Calpulli Tonalehqueh reinstitutes presently, and argues that this process is a site of reinscription and deep personal and cultural learning.

The Revival of Mexica Naming Conventions in México and the United States

In precontact Mexica society, parents consulted many cultural specialists upon the birth of a child. Many precolonial and early colonial sources described these processes (Berdan and Anawalt, 1997; Durán, 1995; Garibay, 1943; León Portilla, 1980; Sahagún, 1992; Sullivan, 1974). Parents consulted the midwife and healer to receive prayers, blessings, and advice for the care of the child. They offered the child's umbilical chord so that it would be buried near the hearth or the field. Parents also paid a visit to the *calpulli* school masters. There they made a commitment to send the child to school and support the work of the institution and the associated *teocalli*. Parents also presented their children to the community. In addition, parents made divinatory consultations with a *tonalpohque*, one who reads destinies. *Tonalpohque* were trained in reading almanacs and divinatory texts (*amochtin*, *tonalamatl*) tied to astronomy and the ancient count (*tonalpohualli*). There were augural texts that could be used for reading the destiny of a person based on birthdate. The text displayed the cosmic elements that belong to the individual. These elements were integral in the naming and rearing of the individual. The practice of consulting divinatory texts and naming individuals based on calendar signs was common throughout Mesoamerica.

Though many texts, specialists, and practices vanished in México's colonial era, knowledge endured through the keepers of the oral tradition. As discussed in an earlier chapter, there was a twentieth-century movement in México to recover these millenary traditions. The *Movimiento Confederado Restaurador de la Cultura de Anáhuac* (MCRA) in México City represented a popular indigenous movement that reinitiated Mexica naming ceremonies in the 1960s and 1970s (Odena Güemes, 1984). Mexican families and individuals arrived at the naming ceremonies to recover their cultural heritage and forge new identities. The *Zamanahuak Tlamachtiloyan* was a descendant of the MCRA. The ZT amplifies the naming ceremonies in México City, investigating their history further, refining the components of the naming process, and executing them at important ceremonial events throughout the year. Kuauhkoatl and others presided over naming ceremonies in the 1980s and 1990s. Calpulli Tonalehqueh would take up this torch in the first decade of the twenty-first century.

The revival of Mexica naming conventions in México coincided with the civil rights movement in the United States, including the Chicana/o Movement whose activists were reconnected to Mexican history, especially with regard to popular visions of an Aztec past. As a symbol of this connection to an Aztec past, Chicanos focus on Aztlan, the homeland of Mexica pilgrims, in countless poems, works of art, scholarly and cultural productions. Many youth born to the activists of the civil rights movement received Náhuatl names like Moctezuma, Cuauhtémoc, Xochitl, and Citlalli instead of ones emanating from Catholic conventions or European influences. Individuals giving their children (or themselves) Mexica names during the last quarter of the twentieth century did so in ways that were less formal than ancient

Mexica traditions. For the most part, parents in recent decades chose from lists of names, identifying mainly with sound and meaning.

Danzantes took a step closer to the ancient rites at the end of the twenty-first century. They took on Náhuatl names with increasing frequency, usually without consultation with any *tonalamatl*, though they did examine their birthdate in the indigenous calendar systems. Furthermore, naming becomes ritualized in dance ceremonies. In Los Angeles, for example, Paztel Mireles led (and continues to lead) a dance group called Cuauhtémoc and has presided annually over naming ceremonies at his Mexica dance group's annual Xilonen ceremony (coming-of-age ceremony of young women). There parents choose a name that is proclaimed by Paztel. Each child is "initiated" into that identity at the public dance ceremony.

Calpulli Tonalehqueh, as a direct descendant of the ZT, took other steps in the revival of the tradition. First as Calpulli Huitzilopochtli and later as Calpulli Tonalehqueh, the group leveraged its relationship to Ocelocoatl to reinstitute Mexica naming processes and formal ceremonies. It is one of the highest achievements of Calpulli Tonalehqueh, one in line with the ideals of the *Mexicayotl* movement (*Conchero* and *Tradición* groups do not have this exact practice). Relative to the scarcity of these cultural specialists in the United States, there are many *tonalpohque* in México available to *danzantes*. In the United States, having direct access to one of the very few *tonalamatl* readers and naming specialists allowed Calpulli Tonalehqueh a unique and pivotal position.

Starting in the mid-1990s and into the present, more than 350 individuals had gone through the naming process with Calpulli Tonalehqueh. In consultation with Ocelocoatl, these individuals received their name options and then established their chosen name formally in a naming ceremony called *in toca in tocaitl*. This ceremony is often held within the larger MNY ceremony hosted annually by Calpulli Tonalehqueh or part of a dedicated ceremony for naming. In many cases, adolescents or adults selected names for themselves. In other cases, parents selected names and consulted the *tonalamatl* for newborns and infants.

In Toca in Tocaitl: Sowing One's Essence

I used the term "naming ceremony" thus far for ease of use and because of popular usage among *danzantes*, though it is not the most accurate translation. *In toca in tocaitl* has been explained to me as "*la siembra de la escencia de su ser*," or the sowing of one's essence. In March 2006, I attended a *huehuetlatolli* Ocelocoatl delivered regarding the *in toca in tocaitl* ceremony (he delivers this talk annually; I also have field notes from that talk because that lecture was prior to my own naming ceremony). There he explained the symbolism, ritual components, and his hopes for individuals preparing to go through the rite. The explanation I give in this chapter is a combination of all the information passed to me by *calpulli* members, including several conversations with and lectures by Ocelocoatl.

The *in toca in tocaitl* process aims for each individual to commence a lifetime of deep personal growth. Again, the ancient Mexica worldview was based on agriculture. In the *in toca in tocaitl* ceremony, a person is compared to a tree. That tree must be planted and given care in order to grow well. Using the metaphor of a tree, Ocelocoatl explained that a person is a seed that germinates, establishes a root network, and grows with a core of strength and fruitful actions. This is why Mexica refers to the ceremony as the sowing of one's essence. Like the seed, each human requires the four elements that create life: earth, wind, fire, and water. Each of us has all the four elements with us throughout our life. Our bodies are made of the elements on the periodic table; we are made of earth and eat all the products of earth. We breath to live, so we are wind. Our body is made mostly of water, so we carry that element. Lastly, our body generates heat; the sun and the universe gives us fire and we carry that energy inside us (when we die our bodies immediately go cold). More than physical growth, however, the *in toca in tocaitl* ceremony involves internal growth. This life way requires continual spiritual reflection.

The Name: A Conjugation of Proprietary Elements

The names that individuals receive are not arbitrary; a consultation of the elements present at the time of one's birth provides their foundation. Many believe that energies present in the environment at the moment of our birth have an impact on our being and, therefore, our destiny in the world. During birth, the first part of the body that passes through the birth canal and encounters the world is the infant's head, with an incompletely formed cranium. Through that opening, a child receives the elements present in the world. In other words, the seasonal cycles, the time of day, the time of year, the phase of the moon, and so on, all factor for that child because they are present at the time of birth and, therefore, "belong" to her or him. A *tonalpohque*, using the divinatory almanacs, can calculate the day—with numeral and day sign, year, *veintena* (20-day month), *trecena* (13-day week in the sacred count)—and many other things such as colors, cardinal directions, spirit birds, tools, plants, jewels, and philosophical concepts

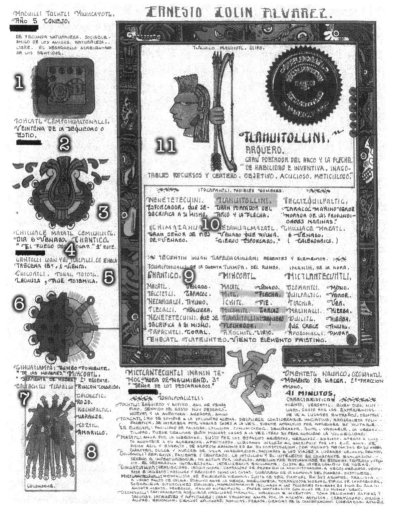

Figure 8.1   This is my own *tonalamatl*, an example of a hand-produced document by a *tonalpohque*.

Notes: The *tonalpohque* takes one's birthday, correlates it with the ancient count, and reads the books of destiny and delivers elements to the individual.

(called *regentes*, Spanish for regents) that belong to the individual. An individual's name emerges from a combination of the elements on this list. The elements not only provide the child with name possibilities, they also signal capacities or aptitudes, personal tendencies, and pitfalls and challenges. The *tonalpohque* transmits all of this information to the child or the parents in order to help them conduct their life or raise their child.

Figure 8.1 is an example of the culminating document of the naming process. It is a record of the calculations, the destiny, and the naming choice the individual receives from the *tonalpohque*. Using my *tonalamatl* as an example, Ocelocoatl found the birthdate fell in the year 5 Rabbit (1), in the *veintena* of *Toxcatl* (2). A full moon was present on the day (3). The day was 6 Deer (4). The day 6 Deer falls in the *trecena* 1 Wind, which is associated with the concept of *chantico* (the spirit of the hearth fire) (5). The bird associated with that day is the owl (6). The cardinal direction that corresponds to the deer is *Cihuatlampa*, the place of women (west) (7). The colors that belong to *Cihuatlampa* are Red, Orange, and Yellow of the setting sun (8). From these calculations, the books are consulted to create a list of elements associated to each of those calculations (9). From all these, a *tonalpohque* can conjugate a list of name possibilities, usually a compound of two or more of the elements. Ocelocoatl devises six of them (10) for each person. He advises consultation with loved ones before choosing the name that will represent the person and signal their destiny. The person chooses a name, and the *tonalpohqueh* or *tlacuilo* designs a pictograph/glyph to represent the chosen name in the Mexica writing convention (11). Finally, the *tonalpohque* outlines the characteristics, aptitudes, and challenges for the individual's personality, which ultimately impact their destiny (12).

Ocelocoatl explains that when one chooses to go through the ceremony, when the name is established, there is no turning back:

Cuando se siembra el nombre, no hay vuelta atrás. Se siembra en la tierra. El saber donde están las capacidades y tendencias de uno, y las áreas de carencia es un compromiso a conocerse mejor. El reto es ser mejor todos los días. No podemos engañarnos a nosotros mismos. Tenemos que darle dignidad al nombre, y ser dignos del nombre. El nombre señala todos los elementos que nos corresponden y ayuda a normar nuestra vida. Requiere el auto-control. El nombre le dice a todos tu destino, tu trabajo en este mundo. Si tu no actúas respetando tu destino, todos lo sabrán. Por ejemplo, si una persona se llama Yolopactiani,

*tiene el corazón contento, y se la pasa enojado, borracho, maltratando
a la gente, engañando, entonces la gente dirá, pues está traicionando su
destino. No le da dignidad al nombre.* (personal communication)

[When a person sows their name (in the ceremony), there is no turning
back. It is planted in the Earth. Knowing where one's capacities and tendencies lie, and one's pitfalls, is a commitment to knowing oneself better.
It is a challenge to be our best self. We can never lie to ourselves. We
have to be worthy of the name, give the name dignity. The name signals
all the elements that belong to us, and helps regulate our life. It requires
self-control. The name tells everyone what your destiny is, what your
job in the world is. If your actions disrespect your destiny, everyone will
know. For example, if a person is named Yolopactiani, meaning S/he
Has a Happy Heart, and s/he goes around angry, drunk, treating people
poorly, lying, then people will say, well, s/he is betraying her/his name/
destiny. S/he is not dignifying his name.] (my translation)

The knowledge of one's destiny and personality becomes a responsibility that one carries forth from the process.

Ocelocoatl will explain the metaphorical meaning of the name
choices a person has in the consultation. All the assembled names are
available, but the individual has to choose one. Ocelocoatl explains
that there are a few methods for selecting. First, people can choose
the name based on sound. Next, people can chose based on meaning.
Others select the name after meditation and consultation with people.
He says that people should dialogue with their heart, and the name
will sometimes choose them.

I chose my name, Tlahuitollini, after consulting with my family
and considering what each implied for my destiny. Tlahuitollini literally means He Carries a Bow and Arrow. It is the name for an archer
and is a metaphor for a teacher. The bow, Ocelocoatl explains, represents raw materials made useful. The arrow represents certainty and
direction. A Tlahuitollini, therefore, is a person who takes materials and makes them useful so that others can have knowledge and
direction. As my *tonalamatl* says, a Tlahuitollini is able and inven-
tive, resourceful and accurate, diligent and meticulous. I had been a
teacher in various arenas in my life and saw that as a good path to
continue on, so I chose the name. This is my destiny and I have to be
the best Tlahuitollini I can be in the world. I make that commitment
to that destiny through the *in toca in tocaitl* ceremony. Every person
who receives a *tonalamatl* and name choices goes through a similar
process.

The Ceremony

After a person chooses a name, they prepare for the ceremony. Ocelocoatl explains that women must come to the ceremony with the following (pictured in figure 8.2):

- a dress (no pants), symbolizing a circle and allowing a connection between womb and earth
- a crown of flowers, usually white or of any variety she likes
- a bouquet of flowers, in the size and amount of her choosing;. this will be a gift for the altar

Figure 8.2   These are images from the *in toca in tocaitl* ceremonies that take place in Calpulli Tonalehqueh.

Note: Ocelocoatl presides over the naming of infants and adults alike with the aid of *cihuapiltin* (venerable women helpers) and *atecocolehqueh* (conch players).

- a necklace or bracelet containing symbols related to her chosen profession, occupation, work, or craft
- a necklace of popcorn (*izquixochitl*), representing abundance
- come barefoot, making a connection to Mother Earth
- memorize the chosen name and its significance
- gifts to give away to everyone at the ceremony

Men are required to come to the ceremony with the following:

- white cotton attire
- an *arma* made by the individual himself, such as a shield, a bow, or an *ayacaxtli*
- a drawing/painting of their glyph
- wearing a red *ixcuaimecatl*
- wearing a necklace of popcorn is optional
- come barefoot
- memorize the chosen name and its significance
- gifts to give away to ceremony attendees

The *in toca in tocaitl* ceremony takes place during the MNY ceremony hosted by Calpulli Tonalehqueh or at other designated ceremonies. First, young children are named, followed by adults and elders, and finally dancers. Candidates present themselves one at a time and are blessed with incense, water, tobacco, and medicinal herbs. Four questions are asked of each individual (or parent[s] if naming an infant): (1) Why do you wish to sow your name? (2) Do you come here of your own volition committed to honoring your destiny? (3) What name are you taking? (4) What does it mean?

If Ocelocoatl is satisfied with the answers, he continues with a blessing of each person. He explains the essence of the person's destiny. He blesses their hands so that they may create useful things, their feet so that they may walk a straight and noble path, their navel so that they radiate energy like the sun, their heart so that they may have strength, and their eyes so that they may see beauty. Ocelocoatl asks each person to pause and look around at the ongoing dance ceremony. He says that all the people are creating energy and harmony for this moment. He explains that the individual must commit to be an upstanding member of the *Danza* community. In the end, the individual proclaims their name four times along with the helpers in the *in toca in tocaitl* ceremony.

The Implications: a Life Guided by Destiny

Members of *Mexicayotl* and Calpulli Tonalehqueh do not intend theatricality or romanticism in the revival of the naming ceremony. They hope that with the knowledge obtained through the process and after the ceremony, individuals and families may be transformed. Adults raise their children with the information as a guideline. Furthermore, individuals who are conscious of their actions are armed with a tool that serves a guidepost for their walk in life; they can evaluate their actions in comparison with their *tonalamatl*. People are now known by new names. The elements that belong to each person are soon used to create ceremonial attire, clothing, art, accessories, and guide a vast number of decisions. Some individuals choose modern or less formal names (e.g., business cards, e-mail addresses, social media accounts, Websites, etc.)

Tonalamatl can have an impact on romantic relationships. The surviving *amochtin* (codicies) make marriage predictions based on the combinations of the numeral assigned to each of the individuals in partnership. The *tonalamatl* forecasts whether the partnership will be auspicious or not. Many couples make consultations to gain insight into their relationships.

Individuals create new identities. There are many *calpulli* members and dancers who are known exclusively by their Náhuatl names and can be more easily identified with the *Mexicayotl* tradition. Individuals are reinscribing themselves.

The Self: Locus of a Palimpsest

The *in toca in tocaitl* process is a different occasion for a palimpsest. The locus of this palimpsest is neither on the societal level nor on group level, it is written on personal biographies. The revival of naming traditions signals important shifts and preferences for communities negotiating minority positionality in the United States and México and reaffirming indigenous identity.

Perhaps all the activities of the *calpulli* are directed to the transformation of the individual. We have surveyed reasons that people give for why they dance, their effort in the group, and why they organize these spaces. They point back to creating a space for themselves, their children, and the future of the community. Establishing the *calpulli* and the *cargos*, organizing the MNY ceremony and the *ensayo* through *tequio*, and creating spaces for *huehuetlatolli* from cultural specialists, all create conditions and occasions for personal identity work.

During the naming ceremony, individuals arrive at the *in toca in tocaitl* with their personal life experience, including previous versions of self. This process provides individuals with materials to make a new entry on their personal biography. With a new name, they are literally reinscribed. The name becomes a marker signaling participation in the *Mexicayotl* tradition and in *Danza*. Moreover, the information provided by the study of one's elements—presented in the *tonalamatl*—can impact the conduct of one's lives. If people are aware of their aptitudes and personal challenges—of their destiny as outlined by this process—they have guideposts for their life's walk. The *tonalamatl* can guide ceremonial attire, art, social relations, romantic relationships, morality, engagement with the mainstream, relations with other *danzantes*, or an infinite number of other life choices. In the identity palimpsest, participants build a bridge between ancestral heritage and a future for themselves and/or their children.

9

A Modern Mexica Palimpsest

México's recent history (last five centuries) is marked by what Guillermo Bonfil Batalla (1996) called the "permanent confrontation between those attempting to direct the country toward the path of Western civilization and those, rooted in Mesoamerican ways of life, who resist." (p. xv) The year 2010 marked the bicentennial of México's independence, and millions of individuals and cultural critics paused to consider what direction the country could take in the face of tremendous social challenges. Can the conditions that arrange for warring drug cartels, widespread poverty, massive emigration, and other current challenges in México be traced to institutionalized colonialism? Bonfil Batalla argued that, though independence from Spain was achieved, decolonization remains incomplete. Instead, all visions of social progress have been organized under a Western framework (p. xvi). Moreover, indigenous models for society are not only ignored but also disparaged and abhorred as backwards, obstinate, or worse. The dominant culture in México has directed a devastating, continual de-Indianization project forcing native communities to change their ideologies, lose their lands, renounce their identity, and abandon their languages and ways of life (pp. 17 and 62).

But just as decolonization is incomplete, so too is de-Indianization. For many, indigenous Mexican culture is seen as something inert, something for tourists, something mired in the past, or something whose vibrancy and historical continuity is fit to be denied. Mesoamerican culture is so profoundly woven into the cultural fabric of México that it is impossible to substitute, erase, or ignore.

In his classic text, *México Profundo: Reclaiming a Civilization*, Bonfil Batalla (1996) conceived *México Profundo* as an intractable component found in the majority of the people and activities of México, a way of understanding the world and organizing human life, which has an origin in Mesoamerican civilization and is expressed today on a cultural spectrum of traits that ranges from internally cohesive to scattered. His text mapped out the presence of Mesoamerican civilization in all sectors of society or what he calls "a panoramic vision of the constant and multiform presence of that which is Indian in México" (p. xv). He also presented occasions when Mexicans deny their origins and embark on a program of cultural substitution instead of cultural development, arguing that this is a feature of a colonial legacy. Finally, Bonfil Batalla of the 1960s looked to the future and signaled the resources Mexican people have to construct a healthy, authentic future that transcends a failing status quo.

Bonfil Batalla's conceptualization and analysis of *México Profundo* illuminates the expressed cultural features and strategies employed by Mexica dancers who are part of the Mexican Diaspora. Bonfil Batalla's definition of *México Profundo* parallels this book's conceptualization of a *Danza* palimpsest. Though Bonfil Batalla focused on México, I contend that Mexican-origin communities living abroad can certainly be counted among the peoples of *México Profundo* because they face similar erasures of their life ways (in the United States, for example), employ similar strategies of resistance, and draw strength from indigenous Mexican cultures. *Danzantes* embody *México Profundo*, and their groups and traditions should be celebrated for their viability and complexity, not just consumed as spectacle, something for tourists, or something marginal in all senses of the word.

Bonfil Batalla (1996) also presented a matrix of cultural strategies employed by minority groups like the members of *México Profundo*, which I explore for the group featured in this ethnography. Bonfil Batalla stated:

> The total and systematic negation of Mesoamerican civilization and the permanent aggression to which it has been subjected have provoked cultural effects of different and varying intensity in different Indian groups. In all cases it has involved changes that reduce the cultural spaces available, that is, the capacity for decision making and the number and quality of cultural elements necessary to carry out any self directed social action…In spite of this long history of domination and the transformations imposed on the cultures of Mesoamerican ancestry, Indian peoples remain. (p. 129)

Bonfil Batalla further stated:

> *México Profundo*, meanwhile, keeps resisting, appealing to diverse strategies, depending on the scheme of domination to which it is subjected. It is not a passive static world, but, rather, one that lives in permanent tension. The peoples of *México Profundo*, continually create and recreate their culture, adjust it to changing pressures, and reinforce their own, private sphere of control. They take foreign cultural elements and put them at their service; they cyclically perform the collective acts that are a way of expressing and renewing their own identity. (p. xvii)

Bonfil Batalla outlined three different paths or mechanisms of indigenous survival: Resistance, Innovation, and Appropriation.

Resistance has often come in the form of violence, but it has also taken the form of reelaborating aspects of culture. Native communities organize against oppression, put into play various forms of social organization, and employ sometimes-latent symbols to subvert colonial regimes (Bonfil Batalla, 1996, p. 131). Countless examples exist (c.f. various rebellions, Mayan talking crosses, the War of the Castes), including the entire modern history of *Danza*, where indigenous people organize activities that carve out spaces of autonomy and protect their traditions, languages, land, and way of life. "The paths of resistance form an intricate web of strategies that occupies a broad space in the culture and daily lives of Indian peoples." (Bonfil Batalla, 1996, p. 132). Resistance became and continues to be a strategy of vital importance in the face of violence, subjugation, ethnocide, and imposition. Bonfil Batalla (1996) explained that the adherence to traditional practices is in and of itself a form of resistance:

> The cyclical exercise of these practices is, on the one hand, a periodic affirmation of the existence of the group, a collective manifestation of its permanence symbolically expressed in the fulfillment *las costumbres*... It is a show of autonomy that preserves space of the activity as a part of the reduced universe of social life over which the group maintains decision-making rights...Finally, these traditional rites acquire new meaning and fulfill functions that may be very different from those they had in previous periods. This process adds contemporary reasons to reinforce other, more profound, justifications for maintaining them. I think of the annual fiestas, the collective rituals, the dances that are carried out. Their importance may be as moments that renew the identity and sense of permanence of the group, and thus the existence of the community itself. (p. 133)

Resistance can be subtle. It can be inner prayer, songs written with double meaning, a glyph on a mural in a sixteenth-century convent, and so on. On the other hand, claiming cultural citizenship through cyclical ceremony can be overtly political. Dancers may take over a plaza, lead protest, organize an online social network, or print their own counternarratives. Indeed, the constant renewal of one's identity incapacitates erasure. Now more than ever, *Danza* can be documented, pictures and videos can be posted online, dancers can "invade" schools and universities, children can be named and educated differently, internal and external structures of colonization can be dismantled. Given the set of resources available in a globalized world, the dance tradition as well as the oral tradition can find new audiences and modes of resistance. Overall, dynamic cultural conservation is not simply resisting change but ensuring survival. Even when forbidden, people have risked their lives for their traditional practices. This has happened without fail (e.g., the Jews of Europe, African slaves in the United States, the people of occupied Tibet, the Quechua of South America), and 500 years of evidence shows *Danza* has been no exception.

Second, innovation is a strategy of *México Profundo*. Internal changes and innovation are compulsory in a colonial situation for subaltern communities. Bonfil Batalla (1996) contended *México Profundo* subtly innovates material, social, artistic, and ceremonial arenas. In the axioms of anthropology, culture is not static; it is dynamic and adaptive. It is through what Bonfil Batalla called "incessant creativity" that *México Profundo* achieves new and useful elements and traditions that go beyond appropriation. It is absolutely clear that Calpulli Tonalehqueh, along with the innumerable dance groups of Mesoamerica, adapt and innovate using contemporary materials and emerging tools in service of autochthonous and endemic millenary traditions. In this text we see Calpulli Tonalehqueh members innovate in education, organizational leadership, material resources, attire, travel and transportation, informal economy, communication, scholarship, and art.

The third strategy of resistance employed by *México Profundo* is appropriation, where a group incorporates and manipulates cultural elements that were foreign and that came from the imposed, dominant culture. For the appropriation to take place, Bonfil Batalla (1996) stated, "it is necessary for the group to take control over those foreign cultural elements, so that it can put them at the service of the group's own ends and its own, autonomous decisions" (p. 135). Later,

communities may acquire the ability to produce, reproduce, and maintain items that were once foreign to them and now cease to be so
(p. 137). The various iterations and forms of *Danza* can be viewed in
this light. Religious syncretism is usually viewed as a simple combination of cultural practices, but it is actually a complex appropriation.
Religious ceremonies and beliefs were imposed, but they have been
reorganized, reinterpreted, and subverted from within, resulting in a
complex product over which indigenous communities have substantial
control (p. 136).

Appropriation and strategic syncretism are common and sen-
sible forms of resistance for minority communities across space and
time. We know, for example, that Mexica elders gave orders (e.g., the
"*Consigna de Cuauhtémoc*," appendix A) to hide traditions using
the "clothing" of the invader. *Danza* in some variations hides meaning, beliefs, and ceremony beneath new Christian saints and rituals.
This practice continues into the present. The *Mexicayotl* tradition, for
example, works to divest its ceremonial practice of elements of the
colonizing civilization from *Danza* while at the same time appropri-
ating modern techniques (e.g., modern attire, Websites, media/social
media, fundraising, sponsorship) to carry out their vision. The presence of "foreign" elements in native Mexican ceremony is cause for
much debate. Bonfil Batalla (1996) noted:

> The presence of cultural elements of foreign origin does not in itself
> indicate weakness of loss of authenticity within Indian cultures. The
> problem does not consist of the proportion of the "original" traits as
> opposed to "foreign" traits exhibited by a culture at any given moment.
> Rather, the question is who exercises control over those traits. (p. 137)

There is no question, given the variance seen in *Danza*, that dancers
control the cultural product. Subordinate and marginalized groups,
like the members of *México Profundo*, manage their appropriation,
and elements are modified, reinterpreted, provided new meaning
beyond the original, and controlled for group purposes (p. 136).

Bonfil Batalla delineated the cultural dynamics of *México Profundo*
and the resistance strategies for their cultural palimpsest. He hoped for
a future of pluralism while acknowledging that the imposed culture
of "Imaginary México" gains ground constantly and the struggle for
indigenous communities to claim space and identity is a difficult one.
Yet, because it has been in development for time immemorial, in this
land, organically, by generations upon generations, *México Profundo*

can always be located, marshaled, called upon, and identified—even in Diaspora—despite all efforts to erase it.

Various questions were posed in this examination of Calpulli Tonalehqueh. One asked if there existed environments of indigenous education constructed today in ways that strategically resist the erasure of traditional Mexica culture? The answer is yes, and the dance/cultural community group under analysis is an example. A second asked how scholars could talk about the influence of precontact Mexica culture in and across the contemporary Mexican Diaspora, and whether it is possible that the *calpulli* offers a version of education that builds a bridge between the deep past and the emerging future of a community caught in situations not of its own making? For answers to these, I turned to the idea of palimpsest as a metaphor for how to understand a difficult present with a hidden but relentlessly powerful past. A third question presented by this concluding chapter involves the match between what Bonfil Batalla (1996) calls *México Profundo* with the subtle march of an educational system brought to life by contemporary participants in a community dance group. Again, the answer to this question is yes, and I use seven cases of palimpsest to help us imagine the potential of community-based education for the endurance of *México Profundo*. Overall, these questions are a way of asking about the appropriateness of a metaphor about a multilayered text with an incompletely erased heritage upon which new texts are superimposed for the description of indigenous education, community organization, and identity work.

Appropriately, palimpsest is a dynamic, plastic, and versatile term. Numerous fields utilize the metaphor to describe phenomena; the palimpsest construct presents implications to numerous fields of scholarship. I bring it to anthropology, indigenous education, and postcolonial studies as a helpful metaphor to describe group activity, cultural traditions, history, and personal identity in a Mexica dance circle. Palimpsest represents a context with multiple layers written over earlier texts, a palimpsest that confronts forces of erasure through strategic construction and rewriting.

Recognizing the palimpsest of Calpulli Tonalehqueh reveals important understandings about the cultural dynamics discussed here. While responsive to the present, palimpsest has a simultaneous relationship with both the past and the future. Members take up a heritage and reconfigure it using contemporary materials while directing their efforts toward a future. There is continuity with the past. The palimpsest concept allows Calpulli Tonalehqueh to build the group in a way that is respectful of the past but responsible to the future and for individuals to recreate themselves through participation in the construction project. Palimpsest leaves room for cocreation, collaboration, and the creative assembly of gathered materials.

Palimpsest specifies a group's total culture and can be understood through the way it circumscribes spiritual practice, art, language, identity performance, organizational structure, education, political economy, cultural citizenship, and so forth. Far too often, members of communities like the one that couches Calpulli Tonalehqueh are intensely concerned with a rigid notion of authenticity or holding on to a past that has either changed or has been partially erased. Instead of rigid and essentialist understandings of ethnicity, identity, or culture, palimpsest reminds us of the complexity of culture. In other words, palimpsest successfully liberates individuals from the constraints of essentialism and unworkable notions of cultural authenticity.

Relief from the pressure of essentialism is valuable to all human groups. Celebration of the ways communities study and reclaim their past, resist erasure, and recreate is valuable as well. This construct may help us appreciate the palimpsest of different contemporary global communities practicing in the United States and abroad. We can identify the palimpsest of B-boy and Krunk dancers, graffiti artists, Tinikling innovators, Step teams, Anishinaabe bicycle makers, Capoeira practitioners, Son Jarocho *fandangueros*, Taiko drummers, jazz musicians, and so on.

The idea of *México Profundo* informs the strategic accomplishments and particular nature of Calpulli Tonalehqueh's palimpsest construction. Reading the work of Calpulli Tonalehqueh through the concept and aims of *México Profundo* builds upon Bonfil Batalla's (1996) scholarly work on *México Profundo*, connects it to palimpsest, and extends it to Mexican-origin communities in the United States. Indigenous Mexican communities successfully resist impositions on their worldview and way of life. The legacy of Mexican colonialism and de-Indianization impacts Mexican-origin communities transnationally. The challenging legacy of these hegemonic projects is exacerbated by similar oppressive forces in the United States, including Native American removal projects, xenophobia against immigrants, assimilationist school designs, and socioeconomic injustice. Recognizing these as a source of social challenge, the people of *México Profundo* become confrontational, hoping to restore and protect cultural pride and community health. Calpulli Tonalehqueh promotes cultural development instead of cultural substitution as the method of advancement in the

US context. Calpulli Tonalehqueh increases the spaces available for modern Mexicas and allies to gather, organize, dance, educate, heal, practice spirituality and move forward together.

The strategies of resistance created and recreated by the people of *México Profundo* are evident in Calpulli Tonalehqueh. First, members of Calpulli Tonalehqueh resist erasure when they organize, denounce historic injustice, actualize their mission, reeducate themselves, and partner with outside nations and communities to build solidarity, alliances, solidarity, and networks of exchange.

Innovation is the second strategy employed by *México Profundo* and consequently by Calpulli Tonalehqueh. When members of Calpulli Tonalehqueh utilize new tools and pioneer elements in the tradition of *Danza*, they help guarantee their perpetuation. Members of Calpulli Tonalehqueh innovate attire, organizational structure, online communication, fundraising, travel, community partnerships, language, and many other elements of their *calpulli*.

The third strategy is appropriation. Members of Calpulli Tonalehqueh take control of and repurpose such things as public and private spaces, electronic communication, media outlets, funding sources, events, organizations, schools, and so forth. These strategies are not different than those of countless indigenous and minority communities in the world. Aboriginal communities have always found creative ways to resist and survive. Calpulli Tonalehqueh is in solidarity with this movement and their work identifies them as part of *México Profundo*.[1]

In sum, the total set of Calpulli Tonalehqueh practices can be understood through the concept of palimpsest. The metaphor of palimpsest is characterized as a text that has visible traces of the past, includes multiple written entries, and reflects its history. The previous layers have been incompletely erased and the diverse layers constitute a whole. Calpulli Tonalehqueh reflects this definition on historical, group, and individual levels. On a historical level, Calpulli Tonalehqueh is embedded in a *Danza* palimpsest written by multicultural pre-Cuauhtémoc indigenous nations and followed by entries from colonialism, Westernization, Christianity and syncretism, loss and reclamation of land, stylistic renewals in the *Conchero* tradition, nationalistic recoveries in the *Mexicayotl* tradition, language, economic, and transnational shifts, and so forth. At the group level, Calpulli Tonalehqueh constructs a palimpsest as it designs its structure, components, education, ceremony, and social relations. At the individual level, identities can be understood through palimpsest as members are transformed, renamed, and empowered through participation in *Danza* and Calpulli Tonalehqueh.

Palimpsest allows us to understand the complex iterations of this modern *calpulli*. Overall, embracing the concept of palimpsest allows people to understand that they can honor and be sustained by the past but move forward dynamically, navigating oppositional forces. They can do this as a collective, untethered by the forces of erasure or essentialism.

Appendix A

The Mandate of the *Huey Tlahtocan* (Great Council) of 1519

Sometimes called the *Consigna de Cuauhtémoc*, this message has been attributed often to the *Huey Tlahtoani* (Great Speaker), Cuauhtémoc, on behalf of the supreme governing council of the Anáhuac Confederation seated in México-Tenochtitlan (sixteenth century). The message was delivered at the end of the wars of resistance to the invasion. The text in Náhuatl and Spanish is taken from Nieva (1969), with my English translation. This message is one of the primary mandates for the *Mexicayotl* movement.

Table A1.1 Members of the *Mexicayotl* movement promote the *Consigna de Cuáuhtemoc* as an ancient mandate

Náhuatl	Spanish	English
Totonal yomotlatih.	Nuestro sol, se ocultó.	Our sun is hidden.
Totonal yoixpolih,	Nuestro Sol se perdió de vista,	Our sun is out of sight,
iuan zentlayouayan, o tech Kabteh.	y en completa oscuridad nos ha dejado.	and it has left us in complete darkness.
Mach tikmatih man Ka okzepa ualla,	Pero sabemos que otra vez volverá,	But we know that it will return,
man Ka okzepa Kizakin,	que otra vez saldrá,	that it will rise again,
iuan yankuiotika tech tlauilikin.	y nuevamente nos alumbrará.	and it will illuminate us again.
Mach imoka ompa Kah mitlan maniz	Pero mientras allá esté en la mansión del silencio,	But while it resides in the mansion of silence,
manzamueliui tozentlalikan, totechtecho kan,	muy prontamente nos reunamos, nos estrechemos,	let us quickly gather, hold ourselves
iuan tozolnepantla, tiktlatikan, nochi intlen toyolkitlazohtla,	y en el centro de nuestro corazón, ocultemos, todo lo que nuestro corazón ama,	and in center of our heart, let us hide everything that our heart loves,
Ki ueyi tlatkiomati.	que sabemos es gran tesoro.	that which we know is great treasure.
Man tikin pohpolokan toteokalhuan,	Destruyamos nuestros recintos al principio creador,	Let us destroy our houses dedicated to the creative force,
tokalmekalhuan, totlachkohuan,	nuestras Escuelas, nuestros campos de pelota,	our schools, our ball courts,
totelpochkahuan, tokuikakalhuan.	nuestros recintos para la juventud, nuestras casas para el canto.	our youth priories, our houses of song.
Man mozelkahuakan tohumeh,	Que solos queden nuestros caminos,	May our roads be in solitude,
iuan man tochanlzakua	y que nuestros hogares nos encierren	and may our homes shutter us in,

Kin ihkuak Kixouaz toyankuiktonal.	hasta cuando salga nuestro nuevo Sol.	until the time when our new sun rises.
In tahtzintzin iuan in nantzitzin	Los papacitos y las mamacitas,	The fathers and the mothers,
Man aik kilkuaukan Kimilhuizkeb 1tel pochhuan,	que nunca olviden conducir a sus jóvenes,	may they never forget to direct their children,
iuan matechuazkeb mo pipilhuan inoka nemizkeb,	y enseñarles a sus hijitos mientras vivan,	and teach them while they live
uel kenin yoko,	como buena ha sido,	how good our beloved Anáhuac has been until now
kin axkan totlazob Anauak	hasta ahora nuestra amada Anáhuac,	
in tlanekiliz iuan tlapeluiliz in tonechtoltiliz uan,	al amparo y protección de nuestros destinos,	in the aid and protection of our destinies,
iuan zan ye nopampa tokenmauiliz iuan tokem pololiz,	por nuestro gran respeto y buen comportamiento,	because of our great respect and good behavior,
okizelibkeb totiachkatzitzihuan,	que recibieron nuestros antepasados,	as given to our ancestors,
iuan tlen totahtzitzin auik yolebkayopan,	y que nuestros papacitos muy entusiastamente,	and that our parents enthusiastically
oki xi nachtokateb toyelizpan.	sembraron en nuestro ser.	sowed in our being.
Axkan tehuan tikin tekimakab in topilhuan.	Ahora nosotros ordenaremos a nuestros hijos.	Now we will guide our children.
Amo kin ilkauazkeb kin nonotzazkeb mo pilhuan,	No olviden informar a sus hijos,	Do not forget to inform your children,
uelkenin yez, kenin imakokiz, iuan uelkenin chikabkauiz,	cómo buena sea, cómo se levantará, y cómo bien alcanzará fuerza,	how good it is, how it will rise, and how well it will gain strength,
iuan uel kenin kiktzon kixtitin ineyika nehtoltiliz,	y cómo bien realizará su gran destino,	and how well it will fulfill its destiny,
inin totlazobtlahnantzin Anauak.	ésta nuestra amada madre tierra Anáhuac.	this, our beloved land of Anáhuac.

Appendix B

Palimpsest in Academic Fields

The following is a compendium of uses of the concept of palimpsest in various academic fields:

- **Archeology.** Archeologists use the notion of palimpsest to describe their field sites and the remains that time has washed over, including the visible traces left by epochs in procession. F. Clarke Howell, in an article about his own documentation of the artifacts in a cave in Turkey, quotes an anonymous archeologist, "For all we know, the archaeological record is just one big palimpsest, incompletely effaced" (1981). Wikipedia offer the following: "Archaeologists in particular use the term to denote a record of material remains suspected of having formed during an extended period but that cannot be resolved in such a way that temporally discrete traces can be recognized as such."
- **Architecture.** Architects sometimes describe the forms they create as speaking symbols or texts (of sorts) to be interpreted. These structures are said to have syntax of their own. Layered constructions are full of meaning and prior constructions are often visible. Consider the following text: "Architects imply palimpsest as a ghost—an image of what once was. In the built environment, this occurs more than we think. Whenever spaces are shuffled, rebuilt, or remodeled, shadows remain. Tarred rooflines remain on the sides of a building long after the neighboring structure has been demolished; removed stairs leave a mark where the painted wall surface stopped. Dust lines remain from a relocated appliance. Ancient ruins speak volumes of their former wholeness. Palimpsests can serve a noble duty in informing us, almost archaeologically, of the realities of the built past. Thus architects, archaeologists and design historians sometimes use the word to describe the accumulated iterations of a design or a site, whether in literal layers of archaeological remains, or by the figurative accumulation and reinforcement of design ideas over time. An excellent example of this can be seen at The Tower of London, where

construction began in the 11th century, and the site continues to develop to this day." (http://www.reference.com/browse/palimpsest)

- **Art, art criticism, and art history.** Many art pieces and instillations make explicit reference to palimpsests. Palimpsest is used as a medium, an art-making process, and/or an analytical tool. Writers such as Hakim Bey (pen name for Peter Lamborn Wilson) critically, and playfully, theorize about theory as well as art from outside academic institutions.
- **Astronomy.** A *Dictionary of Astronomy* defines palimpsests as they are used in planetary astronomy: "An impact crater whose topography has been smoothed by glacier-like flow of the surface. The term was coined for features on the icy surfaces of Ganymede and Callisto. Palimpsests there consist of bright circular features, sometimes at the centre of concentric rings."
- **Chirography.** The study of handwriting alludes to symbolic features in a piece of writing.
- **Classics, theology, and philosophy.** I put these areas together because the use of the term palimpsest by their scholars is closely related. These fields and disciplines refer to the most literal meaning of palimpsest and the manuscripts of antiquity—from early Greek, Roman, Jewish, Christian, Syrian, or medieval writers, for instance. There are frequent references to the monks who created many of the palimpsests, the ancient texts they effaced, and the new, often religious texts they copied.
- **Computer science.** Palimpsest is the word assigned to a process of the tracking of concurrent collaborative editing of hypertext documents in computer programming.
- **Cryptology.** Cryptology is the study of codes and the process of writing and/or solving them. Many code makers and code breakers use the term palimpsest to describe the ciphers or underlying codes in their various encryptions. A famous example of a cipher that has captivated many in the United States is found on an outdoor sculpture, Kryptos, by the American artist James Sanborn at the CIA headquarters (a bastion of codes) in Langley, Virginia. The text on the sculpture is written in code and the keyword to unlock part of the code is "palimpsest."
- **Education.** Palimpsest tropes are part of the discussion of teachers and scholars of education. I have found palimpsest analogies in articles about classroom organization and student writing portfolios, among others.
- **Genetics and genomics.** DNA and RNA sequences are seen as genetic codes/texts, which are written, reproduced, and shared by cells, which can mutate or evolve and to which the palimpsest metaphor can be applied. These sequences are documented, interpreted, and even acted upon as authors by scientists.**Geology, paleontology, and earth science.** From deserts to glaciers to marine shelves, palimpsests are used to describe changing, anthropogenically altered, superimposed, layered, and evolving terrestrial landscapes in geology, paleontology, and earth sciences.

- **History.** Palimpsests are used by historians to describe the multiple truths, documents, voices, texts, precursors, and perspectives available for the examination of events. Many writers have discussed México in these terms. José Rabasa wrote about México City, "On the ruins of the ancient city, México City arises and retains indelible traces of the ancient order for the present. This transformation of reality may be likened to a palimpsest where the text of the conquered furnishes and retains its formal structure in the text of the conqueror. It is not the explorer's accidental and fortuitous mushrooming of colonial entrepôts on a landscape that murmurs and extraneous language. The fuerat, the had-been Tenochtitlan, retains a ghostlike presence in a mnemonic deposit of information about the land despite the city's destruction."
- **Internet.** Internet scholars and bloggers can be found using the term palimpsest to define the pages on the World Wide Web. In a digital world, web pages are written, shared, erased, rewritten, and read. Martin Lessard from Montréal, Québec, has done work to define digital palimpsests, describe the methodology for their production, and note famous digital palimpsests. He cites Wikipedia and other Wikis as digital palimpsests.
- **Linguistics and humanities.** Palimpsest is evoked by humanists when considering modern text forms, editorial theory, authorship, and (re)construction of languages. A book *The African Palimpsest* by Chantal Zabus discusses such things as diglossia, nativization or indigenization ("the writer's attempt at textualizing linguistic differentiation and at conveying African concepts, thought patterns, and linguistic features through the ex-colonizer's language" [3]), linguistic informants, relexification (the replacement of the vocabulary of one language by that of another), deciphering, the linguistic syncretism of colonialism in the scripts of West Africa, and métissage (cultural cross-fertilization), by using the palimpsest metaphor.
- **Literary criticism.** Palimpsest can be applied to the multiple, possibly ambiguous, or complex meanings of literary works. It is a figurative trope that signals layers of meaning in literature itself or as seen in the author's stylistics.
- **Medicine.** Palimpsest can be used for diagnosing or describing "acute anterograde amnesia without loss of consciousness, brought on by the ingestion of alcohol or other substances: 'alcoholic palimpsest.'" Studies on memory within the discipline of psychology also use palimpsest to describe a certain brain operation related to memory.
- **Native American, African American, Chicana/o, LGBT, and feminist studies.** The palimpsest metaphor has been used to represent (re)readings of authors, the multiple voices and layers, liminal spaces, construction of identities, survival strategies, and so forth, in the literature and other cultural productions of ethnic and gendered communities. In addition to palimpsest, numerous other terms allude to, are analogous with, or serve

similarly to the palimpsest metaphor I am trying to develop. I have more familiarity with Chicana/o and Native American studies, yet I can testify to a multitude of terms from all of these fields that are attractive in an interplay with ideas like "palimpsest" (e.g., transculturation, hybridity, multiplicity, liminality, heterogeneity, mestizaje, transborder, transnational, diaspora, embodiment, performance, ceremony, poetics).

- **Urban studies.** For scholars such as Andreas Huyssen, Renato Rosaldo, and José Muñoz Millanes, cities are seen as living organisms of social encounters, layers of physical and living structures, and landscapes of historical iterations. In other words, cities are palimpsests. (Millanes and Huyssen use the term explicitly.) In Andreas Huyssen's *Present Pasts: Urban Palimpsests and the Politics of Memory*, the monuments, cityscapes, and buildings of places like Berlin and Buenos Aires are discussed as palimpsests and in terms of public memory and history.
- **Zoology.** W. K. Gregory and H. C. Raven's work entitled *The Monotremes and the Palimpsest Theory* (1947) launched a debate about the classification of certain species of animals (monotremes [mammals that lay eggs among other things] that share characteristics with different classes of animals) that continues into the present. Many more articles from animal scientists and geneticists make frequent reference to Gregory and Raven's use of palimpsest to describe the genetic relationships and evolution of animals as they are classified.
- **Palimpsest in popular culture.** The notion of palimpsest is not exclusively the domain of university scholars and doctoral dissertations. I have come across explicit palimpsest references in literary works, poems, songs, art pieces, andso on.

Appendix C

Gathering Materials, Experiences, and Interpretations

This appendix outlines the gathering of materials, experiences, and voices to inform this text.

When I embarked on this ethnography, I was a student in the field of education and the discipline of anthropology as well as a *danzante*. I set out on an ethnographically inspired study where I could stay immersed in my community and investigate the dynamics of that particular culture. I started with general questions about the cultural transmission in the group in which I was active, Calpulli Tonalehqueh. Some of my first questions were: (1) How does this group organize teaching and learning? (2) Why do people join and stay in *Danza*, that is, what is in it for them? (3) How are people transformed through their participation in *Danza*? In tandem with the early part of my time in the field, I was immersed in scholarship about Chicana/o and Native American identity, culturally responsive education, and Mesoamerican studies. My time in scholarly conversations with peers and mentors brought me the ideas that would become part of my conceptual framework. Originally I designed a study of *Danza* in a cultural studies framework, studying *Danza* as a commodity on the "Circuits of Culture," but reflection upon the lived activity in Calpulli Tonalehqueh brought the current concept of palimpsest into relief as a better descriptor for the work being done through the *calpulli*. I had been a veteran dancer and member in Calpulli Tonalehqueh and generally knew how the group operated, but through a more focused quality of attention, the questions that would guide this book crystallized. I held my original questions in the background, but through my time in the field, the following questions emerged: (1) When are environments for a modern Mexica education constructed? In other words, at what times does this group mobilize resources for cultural transmission and socialization? (2) When is palimpsest? In other words, at what times is the metaphor of a multilayered text with an incompletely erased heritage upon which new text is superimposed apt for group productions?

My approach to answering those questions involved long-term ethnographic fieldwork, including deep participant observation and the gathering of various materials and engagements in the *Danza* universe surrounding Calpulli Tonalehqueh. About ten years of *Danza* and two years of direct participation with Calpulli Tonalehqueh took place before I entered formally into researching for this book. The nucleus of the research culled for the book took place over the next four years (winter 2007 to winter 2011). After this time, I spent two years writing, in archival research, and doing follow-up, always in continual membership in the group.

One of the challenges of my research was negotiating the multiple roles I played. At various times—sometimes simultaneously—I was an enthusiast, dancer, leader, apprentice, spirit practitioner, scholar, recorder, observer, or critic. At the same time, I became an archival researcher of both the academic/historical archives of *Danza* and the living archives found in the oral tradition. I had multiple points of entry into the phenomenon of *Danza* inside Calpulli Tonalehqueh. One benefit of my membership was certain levels of trust and access that outsiders could not easily obtain. One challenge of the multitude of positionalities is that this book is layered with my reviews of literature, my lived experiences and observations, my gathering of people's interpretations, and my conclusions about the connections between them all. I have done my best to signal to the reader which hat I am wearing, but I acknowledge that this type of challenge is not easily overcome.

Some studies select informants through random selection, snowball techniques, or other methods. I felt it appropriate to not exclude any informants at the outset of the research. I left my informant selection open at the beginning of the study, talking and observing everyone I came across. The key informants revealed themselves in the course of the study. As these individuals emerged organically, they grounded the research. All the people who participated—even marginally—informed the construction and movement of Calpulli Tonalehqueh, but as I received clarity about what was important to this group and as key informants revealed themselves, I spent more focused research time with and on them.

I had formal structured conversations and informal interviews with more than 50 dancers and Calpulli Tonalehqueh members for this book in addition to approximately 30 individuals who participated in the *Danza* universe but are not directly associated with Calpulli Tonalehqueh. Of those 80 or more individuals, about 20 became key informants. I digitally recorded (audio/video) interviews, made field notes of interviews and phone conversations, and collected electronic correspondence with the key informants. The information obtained through these interviews informs the entire book.

Before this book's research began, I had participated in approximately 250 *ensayos* (weekly dance practice ceremonies) with four dance groups, 80 of those with Calpulli Tonalehqueh. All of this spread over a period of about 12 years. During the days of my research, I participated in about 200 more *ensayos* with Calpulli Tonalehqueh. Of these, I videorecorded 20 and created transcripts. I selected one *ensayo* of those 20 to serve as an exemplar. The account of that *ensayo* (January 2008) is the subject of chapter 6. I selected that *ensayo* because it took place during a period of time when I estimate Calpulli Tonalehqueh was consolidated as a group and thriving in its mission, and because it featured a subceremony tied to the evaluation of an individual achieving a promotion in rank within the group.

In addition to dancing at *ensayos* with Calpulli Tonalehqueh, I attended numerous business and planning meetings with Calpulli Tonalehqueh. In their mission of cultural diffusion, the group had formal meetings for planning, fundraising, evaluating, and numerous creating events and ceremonies. In total, I attended more than 50 meetings called by the leadership of Calpulli Tonalehqueh. For the purposes of this study, I collected agendas and took field notes at 25 meetings. Information from these meetings informs chapters 3, 4, 6, and 8 of this book, but especially chapter 5.

I analyzed virtually all e-mail correspondences from Calpulli Tonalehqueh in which I was included. This method of information sharing, discussion, and organizing is key for the group. By the time of this book's completion, I had collected approximately 887 e-mails having to do directly with Calpulli Tonalehqueh business. During the focused research window for this book, I collected and reviewed about 534 e-mails. I analyzed e-mails for patterns, gleaning information about the types of issues discussed. Additionally, I looked for the themes that were most important to *calpulli* leadership, such as how the *calpulli* was organized, language use, group organizational tools (e.g. agendas, spreadsheets, calendars, etc.), and so forth. Much of this analysis is not included in this text because it fell outside of its scope, but the e-mail correspondences did particularly inform chapters 2 and 3.

Through my research, I discovered that formal community lectures are a key part of educational environments Calpulli Tonalehqueh builds. *Danzantes* invite various elders, especially Ocelocoatl Ramírez, to deliver lectures on various topics of interest. More than ten of these lectures are scheduled each year. In total, I attended more than 30 of these lectures. I have field notes from 15 of them. In addition, I reviewed several others that have been posted at video-sharing Websites (YouTube). I videorecorded five of the lectures during the focused time of information gathering for this study. Of these five, I transcribed two, one on education, another on human sacrifice. Chapter 7 features the lecture delivered by Ocelocoatl Ramírez on human sacrifice. Appendix D is the content summary of this lecture.

There are numerous other events that I attended as a member of Calpulli Tonalehqueh during this research. It is difficult to quantify these experiences, but I attended more than a hundred and they include art and music workshops hosted by the *calpulli*, art expositions, participation in ceremonies hosted by other groups, *ensayos* hosted by other groups, community presentations, visits to correctional facilities for powwows, *temascal* (sweat lodge) ceremonies, naming ceremonies, death memorials, weddings, *Hamblecha* ceremonies, potlucks, *Yuwepi* ceremonies, road trips, and so forth. These experiences cannot be discounted from informing every chapter of this study—and the majority of the experiences did not make it in to the book—but they particularly inform chapters 2, 3, 6, and 8.

During my entire time of participation in research and with this group, I collected hundreds of photographs, dozens of video clips, a handbook, and various documents produced by Calpulli Tonalehqueh. The pictures and figures included in this book are all mine, except in the cases of Fair Use or otherwise noted and used with permission.

As a participant observer for two years prior to beginning this study, I brought my own experiences including tacit understandings of the history and dynamics of this dance circle. These experiences led me to develop initial questions for the study, which I used as a lens to decide which materials and experiences I needed to collect to give greater insight. Additionally, I was immersed in the literature, and several key conceptual frames emerged. I reflected on the experiences I had in the field and then focused on the three concepts that I developed into a conceptual framework for this study. The conceptual framework provided a focus for identifying further materials and experiences that would help me to better answer my refined study questions. After gathering the necessary materials and experiences, I set about the task of analyzing the items. After an initial analysis, I developed more structured interview questions. The chapter themes, titles, and the sequence emerged after reflecting on the patterns from the interviews and field notes. I noticed, for example, that the concepts of *calpulli* and *tequio* came up with great frequency as members discussed the mission of the group, that a monumental amount of collective effort was poured into the weekly *ensayo* and the MNY ceremony, and that members referenced the workshops and lectures as spaces where they acquired important perspectives on how to participate more fully in the *Mexicayotl*. Moreover, I noticed the area that brought the most consternation, for instance, deciding group structure, managing the *cargos* and *palabras*, and reconciling the competing ambitions of the group leaders. I also noticed how central and transformative the process of acquiring a Náhuatl name was for individuals. In all these parts of the total *calpulli* environment, I saw educative spaces and spaces where people were constantly looking back to the past in order to construct the *calpulli*, activity that evoked the metaphor of palimpsest.

After organizing and analyzing the interview and field notes, I further analyzed the materials over the next two years—agendas, recordings and transcriptions, e-mails and workshops, and conversations—using the lens of the conceptual framework and the study questions to develop insights, understandings, and conclusions to report in this ethnographic account.

In order to provide an ethnographic account of the spaces carved out for education and of the locations of palimpsest in the Calpulli Tonalehqueh, I organized the chapters purposively. Hence, this ethnographic account is organized from the larger to smaller scales, with the broader societal concepts of *calpulli* and *tequio* in chapters 2 and 3, respectively, followed by concepts that operate on the group level in *tlacahuapahualiztli, macehualiztli, cargos,* and *huehuetlatolli*. I conclude with a chapter on the *in toca in tocaitl* (naming ceremony) as it refers to a palimpsest at the individual level. In all chapters, a historical treatment of each term begins the chapter and is followed by how members of Calpulli Tonalehqueh gather the ideas around the concepts and reauthor them contemporarily.

Appendix D

Content Summary: Calpulli Tonalehqueh
Ensayo January 2008

The following is a content summary of one *Danza ensayo* with Calpulli Tonalehqueh. It took place in January 2008. Information is taken from my field notes and videotapes of the public ceremony. This *ensayo* was held at the Latino College Preparatory Charter High School cafeteria/theater on the campus of the National Hispanic University in San José.

Table D1.1 Transcript of events from a Calpulli Tonalehqueh *ensayo* from January 2008

7:25 p.m.	Dancers arrive at about 7:15 p.m. Mitlalpilli leads a group of dancers that has arrived early in a step-by-step review of the *Tezcatlipoca* dance. Zihuayaocuicatl is on the drum with Mitlalpilli. Included in the group of dancers are several members of the *Grupo de Guerra* and some beginners in a row behind the experienced dancers. Some young dancers, including Yoli, are there in the second week of *Danza*. The dance starts and stops on four occasions, for errors, review of step, for modeling, and explanations of nuances in steps. They achieve the whole dance on only one occasion. The *calpulli* leadership has been making more concerted efforts to be at the *ensayo* early and to bring their *armas*, or ceremonial weapons, at the behest of Mitlalpilli. In the meantime, about 23 other people are on the periphery of the room, getting ready for the official start of *ensayo*. They stretch, socialize, and watch over young children.
7:36	This opening session ends with a huddle and more instructions from Mitlalpilli. He informs everyone that Texcallini will be giving her *palabra* today and Cihuachimalli next week. He also wants the last four dances of each *ensayo* to be given to group members to do the four core dances of the group. In recent months, Mitlalpilli devised a system whereby people prepare the four core dances of the group and present their mastery of the dances along with their public commitment to the group. Texcallini was one of the first to do this. Tonalcoatzin, Cihuachimalli, Atezcazolli, and Cuauhxihuitl are others undergoing this course. This new system has become known as "testing" among the dancers as they feel it is an evaluation for entry into the *Grupo de Guerra*.
7:42	Ceremony is about to get underway. People arrange drums. Nauhxayacatl has set up the *momoztli*, or center altar, earlier in the evening. Children run around, including Ollinteotl. Xochicuauhtli sets up his music amplification system in the corner of the room. Crystal and Cihuachimalli take charge of the circle's door. Drums start and signal everyone to come in. A circle forms and is aided by Mitlalpilli. About 20 people form the circle at this point, and about 17 people are outside the circle, observing or getting ready. Tekolpoktli, Atlaua, and I kneel at the *momoztli* to take up our conch shells. We wait for Mitlalpilli to finish greeting dancers and get some feathers to begin the invocation.
7:45	Mitlalpilli leads the invocation of the four directions. Each direction is greeted in Náhuatl and permission is asked for the ceremony. The invocation starts in the east (Tlacopan), followed by the west (Cihuatlampa), north (Mictlampa), south (Huitzlampa), earth (Tonantzin), and sky (Omeyocan). Conch sounds, assigned drum beats, incense, and clockwise body turns accompany the invocation.

200

7:50	Tekolpoktli begins a warm-up of the dance. Atlaua places dancers in the circles. About 40 dancers are in the circle now. More come in through the door. Twenty-nine people are outside the circle. Many dancers from other dance groups come to visit the ceremony, including Belen, Tezcacoatl, Jesús, Citlalcoatl, Iztacoatl, Nico, and Vanessa.
7:53	Because there are slightly more people attending than usual, Atlaua makes three concentric circles (sometimes two would suffice). Frist dance of the night is given to Citlalcoatl from the Ixtatutli (White Hawk) dance group in Watsonville. He offers the dance called *Mázatl* (deer). He offers the dance at a faster pace than average, but gracefully and with multiple choreographic variations. There are four drummers: Zihuayaocuicatl, Xochitecpatl, Mitlalpilli, and me. Two other drums are open.
8:00	Tlacotonalli gets the second dance. He offers *Iztacuauhtli*, the white eagle. About ten more people enter the circle after waiting a bit for Nauhxayacatl to bring the *copal* incense to the door.
8:04	Carolina gets the third dance. She offers *Tonantzin* (our precious mother), a dance for Mother Earth, at a quick tempo. Some members of the Yaocuauhtli group enter. Mitlalpilli goes around the circle four times to organize and greet.
8:07	Tezcacoatl offers the third dance: *Chichimeca*. There are about 50 dancers in the circle. Atlaua continues to find places for dancers. There are about 15 males, 35 females in the circle.
8:15	Xochinecuhtli gets the fifth dance. Mitlalpilli helps some of the beginners space themselves in the circle. The drummers make three attempts to ascertain the drum beat Xochinecuhtli wants. Techimalli is also on the drum. He is about two or three years old. Temaquizcuini joins Xochicuauhtli on the musical instruments.
8:19	Tekolpoktli selects Melissa to offer a dance, the sixth of the night. She offers a dance that some call *Ehecatl*, the wind. She expedites the dance by about 200 or 300 percent. Dancers continue to arrive. At this point, there are representatives from about seven different dance circles present.
8:23	Nico gets the next dance. He comes with a young boy I believe is his nephew who is a brilliant 5-year-old. Nico offers the *Mixcoatl/Apache* dance. The dance has steps that are more theatrical and whose representations are more easily identified than other dances. It represents a hunting sequence.
Tape 2–8:27 p.m.	Iztacoatl leads the dance. A few of her group members come up to join her. They lead the circle in the dance *Tletl*, fire.

continued

Table D1.1 Continued

8:35	Atlaua offers short *permiso* dance to initiate this segment of the ceremony: the "test." After Atlaua is done, Mitlalpilli halts the activity and welcomes everyone once again. He announces that Texcallini will give her *palabra*, her commitment to the *calpulli*. Texcallini comes to the center and dancers cheer. She offers a short speech, thanking everyone for their support on her path in *Danza*. In short, she discusses how being a dancer and having the discipline has helped her to be a betterfriend, teacher, dancer, and person. Chuy and Xochitecpatl come off the drums. Atlaua and I come back on the drums with Mitlalpilli and Zihuayaocuicatl. Another little boy, probably about three or four years old, joins us on the children's drum. We follow Texcallini on her first dance, which is *Yaotecatl*, a warrior dance. It is great to see so many beginners, some in their second practice, dancing. Texcallini offers a long dance, taking us to about 8:47 mark. Nauhxayacatl dances this one. For Texcallini's second dance, I come off the drum. She leads *Tezcatlipoca*, the dance that represents a smoking mirror, our memory/ intelligence. Here we see the dance that the group was going over in the beginning.
8:52	Mitlalpilli and the *Grupo de Guerra* surround Texcallini and give her feathers and hugs. She is one of the first people to go through this process in Calpulli Tonalehqueh. The group is relatively new and the other dancers in the Grupo de Guerra were grandfathered in. Tekolpokotli and Mitlalpilli discuss what to do next. They decide to go for two more dances. Atlaua will lead the next one, the twelfth of the night. He shows the drummers how he wants the beat. He offers the dance called *Huitzilopochtli*, human willpower.
9:01	Tonalcoatzin and Tekolpoktli offer the final dance as a pair: *Huilotl*, the dove. Some of the dancers in the circle also dance as pairs.
9:05	The dance portion of the ceremony closes with Mitlalpilli and the *Grupo de Guerra* rotating around the circle, sending the indicated spirits of the four directions off. It is the same as in the beginning of the ceremony, but instead of calling elements in, they are thanked and sent off.
9:11	Mitlalpilli asks Teddy Yohuac, Standing Bear Butler, a dancer in the *calpulli*, if he would offer a song from his tradition/ language. Mitlalpilli announces that he would like to do a giveaway to some of the *calpulli* members who have been working hard. Mitlalpilli gives a short speech about how *Danza* in San José has grown in the past 20 years, whereas previously *ensayos* used to attract 10–20 dancers and now we have more than 50 inside the circle alone. Also, there are many more groups rising in the area. He wants to recognize some of the leaders of the group with handkerchiefs from Chiapas state in México. Also he wants to do a giveaway of feathers. He calls a few of members of the *Grupo de Guerra* up. Afterwards, Standing Bear offers a song, with little Techimalli by his side, playing a rattle.

202

9:17   With the main ceremony being over, many people leave. There is a lot of noise and commotion. The *Palabra* session is the last activity of the night. People sit in a circle and, clockwise, are encouraged to share their thoughts. Approximately 34 people stay for this activity in the circle. About 9 people stand on the margins waiting for the dancers to finish this session. Many people chose to not speak, offering the word "Ometeotl" before passing on their turn. A summary of the comments made by the people who get into it, the *palabra* follows:

Atlaua talks about achievement in *Danza* requiring many trials. He appreciates those people who get into it. He talks about respect for feathers, for his son's battles at a young age, and apologizes to all those who did not get a turn to lead a dance tonight.

Tlacotonalli (in Spanish) says he likes coming to the *ensayo*. He appreciates people opening their hearts and working to hold on to their traditions.

Xochitecpatl (in Spanish) introduces a new dance group that he has formed. He says that they are a small circle but they are growing and looking forward to working with other established groups of the area. He and Iztacoatl are the leaders.

Tonalmitotiani (in Spanish) thanks Mitlalpilli for having the doors open, and Carol and Victor for inviting him into the *Danza* lifestyle.

Iztacoatl (in Spanish) talks about how she felt welcome at Calpulli Tonalehqueh since the first time she visited, even though she did not know anyone. She takes Atlaua's words to heart. She knows how powerful it is to help raise children and see them overcome obstacles. She implores everyone to keep struggling to make sure that they remember their culture and thanks everyone who has ever worked for the perseverance of our traditions.

Tekolpoktli says that he appreciates Texcallini's work in the circles and thanks everyone for coming.

Zihuayaocuicatl offers a prayer of gratitude for humility and for her life.

Two visitors, twin brothers, thank the group for allowing to visit and say they are happy to be here.

Texcallini (in Spanish) thanks everyone for their support and for lending her energy when she needed it.

Xochicuauhtli thanks Mitlalpilli for the feather bequeathal. He adds that he is impressed by how quickly Texcallini progressed in her learning of dances and in her commitment to the group. He is thankful to her example.

Atezcazolli congratulates Texcallini.

Citlalcoatl thanks everyone for the ceremony tonight, especially Calpulli Tonalehqueh for hosting.

Belen's mom (in Spanish) thanks everyone for opening the doors to the circle tonight.

Teddy offers a prayer that the Creator give everyone exactly what they need, how they need it, and in a way they will love and understand it.

Mitlalpilli (in Spanish) closes with a short speech saying we are all part of a worldwide movement. *Danza* is happening all over the United States. Groups may be big or small, but they are doing crucial work. We also have to recognize, beyond just dancers, people who work behind the scenes. He thanks everyone for coming.

9:35   People pack up and leave. The tables and chairs of the cafeteria are put back into place. Socializing and casual conversations happen.

Appendix E

Content Summary: "The Myth of Human Sacrifice" by Ocelocoatl

This appendix provides the content summary of the lecture *El mito del sacrificio humano* [The myth of human sacrifice]. The lecture was delivered at the Center for Training and Careers, San José on December 23, 2007, by Ocelocoatl Ramírez. (Content summary comes from videos and notes by Ernesto Colín. Translation by Ernesto Colín.)

Table E1.1 Summary of a lecture hosted by Calpulli Tonalehqueh

Time	Slide	Content Summary
0:00	–	Ocelocoatl opens in Náhuatl, thanking and welcoming audience.
1:15	–	"*Estamos encontrando nuestro verdadero camino. Ya esta escrito. Nadie lo va a evitar. Nadie lo va a detener.*" [We are finding our true path. It is written. No one can avoid it. No one can stop it.] Ocelocoatl discusses the emancipatory value of this work. He is presenting investigation that has been done by many.
2:16	–	Video of an open-heart surgery. Former Calpulli Tonalehqueh member, Cuauhtlequetzqui, received permission from the surgical staff and patient. He is a medical technician who operates the artificial heart apparatus during surgeries at his hospital. Video is important for the proof. It is said that the Aztecs sacrificed a virgin, a victim with one blow, and that a priest would take out a beating heart.
5:00	–	A video plays. Camera focussed on patient's chest and hands of the medical team. First pass with a scalpel. Second pass with a laser scalpel to cauterize. Three more passes for a total of five passes, depth of one half inch. Electric saw used to cut sternum. High velocity for 1 minute. Apparatus to hold the rib cage open. Artificial bypass for main artery. Video ends.
12:00	1	*Antropolocos* say the Mexica gave human sacrifices to the sun so that it would walk the sky and illuminate, that the sun required hearts, like a God: vain, thinking, humanized. In Deuteronomy (Bible), God tells Abraham to kill his own son to prove faith. Archangel stops him. Otherwise he would have done it. The idea of human sacrifices already existed in this worldview. There is an altar, with a dagger, etc. There is an ancient tradition in the Middle East to sacrifice a lamb to ask God for things. Every week at Mass, a priest tells the congregated to drink this blood and eat this body, and Catholic doctrine has it that through Transfiguration, these are literally the blood and body of Jesus. "So, who is sacrificing? Who is eating flesh and drinking blood?" The idea was transferred. Europeans could not conceive that a nation could grow without Gods. "There is a claim of polytheism. God of fire, war, corn, death, river, etc. A Pantheon!" "Lies upon lies; they have imposed a Hebrew, a Judeo culture and religion. A culture based in pastoral life. We are an agricultural society and culture. More advanced! We invented corn."

206

		Genesis, John. When God created earth and all things in six days, he forgot to make the American continent, and the nations of Red people. The bible only mentions three races. White, Black, Yellow. "In 1492, the 'discovery' of America. They call us the 'New World.' What they discover is their ignorance." God forgot to create the turkey, the hummingbird, the cempoaxochitl, the cuetlaxochitl. Wheat, rice, and millet all grow naturally. Corn is an invention of 10,000 or more than 30,000 years ago. It is hard to know exactly. So who is the old and who is the new world? So yes, Aztecs were concerned about the sun. They were not concerned about it rising, but about its movement, which creates the four seasons, the four climates, and marks time. It tells us when to plant, when to harvest, when to prepare the land, when it rains. So it was necessary to study the sun.
21:45	2	Image of the *Huey Teocalli*, the Templo Mayor.
22:00	3	*Teocalli* was designed to mark the spring equinox
22:14	4	*Voladores*. 4 × 13 rotations = 52. This marks a solar rotation.
22:38	5	The astronomical observatory at Chichen Itzá. Shows we had the study of cosmic bodies. Not just the sun. All of them.
23:15	6	We had underground observatories. Cave marking the spring equinox.
23:32	7	Same.
23:50	8	The observatory. Made more than 1,000 years before any European came here.
23:56	9	Top view of a cave observatory. Many of these were covered by friars. They saw people going into the caves. They feared that satanic rites were going on. Witchcraft. Paganism. It was an observatory. To make it, one requires geometry, trigonometry, and astrophysics.
2:5:18	10	Teotihuacan. It is the *tzacualli* representing the moon. The design represents the phases of the moon. The *teocalli* set around it represents the Pleiades. The cities are cosmic maps and represent a deep knowledge of the cosmos.

continued

Table E1.1 Continued

Time	Slide	Content Summary
25:40	11	Phases of the moon control tides and humans. We are 85 percent water. If the moon influences all water on earth, if it moves the tides, then imagine what it does to humans. There are certain times when humans are deeply affected by lunar gravity. Temperament becomes irritable. That is where the word "lunatic" came from.
26:40	12	*Teocalli* sets mark the solstices and equinoxes with towers.
27:06	13	From the Laud Codex, the idea of *Pabtecatl*, or medicine. The books record our knowledge of herbology, medicinal plants, flora, the days, the offerings, the hummingbird. Take note of the style of the drawing. The outline is perfect. The graphic detail, color, figure is in profile, personified form, no eyebrow, two-dimensional.
28:47	14	Tezcatlipoca image from the Laud Codex. Tree made of smoke. There is no eye; figure is looking inward, has a mirror on its neck to represent the idea of memory. Smoke on top of its head to represent thinking. "Observe! There are hearts, blood, and a head. Simple [sacactically]. The anthropologists say those are hearts from sacrifice, and blood offered, and the head of a decapitated victim…This image *actually* speaks about one's inner essence, what is in one's heart. Blood represents life. Face represents identity. *In Ixtli, in Yollotl*. The face, identity, and to have feelings, senses, an essence. It is a metaphor. When we say, 'with our heart in our hand,' we didn't literally take it our of our body and hold it in our hand!"
32:17	15	The image of *tlaloc* from the same codex. It means "earth's drink" or "earth's liquor." That is why it is important to know the language. Because people will say "it's the God of Rain." First of all, rain is *quiabuitl*. How do you say "God" in Náhuatl? The answer is "God." How do you say "elephant"? Answer is "elephant." How do you say "giraffe"? Exactly. The words do not exist because the Mexica never knew an elephant, a giraffe, or any God. Word for God does not exist. Consequently the idea of a God did not exist. This is *tlaloc*, personified. It shows the days of rain, groundwater, a lightning rod, in the form of a white serpent. Look at the style, color. Look at the capacity for synthesis in the images.

| 34:15 | 16 | The sun from the Borgia Codex. |

"The Sun! Please look at the Sun! Red. Perfectly straight rays. With lots of flags because of all the causes it supports. It's what gives personality. What makes objects visible. It's what battles. Because it always rises and sets at its exact time. It is never early. Never late. Punctual; not like us who say, 'wait, Mexica, we are over here jotting this down.' No, no, no. The sun comes out and no one can stop it. And it sets and says, 'see you later, tomorrow.' And you know what? It will always come out the next day. That is why it is shown with its weapons, of energy, because it's the rising eastern sun. Look at how it is. Observe it because further ahead we will compare them, and you yourselves will say if it is true or not. See that the the figures are flat. They have no shadow. They do not have perspective, or, they are not drawn with an angle, they're flat, shown in profile. There it is."

35:32	17	Venus in the daytime as *tlahuizcalpantecuhtli*.
35:40	18	Venus but in its nocturnal phase as *xolotl*.
35:59	19	*Xiuhtecuhtli* (fire) from the Codex Fejérváry-Mayer. Style shows four corners of the universe.

The number four is important. There are four seasons, directions, limbs, heart chambers, colors, elements, everything.

Nahui ollin (four movements) signals the creation of the universe.

We can never stay still. The earth is moving something like 30 miles per second. The earth rotates on its axis. The earth goes around the sun. The sun rotates around in the galaxy. The galaxy is expanding and in orbit.

Like Galileo said, "Nonetheless it moves!" and they were going to burn him alive.

All this is contained in the codices, the *amochtin*.

Each direction has a pair represented. The days are counted. 13 × 20 all the way around for a total of 260 (the days it takes for the gestation of a fetus).

All the symbols were misinterpreted: blood, cranium, devils.

| 39:53 | 20 | Here is the same image, but the Mayan version. Shows the moment of birth, not human sacrifice. |
| 41:40 | 21 | The concept of *ometeotl* from the Borgia Codex. |

"You are me. Above, below. Front, back. Left, right. Man, woman. Hot, cold. Wet, dry. Good, bad. Live, die. Here, there. Life and Death together. Because as we live, we are on our way to our death." Europeans saw this as demonic.

continued

Table E1.1 Continued

Time	Slide	Content Summary
41:43	22	Tezcatlipoca from the Codex Fejérváry-Mayer. The dots are the 13 day counts. $13 \times 20 = 260$.
42:43	23	A human with the day signs and lines. Our books were burned and new images were drawn. But this is a distortion. The counts are gone. They changed the places to where they point. They took out the metaphors. If we go back to the previous slide (22) we see the reed is connected to the penis, which is logical; the reed is used for planting seeds, the metaphor for the penis. Back in slide 23 the penis is linked to the serpent. The penis and serpent represent sin for the Europeans. Remember the story of Adam and Eve. (Ocelocoatl quotes the Genesis story.) This image has eyebrows, has muscles like the model of Da Vinci. Praxagoras. Man as the measure of all things. Bible says that God created everything and decided who it was all for, so he created man in his own image.
48:10	24	Mixtec version of Tezcatlipoca concept.
48:20	25	(Supposed to be a video of book and regalia burning by friars and soldiers. Does not play but Ocelocoatl explains.) In Yucatan, book burning took three days and three nights. In Texcoco, book burning took four days and four nights.
52:58	26	After the burning of books and the death of many of the Mexica community elders, the friars wrote and commissioned many new books. This is what people have to study and understand history. Compare (1) the way the blood runs; (2) the perspective drawn in, crooked teocalli; (3) the heart that shoots out whole after a stab in the chest; and (4) the eyebrows.
54:13	27	Image of *mictlantecuhtli*. There are body parts in the bowls. People are feasting in front of a god. Anthropophagic scene used as evidence for human sacrifice.

55:01	28	Apocalyptic scene. European print. Points out that Mexica were depicted in European texts as hair, ape-like men, with chalices in the air, and sexy light-skinned women in foreign attire dance over a sacrificial victim. Fantastical imaginings that circulated the world.
55:57	29	This image is of Moctezuma and some more human sacrifice. It is even marked with Spanish text, saying "Chapter 23." Shows European elements on the figures, like hairy men, a Greek chorus, a sawing tool used for the sacrifice that never existed in México, perspective, shadow, and three-dimensional.
57:15	30	One of the most popular drawings of the supposed human sacrifice.
		First, we can look at the sun and remember the precontact image of the sun we saw earlier. This one has a face and squiggly rays in the European style, whereas the original had eight straight rays, marking the four directions, solstices, and equinoxes.
		The drawing has a flint knife and a beating heart emerging, compared to the video that opened the presentation where we remember how difficult it is to get to the heart through the sternum and how tough the arteries are. Three laser scalpels, electric saw, rib cage opener, machines to keep heart beating.
		As if the sun was capricious, moody, and required hearts to keep illuminating.
		We can look at the *tonalmachiotl* (Mexica sun stone) that records the 104-year rotation of the sun, which is more than a person's usual lifetime. So how would anyone fear that the sun was not going to come back out? It also accurately predicts eclipses, equinoxes, solstices, etc. All perfectly predictable.
58:56	31	Slide shows a codex of annual events. Original was written over. Then, the second writing was noted as erroneous, scratched out, and rewritten. Layers of errors.
1:00:15	32	Archeological dig at the Templo Mayor in Mexico City. The director of the museum, Eduardo Matos Moctezuma, declared that the finds were proof of human sacrifice.
		Found clay pots with human bones.
		The site was meticulously recorded, to the degree that even a pollen analysis was done.

continued

Table E1.1 Continued

Time	Slide	Content Summary
1:01:27	33	Clay pot with lid and human remains of a child, from the Templo Mayor dig.
		Sarcastically, "Of course, it is common sense. A clay pot is for food, human bones equal food. Here they had *pozole* made with a baby!…yesterday we had the winter solstice. Lets see, who wants to give their child so we can all have communion?"
		Used as proof of human sacrifice, but it was a burial.
		We call the earth, *tonantzin*, "our precious mother."
		We have the entire periodic table of elements inside our bodies. He names several gases and elements.
		We are "born" from earth, that is why we call it our mother.
		So when we die, we are bundled in cloth, in a fetal position and are put in the ground, sometimes in clay jars.
		It means that we are returning to Mother Nature.
		The body is fully intact. If we were cannibals, then the pieces would be chopped up and divided.
1:05:36	34	Codex image in three panels: sacrifice and anthropophagi.
		Ocelocoatl admits he is speechless about the image.
		Points out the clay pot and people feasting on body parts.
		Points out the curly hair on the subjects. They look like Greek myths.
		Someone is eating a human leg whole.
		Points out the representation of fire is much different than the ancient books.
		And this is what they use for proof.
		Asks the audience if they know where the word "cannibal" comes from. It comes from Christopher Columbus. He came to the islands and perpetrated massacres.
		On the beach, he found the clay pot burials. He asked the people what they called it, they said *Carib(es)*. Columbus took the story of the human remains in the clay pots back to Europe, calling it *Caníbales*. The term was coined, the myth perpetuated: cannibals and cannibalism.
1:09:13	35	Another postinvasion codex depicting human sacrifice, *mictlancihuatl*, tongue piercing, ear piercing.
		Another look at this style, not made my Mexica.
		Several books like those of Vaticano, Rios, Tudela were like this.
1:10:00	36	Sacrifice scene at *teocalli*.
		Imported sun, body parts thrown from teocalli, perspective, oddly shaped teocalli, bear hands to rip out a heart.

1:10:45	37	Now sacrifice scene is with a sword in this print. Swords did not exist. Illustrated heresay. Again, the scale of the teocalli, the eyebrows.
1:11:18	38	Sacrifice scene print, published by INAH (*Instituto Nacional de Antropología e Historia*) in 1997 as the lead image to promote the exhibition of the findings of the dig at the Templo Mayor. It is a European lithograph. Our own national institutions perpetrating the myths.
1:12:07	39	Print made in Europe of sacrifice scene. Based only on European stories taken back, illustrators made these images. These were not made by witnesses, nor were they based on sound research. Totally stylized. A romantic vision of sacrifice. Demons. Greek tunics and attire. Bald, white, figures. Craniums, body flung downstairs, a dagger. We draw conclusions from such poor sources.
1:13:23	40	Video that does not run of book burning.
1:13:36	41	*Teocaltin* (temples), represented as European castles. Walls covered in serpents, as if this were a bad thing. The *tzompantli* (altar of time) depicted. *Danzantes* in the courtyard. Sacrifice at the *teocalli*.
1:14:27	42	The *tzompantli* (altar of time) misrepresented as a bunch of craniums between stakes. Representations of *Tlaloc* and *Huitzilopochtli* concepts. Greek columns.
1:14:53	43	*Chicomecoatl* (seven serpents) figure in relief on a stone carving. This was sited by the colonial writers and others after them as proof. A woman with seven snakes as a head. This cannot be taken literally. Seven serpents is the representation of the concept of harmony, cosmic harmony. The rainbow has seven main colors. Music has 13 primary notes, the seventh note is in the middle, dividing the six higher notes from the six lower ones. Women have four phases in their fertility cycle, or menstruation cycle, each for seven days. $4 \times 7 = 28$ (a lunar cycle). These are concepts, not something physical or real.

continued

213

Table E1.1 Continued

Time	Slide	Content Summary
1:16:55	44	Book cover of David Carrasco's (1899) *City of Sacrifice: The Aztec Empire and the Role of Violence in Civilization.* The cover image is again of the *tzompantli*. Carved craniums on a *teocalli* façade. It is an alter to past epochs. It is a script for remembering history and counting time. The craniums represent a "time" that has "died" or come to an end.
1:17:39	45	Image of a falling *teocalli* again.
1:17:46	46	A more recent illustration. A figure holding a human heart to the sky. A poster like many that have been done. Artists complicit in myth making.
1:17:56	47	Outline of a Mayan carving made on a large golden disc at Chichen Itzá. Depicts people holding a man down and an object being taken from his belly by a lavishly dressed individual. The midsection is split open. A serpent flies overhead with a human figure falling out from it toward the ground. This is taken as proof of human sacrifice.
		"If this is taken to be literal, then I ask, what is with huge flying serpent with the person falling out of its jaws? The scholars then would say, 'oh, well that is a concept, not literal.' Right! In the same what that serpent is a 'concept,' this down here, the man being held down, is also a 'concept.' It represents the death of a part of one's personality. It is letting go of things that are not helpful for your life, or for your renewal.' The man is getting help in doing that. It is not his chest that is open, nor his heart cavity. It is his solar plexus. The solar plexus is the place where our energy is manifest. Energy enters the cranium at birth before the bones are set. Then it lives in the solar plexus. Then it leaves the feet. That is why when we die we say, 'he kicked it'; because the energy zooms out of our legs and they kick, get stiff. That is why it is called the *solar* plexus. It radiates energy."
1:20:04	48	Glyph showing the same thing from the Laud Codex. This is a precontact text. No one is holding the person down. His arms are free. The stabbing figure has symbolic attire. It is the act of transcendence, the death of ego, of vanity.
1:21:04	49	Back to the Magliabechi Codex image. Feast of body parts.

1:21:17	50	A *Xipe Totec* stone figure.
		It is said that priests would wear the skin of sacrificial victims, usually virgins.
		Even the idea of a virgin is a Western notion.
		The statue is said to be proof of skinning, flaying.
		"But it is simple. This represents Regeneration. Did you know that in our lifetime, we change-regenerate *all* our skin at least ten times? And not only us; all of nature renews itself, annually. Look at the hills. In the winter, the plants die, turn yellow, and then the rains come and turns them green. The 'skin' of the hills turn green! A lot of the dust found in your home is skin cells that have sprinkled off. It is a concept!"
1:23:30	51	Back to another view of that one.
123:40	52	Image of Mel Gibson directing the film *Apocalypto*.
		Ocelocoatl tells of how Gibson came to México looking for help and to Ocelocoatl's group to consult on the movie. In short, Ocelocoatl asked him for details on the film, which Gibson would not provide. The process went on for two years. Ocelocoatl had high hopes, because he had been impressed with the *Braveheart* film. He hoped that Gibson could do something for our people. Ocelocoatl asked for a script, Gibson refused. Another time, Ocelocoatl said he needed at least a vision for the film, a summary, and Gibson said only that it was not for the faint of heart. With that, Ocelocoatl knew where Gibson was going with the film. It was going to be gore and violence and shock. Ocelocoatl refused to help out. Gibson tried to persuade him with fame and money. Then he offered to cast him in a lead role as a priest. Ocelocoatl refused. He said that he would offer to consult for free if only he could see the script and assist with getting the history correct. Gibson offered thousands of dollars to build a community center for Mexica arts and elderly care. Ocelocoatl was tempted because this had been one of his dreams.
1:30:01	53	Scene from the movie *Apocalypto*.
		Ocelocoatl relays his reaction after seeing the film.
		"More of the same. More of the same. Let's not humor it, give it more importance than it deserves. I react the same as I do with the Superman and Spiderman movies. It's fantasy. They can make this stuff up all they want. People didn't even like the film. It tanked. [joking] The ancestors cursed it!"
1:31:43	54	Florentine Codex ball court scene.
		This is postinvasion. The ball game was actually about the sun, coming and going.

continued

Table E1.1 Continued

Time	Slide	Content Summary
1:33:54	55	Florentine Codex scene of a captive being held by the hair.
		There are many myths about war making.
		Actually, the goal of wars was to take captives, not to kill.
		Killing is easy. Capturing is much harder.
		He who captured 1 was ranked *tequihua* and could wear red feathers.
		He who captured 2 was *teachcau* or *achcautin*.
		He who captured 4, a *cuauhocelot* or *cuauhteca*, the elite warriors. Captures with not kills.
		Supposedly, the captives were taken to be sacrificed, but this is incorrect.
		There is the story of *Tlahuitocolleb*. He is a fifteenth-century general from Tlaxcala. He is captured in a battle and brought back to Tenochtitlan. He choses to go through a trial, where he is tied to a rope on a stone platform. They give him used weapons and send warriors up to fight him. He defeats 15 warriors and he is given gifts and his freedom. He decides to stay and even leads other military campaigns. But he never returns to Tlaxcala because he was captured, thus he had lost his dignity.
		The battles were demonstrations, of strategy, skill, discipline, physical fitness, of the *telpochcalli* graduates. Captives were brought to spar with the students at the *telpochcalli*.
		Then there are the poems that have survived. Like the one from Nezahualcoyotl who says, he loves all these beautiful things in nature, but he loves his fellow man more. "How is it possible to sacrifice people under that kind of ideology?"
		The other proof is the axiom: *Tehuatl tinehuatl, nehuatl itehuatl* [You are me. I am you.] Meaning that if I hurt you, I am only hurting myself. "How are you going to kill someone who is your other you?"
		There is also the saying, "let me get to know you so I can know myself."
		Also, from a linguistic standpoint, the verb to sacrifice does not exist. The word for priest did not exist. If the word does not exist the idea did not exist. And if the verb does not exist, then the place designated for the verb does not exist (the sacrificial altar, etc.), and if the verb does not exist, then a perpetrator of the verb cannot exist or a victim of the verb cannot exist. The verb *nezahualli* means to fast. There were no priests. The word for high scholars, the elders they called priests is *tlamacazque*, meaning the person who knows, the wise person.

1:43:54	56	*Apocalypto* scene concerning slavery. Slavery did not exist. What did exist is debt. Debt that could be paid with work. People would gamble. For example, *Pabtolli* game. They would wager posessions, and then when those ran out, they would gamble themselves, but not literally their own selves, but their labor. When they lost they owed work to someone. And that work could be traded or transferred. But once the debt was paid, the person was free to go. When a person owed work, they put a wooden necklace on to designate it. The Spaniards saw this in the market and said, "Yup, there is slavery." But they are the ones who enslaved and brought slaves. It was already in their worldview.
1:45:22	57	*Apocalypto* slaves painted blue, being led to their sacrifice after being hunted for this purpose. This is nonsensical. Turquoise represents time. It represents the solar year, time. It represents the preciousness of water, fertility, life. But the movie distorts everything.
145:53	58	*Apocalypto* priest on top of *teocalli*. Gibson portrays the people as fanatical zombies. Like the Romans in the coliseum. That was his vision. An ignorant public being manipulated by twisted priests and rulers.
1:46:30	59	*Apocalypto* close-up, priest close-up. "It is a shame. Some of my students helped with the jewelry and headdresses. They took the gigs making the outfits."
1:47:00	60	Comic strip of *Apocalypto* characters holding Mel Gibson over a cross ready to sacrifice him. Also, a line of captives behind, including George W. Bush, Vicente Fox, Arnold Schwarzenegger. "[joking] There is a long list!…of people we would like to sacrifice."
1:47:17	61	Florentine Codex scene of bonfire out of the empty chest cavity of a sacrificial victim. This is where the new fire was supposedly lit. If only they knew what that ceremony (ew fire) was really all about. This has nothing to do with it. Last thing to say is that if human sacrifice was so central in our culture, so pervasive, it would survive until today, in the language, in the rural communities, in substitution, something. But it does not. Not like *Danza*. It has been changed but still remains. Human sacrifice is an absolute lie. Words of gratitude. End

Appendix F

Basic Structure of the Prayer Used to Open and Close a Calpulli Tonalehqueh *Ensayo* or Formal Ceremony

Table F1.1   General transcript of the prayer used to open and close a dance *ensayo* or formal ceremony.

Axcan totlahpaloliz in tlaubcopa chanehque	We greet the guardians of the place of light (east)
In tonatiub iquizayan, xochicuepopan	Direction where the sun rises, where the red and black ink blossoms like a flower
In tlilli in tlapalli, iyeyan in quetzalcoatl	Region of the precious wisdom
Totlahpaloliz ce	Our first greeting
Axcan totlahpaloliz in cihuatlampa chanehque	We greet the guardians of the place of women (west)
Iyeyan in yaocihuab, cuauhtemotzinco	Direction of the venerable eagle that descends
In tlatlaubqui tezcatlipoca, in mixcoatl	Region of the red Tezcatlipoca, the cloud serpent
Totlahpaloliz ome	Our second greeting
Axcan totlahpaloliz in mictlampa chanehque	We greet the guardians of the place of quiet and rest (north)
Iyeyan in yayauqui tezcatlipoca,	Place of the mirror's smoking
Itzebecayan tequibtoc toxayac	Region of the obsidian wind that cuts our face like knives
Totlahpaloliz yei	Our third greeting
Axcan totlahpaloliz in huitztlampa chanehque	We greet the guardians of the place of the thorns of light, the infinite stars (south)

In ueyi yaoquizqui huitzilopochtli	Region of the warrior Huitzilopochtli, the portentous Tezcatlipoca
Icaltzinco, iyeyan in tetzahuitl tezcatlipoca	The hummingbird that opposes, our willpower
Totlahpaloliz nahui	Our forth greeting
Axcan to tlahpaloliz in hueyi xihctli in cemanahuac	We greet the great center of the world, the great naval
In huel mahuiztic, huel tlazohtli to tahtzin tonatiuh	To our welcomed and beloved father sun
In totonamitl, xiuhpiltontli, in cuauhtlehuanitl	The one who creates warmth, our beloved son, a small ray of light, ascendant eagle
Totlahpaloliz macuilli	Our fifth greeting
Axcan totlahpaloliz huel mahuiztic, huel tlazohtli totlahnantzin anáhuac	We greet our welcomed and beloved land of Anáhuac
In coatlicue. in chalchiuhtlicue	The skirt of serpents, the precious turquoise skirt
In tlaltecuhtli in tlalcihuatl	The essence of duality in our earth
Totlahpaloliz chicoaze	Our sixth greeting

Notes

Author's Preface

1. Other works that influenced the book's research and format include: Aguilar (2009), Ceseña (2004), E. G.-M. Maestas (2003), Martínez-Hunter (1984), and Powell (2003).
2. For more on the methodological approach, data collection, data analysis, and sequencing decision made for this book, see appendix C.
3. I italicize *palimpsest* on first use as needed for emphasis or as dictated by formatting requirements of the citation style.
4. In this book I use the adjective pre-Cuauhtémoc to describe any historical occurrence in México prior to European invasion. Cuauhtémoc was the last *Huey Tlatohani* (Speaker of the Great Council) of the México-Tenochtitlan Confederacy and led the resistance to European invasion. I privilege this term over others that scholars use to mark this era of history, like precontact, pre-Columbian, prehispanic, and so forth, which often center on Europeans. *Anáhuac* is a Náhuatl term I will use for what is commonly referred to as North America. It is roughly translated as, "land that on its four sides is surrounded by water." Anáhuac is the Mexica term that includes the modern state of México. I use the term in place of the terms such as North America, Mesoamerica, Aridoamerica, and Oasisamerica.
5. By my count, at least 25 fields and/or disciplines utilize the term palimpsest, often in quite distinct manners. All of them are helpful in creating a deeper understanding of the metaphorical use of palimpsest as a frame. For a set of fields in which I find the use of palimpsest, see appendix B.
6. The *cuicacalli* and *mixcoacalli* were two schools of song and dance. They were ancient Mexica educational institutions, the first for children and the second for professional artists.

1 A *Danza* Landscape

1. Zepeda-Millán (2011) states, "In the spring of 2006, up to 5 million immigrants and their allies took part in close to 400 demonstrations across the

country in protest of proposed federal anti-immigrant legislation (H.R. 4437). The unprecedented level of immigrant activism captured the nation's attention with a series of mass marches and an array of other forms of dissent ranging from hunger-strikes and caravans to boycotts and candlelit prayer vigils...Through the formation of broad coalitions, the utilization of pre-existing local resources, and ethnic media outlets, immigrant rights activists organized the largest coordinated mass mobilizations in American history."

2. Mexica is the name of the Náhuatl-speaking indigenous nation of Central México more commonly known as Aztec. Technically and mythically, Aztecs are the ancestors of the Mexica, before they migrated out of the Aztlan region over hundreds of years down to the Lake Texcoco region in México to found the city of México-Tenochtitlan, now known as México City. In common parlance, the terms *Aztec* and *Mexica* are interchangeable. I refer to that nation of people, past and present, by the name they call themselves, Mexica, except for times when common practice, quotations, informants, or scholarly works refer to them as Aztec(s).

3. *Danza* is a shorthand term that refers to any tradition of dance rooted in the ceremonies of pre-Cuauhtémoc Náhuatl-speaking peoples from the area in and around what is now México City. In the colonial and modern eras, the dance tradition practiced by Mexicas has seen many changes and is expressed with many variations. These variations include *Danza Conchera, Danza Mexica, Danza Azteca, Tradición, Danza Azteca-Chichimeca, Chitontequiza, Macehualiztli, Mitotiliztli,* and many others, depending on regional, ontological, and organizational differences. In this book, I use the term *Danza* as an umbrella term for the various types found in the United States, México, and beyond. When necessary, I use more specific terms. Additionally (as in the academy and in popular use), *Danza* is distinguished from *baile* (also dance) to underscore the collective, spiritually based, and traditional practices of *Danza* rather than more secular dances (*bailes*), which are usually executed in pairs and go with popular genres of music.

4. Chapter 6 of this book explores the components of dance and ceremony in Central México at the time of European contact and reviews the colonial accounts of Mexica dance in some detail, a few details are important in this section in order for readers to contextualize the building materials taken up by Calpulli Tonalehqueh.

5. See Clendinnen (1990) for her review of problems of Spanish texts, including the fragmentary records that were kept, the lack of "official" histories taken, the idiosyncrasy of perspectives and observations provided by friars, and the general disagreement upon the nature of what they observed. She says we cannot work from the conclusions of these men. She also points out problems with relying on the scarce accounts by native recordkeepers in the early colony as other scholars attempt.

6. In México alone, there are nearly 200 different indigenous groups, each with their own language or language variant, dance, and cultural elements. In this book, I took a US group whose members claim a Mexica identity. They carved out a modern Mexica community in a contemporary US context. I apply ethnographic methods to their dance, which relies on both the past and present.

7. Quotations in this book are left in their original language, so that readers familiar with these languages can reference the original words in addition to my English translation.

8. The collective nature of *Danza* is still a primary characteristic today. *Danza*, by nature, cannot be done alone. Central to the practice is its public, largely open, and coconstructed nature. Huerta (2009) and Luna (2011) use Benedict Anderson's (2006) construct of "imagined communities" to understand the complex and collective identities formed by *danzantes*. Huerta, in particular, contends that *Danza* communities exist on at least two planes: as transnational imagined communities and as a community that imagines its linkages to the past collectivity of dancers in pre-Cuauhtémoc México.

9. Another excellent treatment of indigenous forced adaptation comes from Florescano's (1999) *Memoria Indígena*, which is a study of indigenous reconstruction after the invasion.

10. As evidence of this point, one can look to the work of Sánchez Jímenez (2009) who describes the mixture of ancestral Nahua ceremonies with popular Catholicism in the annual Corn Dance in the state of Hidalgo, México.

11. With the indigenous population decimated and the imperial government needing for labor for construction, agriculture, mining, and so on, African slaves were imported in great quantities into México. In México City, native Mexicas and African slaves were segregated into ghettos. Exchange between these groups at that time was certain. African influences in *Danza* during the colonial period have not been identified (to my knowledge), though there is a growing body of work on the ways that the African presence in México has influenced music, dance, and so on, in other regions of México.

12. The superimposed patron saints would become central to Aztec dance into the twenty-first century.

13. Authoritarian parish priests continue to hold sway over *Danza* ceremonies in more recent times. In the mid-twentieth century, Martha Stone (1975) participated with *Conchero* groups in México City, and her account describes several scenes where the decision-making power of parish priests over timing, space, conflict resolution, and so on, was wielded over the ceremonies in which she took part near the town of Chalma and México City. In the twenty-first century, families that have celebrated *Danza* ceremonies for generations upon generations must negotiate the terms, timing, location, and protocols of major ceremonies with church leaders (Beto Jímenez, a friend, informant, and *General* of a well-known *Danza* family in México City, personal communication).

14. See, for example, folding screens available in the permanent collection of the Los Angeles County Museum of Art and a folding screen included in the *Aztec Pantheon and the Art of Empire* exhibit that came to the Getty Museum in Los Angeles in summer 2010. Yolotl González Torres (2005) describes other works of art of the colonial era that show the changes imposed on *Danza*, each is like a snapshot.

15. Renée de la Torre (2009) studied the extensive variation of dances that are in practice in Guadalajara, Jalisco, México, some of which are kin to *Conchero* traditions. She explores Mexica dance as well, but also includes *new age*, *sonajero*, *lancero*, *Chichimeca*, *Apache*, and other dance traditions that have

emerged in that region as a result of vigorous hybridity and innovation in traditional dances.

16. For more on attire and instrumentation, see, for example, Y. González Torres (2005), Martí and Prokosch Kurath (1964), Medina (1970), Montes de Oca (1926), and Toor (1947).
17. The resistance to this change is ironic: *Conchero* dancers saw the reclamation of pre-Cuauhtémoc attire as something inauthentic to *Danza*.
18. There are at least two other studies of the *Mexicayotl* movement in México City, one by Vásquez Hernandez (1994) and another by E. González Torres and Martínez (2000).
19. The MCRA is still alive and well. Its cultural diffusion efforts are aided by a Website, http://www.movimientoconfederado.com.mx, launched in 2009. The Website includes writing from Nieves, philosophical essays from current *danzantes* and scholars, information on ceremonies and events, and a new initiative to coordinate and unite dance circles that identify as *Mexicayotl*. The children of the Nieva family, whose stated objective is to continue to diffuse the millenary Mexican culture, now head the group.
20. Calpulli Tonalehqueh exemplifies the lasting impact of the *Mexicayotl* movement (and I argue their practices successfully answer many *Mexicayotl* critics).
21. Several centuries have passed and leaders of the *Mexicayotl* reference this decree as the supreme mandate of the movement. The entire text is found in appendix A. Calpulli Tonalehqueh references the mandate with frequency as a guiding message.
22. I also acknowledge that there are many important centers, activists, and movements that postdate the ZT and do not receive adequate focus in this book but are important, like the Universidad Náhuatl in Ocotepec, Morelos, México, which is university founded to teach Náhua language and culture and becomes an important site for Chicana/o scholars and *danzantes*. Mariano Leyva Dominguez founded it in 1989. He was also the founder of the famed Mascarones indigenous theater group in the 1970s that was the precursor the Teatro Campesino group of California.
23. At that event, the ZT receives a contingent of Mexican American activists led by Reies López Tijerina who are connected to the Chicano Movement in the United States. The connections between the various continental civil rights movements are always active. That year, 1978, is also important as the ZT was featured in three US newspapers: *The Pueblo News*, the *Sacramento Bee*, and the *New York Times*, where *Danza* is featured on the front page of that periodical for the first time in its history (Mendoza "Kuauhkoatl," 2007).
24. The ZT's popular *Mexicayotl* ceremony in honor of Cuauhtémoc is repeated annually in Ixcateopan into the present on February 23. The ceremony is duplicated in Los Angeles, San José, San Francisco, Tijuana, and beyond.
25. At this Congress, the ZT was put into contact with Angelbertha L. Cobb, an indigenous leader and dancer in California who would mentor many of the California *danzantes* after that point. Her biography and significant contributions are featured in Luna (2011).

26. Miquiztli and Totocani would later advise and participate with Calpulli Tonalehqueh in California from 2009 into the present.
27. In attendance were dance groups headed by Nina Legrand, Felipe Aranda, Andrés Segura, Teresa Mejía, Cruz Hernández, Leonidis Flores Álvarez, Polo Rojas, Luis Alonso, Rey David Peñaflor, Felix Galicia, Carlos López Ávila, Eustolia González, José González Rodríguez, Marcelo Mexolan, and others. Roll calls are often important in *Danza* and this is why I included the information here. Full details of the event can be found in the institutional history of the ZT compiled by Kuauhkoatl.
28. For the exact agenda, see Mendoza "Kuauhkoatl" (2007).
29. For more on the New Age or neo-Azteca movements, see Argyriadis et al. (2008), de la Torre (2008), and Susanna Rostas (2009).
30. Sometimes spelled Yeskas, Illescas, or Llescas in various sources.
31. For an excellently detailed chronology of the migration of *Danza* to the United States, see Luna (2011).
32. Figure 1.1 displays the lineage and connection between some of the individuals who brought *Danza* to the United States and the members of Calpulli Tonalehqueh. I am at the center of the figure.
33. This ceremony is connected to the Mexica concept of Huitzilopochtli (in one of its aspects, symbolized by a small hummingbird or young warrior, representing the moment when the earth's tilt causes the sun to be deepest in the southern hemisphere before cycling back up to create spring).
34. This ceremony marked the beginning of the Mexica solar year in March.
35. In chapter 8, I explain the naming process in more depth.

2   *Calpulli* (An Alliance of Houses)

1. Sometimes cited as Alonso de Zorita.
2. For a meta-analysis of the scholarship on *calpulli*, see Escalante Gonzalbo (1990).
3. Eulalia Guzmán (1989) has made this clear in her meticulous review of the letters written by Hernán Cortés to the Spanish crown. She finds egregious inaccuracies and self-serving falsities. Printed copies of this piece of scholarship are extremely scarce.
4. From my field notes. Lecture delivered in Spanish by Ocelocoatl Ramírez, November 27, 2005, in San José, California. Any errors in the quotation are mine.
5. Nieva (1969), a colleague of Romerovargas Yturbide, included a chapter on *Kalpulli* in his seminal *Mexicayotl* text. He agreed with Romerovargas Yturbide on every aspect of his description of *calpulli*, using the nuclear family as a model for geopolitical governance, the ideology of *Tloke-Nauake* (meaning together and close, or duality) as a base, having the characteristics of democracy, reciprocity, self-sufficiency, mutuality, communalism, and showing how it is replicated up to the state level of social and political regimentation (pp. 107–122). Guzmán (1989), another *Mexicayotl* scholar, also provided a

noteworthy treatment of the concept of *calpulli*. She agreed with Nieva and Romerovargas Yturbide but added that the *calpulli* system is ancient, resists racism, and is centered on the wisdom of elders.

3 *Tequio* (Community Work)

1. For scholarship on the various types and characteristics of *calpultin*, beyond what has been cited here and in chapter 2, especially about the confederation of *calpultin*, see Guzmán (1989), Klor de Alva, Nicholson, and Quiñones Keber (1988), León Portilla (1999b), and Romerovargas Yturbide (1957, 1978).
2. Sometimes called the Azteca/ MNY ceremony, *Año Nuevo Mexica*, or the *Yancuic Xihuitl* ceremony.
3. The calendar of ceremonies is a palimpsest layered with modern ceremonies on top of ones from the *Mexicayotl* tradition, on top of syncretic Catholic/ Mexica ones, on top of ancient Mexica ceremonies.
4. *Ensayos* are, in essence, rehearsals and education occasions in preparation for the formal ceremonies of the year (see chapter 6).
5. As stated in chapter 1, many *Danza* ceremonies, especially those in the *Conchero* tradition, begin with a *velación*, an all-night vigil of prayers, music, ceremony preparation, and guest reception before the next morning's dancing. Calpulli Tonalehqueh has deviated from this formula largely because the modern *velación* paradigm is so imbued with Catholicism. The absence of a *velación* is often cited as a failure of Calpulli Tonalehqueh, which chooses instead to open their MNY with an intertribal sunrise ceremony.
6. *Tlacatecatl* is a high rank given to a person who oversees several groups. See chapter 5 for more on ceremonial and administrative ranks/roles.
7. The components and logic of the *momoztli* are discussed in chapter 6.

4 *Tlacahuapahualiztli* (The Art of Educating a Person)

1. Some consider Bernardino de Sahagún the world's first ethnographer because much of his written work was based on direct interviews with native informants in early colonial México (c.f. Jose Jorge Klor de Alva, Nicholson, & Keber, 1988).
2. Part of the Codex Mendoza, written around 1540, depicts some child-rearing techniques of Mexica parents pictographically, from birth until the age of 15.
3. Also, his propositions on Mexica education and dance have been documented in a lecture given in March 2009 entitled "Elementos y simbolismo de la danza guerrera mexica" as well as in several other conversations I had with him.
4. Mexica school designers' rationale for community service is similar to that of contemporary school reformers who argue the inclusion of community service hours for PK-12 schools (e.g., community benefits, promotion values like caring for elders, staying humble, democracy, etc.).

5. In Calpulli Tonalehqueh and in the larger *Danza* universe, children are often called *semillas*, seeds. Agricultural references are commonplace in Mexica rhetoric and poetry. This idea calls on parents to nurture their children like trees, to be fruitful with a strong core and strong roots.
6. Plural of *cuicacalli*.

5 *Cargos*

1. Other studies show that the *cargo* system was important throughout indigenous communities in México. For example, the classic text by Evan Z. Vogt (1970) made the *cargo* system of the *Zinacatecos* familiar to US anthropology undergraduates. Many indigenous nations have similar leadership structures and rotating community office.
2. For a discussion of the misunderstandings evoked by Spaniards familiar with feudal, imperial, and other Western forms of sociopolitical arrangements as well as later progressive evolutionist frames of reference, see Moriarty (1969).
3. Currently, I am on this council, as I have moved to Los Angeles away from the group. I visit various groups and ceremonies and act as ambassador or carry the *palabra* (word) of the group
4. At that 2007 meeting, I was nominated and selected to be the *Tlahuizcatecatl*, the bearer of the insignia. I carried that *cargo* until I moved to Los Angeles where I was transferred to the *painales* council/group.
5. Some of the roles developed by Calpulli Tonalehqueh in consultation with Ocelocoatl are different from those outlined by Guzman (1989) and others.

6 *Macehualiztli* (The Art of Deserving)

1. Calpulli Tonalehqueh, when programming their MNY ceremony, considers this information when including representatives from other nations, and entertainment, merchants, crafts, and so forth. See chapter 3.
2. The Mexica solar year consists of 18 months of 20 days each, called *veintenas* in Spanish, plus 5.25 extra days called *nemontemi* that complete the 365.25-day orbit around the sun.
3. For example, the day One Flower, no matter what time of the year it fell, was a special day for the arts (music, dance, poetry, weaving, sculpture, feather work, etc.).
4. Modern-day ceremonies in México and the United States usually last from one afternoon to four days. Calpulli Tonalehqueh has ceremonies that last a few hours to two days.
5. All of these formations still exist in modern Mexica dance.
6. For the typical set of prayers offered to open the ceremony, see appendix E.
7. The comments about this *cargo* are a product of interviews I did with various *saumadoras* (*chicomecoatl*), observations, and *huehuetlatolli* (lectures) I attended with elders.

8. *Ometeotl*, from the Náhuatl words *ome* (two) and *teotl* (force, energy), is a reference to the supreme force in the universe, which is seen as a duality, much like the Ying and the Yang of Chinese cosmology. Mexica belief dictates that nothing in the universe exists without its duality. Infinite examples exist, like night-day, man-woman, in-out, left-right, up-down, spiritual-material, wet-dry, and so on. In the *Conchero* tradition, one's *palabra* initiates with the phrase *El es Dios,* in acknowledgment of God. Dancers in the *Mexicayotl* tradition generally reject this phrase as a Christian imposition and as a term that does not acknowledge the female part of the dual nature of creation.

7 Decolonial Pedagogy

1. The mission statement of the Getty museum includes furthering knowledge of visual arts and promoting critical seeing through the use of its extensive collection. The Getty Villa (on a nearby site from the main museum) houses more than 44,000 works of art from the museum's extensive collection of Greek, Roman, and Etruscan antiquities, of which over 1,200 are on view when the Aztec exhibit runs.
2. Many scholars support Ocelocoatl's thesis about the fabrication of human sacrifice among the Mexica. Notable are Fernández Gatica (1991), Gómora (2007), Hassler (1992a, 1992b), Lira Montes de Oca (2004), and Meza Gutiérrez (1993).
3. Outside of academia, the contention that the Mexica sacrificed humans and practiced anthropophagous rituals is commonplace in the worldwide popular imagination, including in México. A review of popular art, films, and other arenas exposes that there is very little questioning on the subject.
4. This idea refers to the principle of linguistic relativity. Because the Hopi language does not have a preterit verb tense, the way the Hopi conceive time is fundamentally different from other cultures that do have past tenses. For the Hopi, the past, ancestors, and the like are ever present.
5. Cortez, who led the invasion, lived in México for a significant period of time and wrote extensively, but never mentions human sacrifice. Doctor Francisco Hernández, who was the chief royal physician in Spain and sent to México to do an inventory of medicine and curing techniques in 1570, wrote 16 volumes of religious and medical practices. He never mentions human sacrifice. He does mention ritual piercing and ritual bloodletting, which were well documented in pre-Cuauhtémoc books and carvings.

9 A Modern Mexica Palimpsest

1. There are social scientists and scholars in cultural studies who have presented concepts that have a high degree of congruence with palimpsest of cultural identity (see transculturation, hybridity, multiplicity, heterogeneity, *mestizaje*, *nepantla*, etc.). *México Profundo* presents important points of contact with these ideas.

References

Acosta, J. d., Mangan, J. E., & Mignolo, W. (2002). *Natural and moral history of the Indies / Uniform Title: Historia natural y moral de las Indias. ca. 1590. English* (F. M. López-Morillas, Trans.). Durham, NC: Duke University Press.

Actas de cabildo de la Ciudad de Mexico. (1889). Mexico: Edicion del Municipio Libre.

Adler, M. J. (1982). *The Paideia Proposal: An Educational Manifesto.* New York: Macmillan.

Adler, M. J., & Van Doren, G. (1988). *Reforming Education: The Opening of the American Mind.* New York: Macmillan.

Aguilar, M. E. (2009). *The Rituals of Kindness: The Influence of the Danza Azteca Tradition of Central Mexico on Chicano-Mexcoehuani Identity and Sacred Space.* PhD, Unpublished Doctoral Dissertation, Claremont Graduate University and San Diego State University, Los Angeles and San Diego.

Álvarez Fabela, R. L. (1998). La danza de los concheros en San Juan Atzingo. In E. A. Sandoval Forero & M. Castillo Nechar (Eds.), *Danzas tradicionales: Actualidad u obsolencia?* (1a. ed., p. 203). México: Universidad Autónoma del Estado de México.

Anderson, A. J. O., & Talamantez, I. M. (1986). Irrepressible sorcerers: Verbal art in colonial Nahua society. *New Scholar, 10,* 135–143.

Anderson, B. (2006). *Imagined Communities: Reflections on the Origin and Spread of Nationalism* (2nd ed.). London: Verso.

Appadurai, A. (1996). *Modernity at Large: Cultural Dimensions of Globalization.* Minneapolis: University of Minnesota Press.

Argueta López, M. G. (1998). La danza de los concheros: su difusión y permanencia en toluca, estado de méxico. In E. A. Sandoval Forero & M. Castillo Nechar (Eds.), *Danzas tradicionales: Actualidad u obsolencia?* (1a. ed., p. 203). México: Universidad Autónoma del Estado de México.

Argyriadis, K., Torre, R. d. l., Gutiérrez Zúñiga, C., & Aguilar Ros, A. (2008). *Raíces en movimiento: Prácticas religiosas tradicionales en contextos translocales* (1st ed.). Zapopan, Jalisco; México, DF; Tlaquepaque, Jalisco: El Colegio de Jalisco; Institut de Recherche pour le Développement : Centre d'Études Mexicaines et Centraméricaines: CIESAS; ITESO.

Armstrong, E. G. (1985). *Danza azteca: Contemporary manifestation of danza de los concheros in the United States.* MA Unpublished Thesis, University of California, Los Angeles, Los Angeles.

Bandelier, A. F. (1878a). On the distribution and tenure of lands, and customs of with respect to inheritance, among the ancient mexicans. Eleventh annual report to the trustees of the Peabody Museum of American Archaeology and Ethnology (pp. 385–448). Cambridge, UK: Cambridge University Press.

Bandelier, A. F. (1878b). On the Social Organization and Mode of Government of the Ancient Mexicans. Eleventh annual report to the trustees of the Peabody Museum of American Archaeology and Ethnology (pp. 557–669). Cambridge, UK: Cambridge University Press.

Benner, S. A., Ellington, A. D., & Tauer, A. (1989). *Modern Metabolism as a Palimpsest of the rna World*. Paper presented at the PNAS: National Academy of Sciences of the United States of America.

Berdan, F., & Anawalt, P. R. (1997). *The Essential Codex Mendoza*. Berkeley: University of California Press.

Bonfil Batalla, G. (1996). *México Profundo: Reclaiming a Civilization* (P. A. Dennis, Trans.). Austin: University of Texas Press.

Bonfíl Batalla, G. (Writer) & V. Anteo (Director). (1965). *¡Él es Dios!* In INAH (Producer). México: SEP.

Brotherston, G. (1992). *Book of the Fourth World: Reading the Native Americas through Their Literature*. New York: Cambridge University Press.

Broyles-González, Y. (1994). *El Teatro Campesino*. Austin: University of Texas Press.

Brumfiel, E. M. (1988). The multiple identities of Aztec craft specialists. *Archeological Papers of the American Anthropological Association, 8* (1), 145–152.

Butts, R. F. (1973). *The Education of the West: a Formative Chapter in the History of Civilization*. New York: McGraw-Hill.

Carrasco, D. (1999). *City of Sacrifice: The Aztec Empire and the Role of Violence in Civilization*. Boston: Beacon Press.

Carrasco, P., & Broda, J. (Eds.). (1982). *Estratificación social en la Mesoamérica prehispánica* (2nd ed.). México DF: Centro de Investigaciones Superiores Instituto Nacional de Antropología e Historia.

Casas, B. d. l. (1981). *Breve resumen del descubrimiento y destruición de las Indias*. Madrid: Emiliano Escolar.

Caso, A. (1954). Instituciones indígenas precortesianas *Memorias del Instituto Nacional Indigenista* (Vol. 6, pp. 15–27). México DF: Instituto Nacional Indigenista.

Caso, A. (1959). *La tenencia de la tierra entre los antiguos mexicanos*. México DF: Instituto Nacional Indigenista.

Caso, A., & Wicke, C. R. (1963). Land tenure among the ancient Mexicans. *American Anthropologist, 65* (4), 863–878.

Ceseña, M. T. (2004). *Negotiating Identity, Politics, and Spirituality: a Comparison of Two Danza Azteca Groups in San Diego*. California. MA: Unpublished Thesis, University of California, San Diego.

Ceseña, M. T. (2009). Creating agency and identity in *Danza Azteca*. In O. Nájera-Ramírez, N. Cantú, & B. M. Romero (Eds.), *Dancing across Borders: Danzas y Bailes Mexicanos* (pp. 80–96). Chicago: University of Illinois Press.

Chance, J. K. (2000). The noble house in colonial Puebla, Mexico: Descent, inheritance, and the Nahua tradition. *American Anthropologist, 102* (3), 485–502.

Clavijero, F. X. (1987). *Historia antigua de Mexico (1780)*. México DF: Editorial Porrua.

Clendinnen, I. (1990). Ways to the sacred: Reconstucting "Religion" in sixteenth-century Mexico. *History and Anthropology, 5* (1), 105–141.

Coe, M. D. (1977). *Mexico* (2nd ed.). New York: Praeger Publishers.

Colín, E. T., Gonzales, M., Ramírez, O., Madrid, T., Hernández, A., & Chavira, N. (2007). *Wisdom, Harmony, Culture: Danza Guerrera Mexica*. Handbook. Calpulli Tonalehqueh. San José, California.

Concilios Provinciales: Primero y segundo: De México, celebrados en la Ciudad de Mexico, en 1555 y 1565. (1769) [cited in Stone, M. (1975) *At the Sign of Midnight*, p. 196–197]. México City: Imprenta del Superior Gobierno.

Cooper Alarcón, D. (1997). *The Aztec Palimpsest: Mexico in the Modern Imagination*. Tucson: University of Arizona Press.

Cortés, H., & Guzmán, E. (1958). *Relaciones de Hernán Cortés a Carlos V sobre la invasión de Anahuac. Aclaraciones y rectificaciones por la profesora Eulalia Guzmán [Diseños de Ignacio Romerovargas Y.]*. México: Libros Anahuac.

Cruz Rodríguez "Tlacuilo," J. A. (2004). *La misión del espinal*. México DF: Centro de Estudios Antropológicos, Científicos, Artísticos, Tradicionales y Lingüísticos "Ce Acatl."

Cuauhtlatoac, C. (2010). "Maestros" speaking for a price at a corporate-sponsored event. Accessed March 2010. Retrieved from <http://eagle-speaks.danza-azteca.net/2010/03/10/maestros-speaking-for-a-price-at-a-corporatesponsored-event.aspx>.

Damián Juárez, M. D. (1994). *La educación en la sociedad mexica: Familia y estado*. Universidad de Guadalajara, Guadalajara, Jalisco, México.

Darvil, T. (2002). Palimpsest. *The Concise Oxford Dictionary of Archaeology*. Retrieved from <http://www.oxfordreference.com/views/ENTRY.html?subview=Main&entry=t102.e2972>.

de Benavente "Motolinia," T. (1951). *Motolinía's History of the Indians of New Spain* (F. B. Steck, Trans.). Washington, DC: Academy of American Franciscan History.

de Benavente "Motolinía," T. (1971). *Memoriales o Libro de las cosas de la Nueva Espana y de los naturales de ella*. Mexico DF: Instituto de Investigaciones Historicas, UNAM.

de la Peña Martínez, F. (2002). *Los hijos del sexto sol: Un estudio etnopsicoanalítico del movimiento de la mexicanidad* (1st ed.). México: Instituto Nacional de Antropologìa e Historia.

de la Torre Castellanos, R. (2009). The Zapopan dancers: Reinventing an indigenous line of descent. In O. Nájera-Ramírez, N. Cantú, & B. M. Romero (Eds.), *Dancing across Borders: Danzas y Bailes Mexicanos* (pp. 19–47). Chicago: University of Illinois Press.

de la Torre, R. (2008). Tensiones entre el esencialismo azteca y el universalism New Age a partir del estudio de las danzas "conchero-aztecas." (www.cemca.org.mx). *TRACE* (December), 61–76.

de Mendieta, F. G. (1980). *Historia eclesiástica indiana*. México: Editorial Porrúa.

del Solar, D. (1963). Nahua Calpulli. Working Papers in Ethnology. Social Relations 249. Seminar of the Ethnology of Middle America. Harvard University, 6, 22.

Dewey, J. (1899). *The School and Society: Being Three Lectures*. Chicago: The University of Chicago Press.

Díaz Cíntora, S. (1995). *Huehuetlatolli: Libro sexto del códice Florentino*. Mexico City: Universidad Nacional Autónoma de México.

Díaz Infante, F. (1982). *La educación de los aztecas: Cómo se formó el carácter del pueblo mexica* (1st ed.). México, DF: Panorama Editorial.

du Gay, P. (Ed.). (1997). *Production of Culture: Cultures of Production*. Thousand Oaks, London: SAGE, the Open University.

Durán, D. (1995). *Historia de las Indias de Nueva Espana e Islas de Tierra Firme* (1st ed. Vol. II). México, DF: Consejo Nacional para la Cultura y las Artes.

Echeverría, R. (2011). Los Huehuetlatolli. Retrieved from http://www.buenastareas.com/ensayos/Huhuetlatolli/2096104.html

Eliade, M. (1967). *Lo sagrado y lo profano*. Madrid: Ediciones Guadarrama.

Escalante Gonzalbo, P. (1990). La polémica sobre la organización de las comunidades de productores. *Nueva Antropología, XI* (38), 147–162.

Fernández Gatica, A. (1991). Los sacrificios humanos. [prologue for Romerovargas Yturbide, I.] *Motecuhzoma Xocoyotzin o Mextezuma el Magnifico y la invasión de Anáhuac: Estudio basado en las fuentes históricas*. Mexico City: Asociación Anahuacayotl de Tlacalancingo.

Flores Quintero, G. (2004). Tequio, identidad y comunicación entre migrantes oaxaqueños. *Médidas et migraciones en Amérique Latine*, (8). Retrieved from <http://alhim.revues.org/index423.html>.

Florescano, E. (1987). *Memoria mexicana: ensayo sobre la reconstrucción del pasado : época prehispánica-1821*. Mexico, DF: Editorial J. Motriz.

Florescano, E. (1996). *Etnia, estado y nación: Ensayo sobre las identidades colectivas en México*. Mexico City: Nuevo Siglo/Aguilar.

Florescano, E. (1999). *Memoria indígena*. Mexico, DF: Taurus.

Garcia Icazbalceta, J. (1971). *Coleccion de documentos para la historia de México* (1er edición, Facsimilar ed.). Mexico: Porrúa.

Garibay K., A. M. (1943). Huehuetlatolli, Documento A. *Tlalocan, 1* (1), 31–53.

Gibson, C. (1964). *The Aztecs Under Spanish Rule: a History of the Indians of the Valley of Mexico, 1519–1810*. Stanford, CA: Stanford University Press.

Gómora, X. (2007). *Juicio a España*. Mexico City: Umbral.

Gonzalbo Aizpuru, P. (1990). *Historia de la educación en la época colonial: El mundo indígena* (1st ed.). México, DF: Colegio de México, Centro de Estudios Históricos.

González, A. (1996). Los concheros: La (re)conquista de México. In J. Jáuregui & C. Bonfiglioli (Eds.), *Las danzas de conquista* (1st ed., p. 461). México: Consejo Nacional para la Cultura y las Artes: Fondo de Cultura Económica.

González Torres, E., & Martínez Acevedo, V. (2000). *Inkatonal: La casa del sol. Iglesia del movimiento de la mexikayotl*. Unpublished bachelors thesis, Escuela Nacional de Antropología e Historia, Mexico City.

González Torres, Y. (1985). *El sacrificio humano entre los mexicas* (1a ed.). México: Instituto Nacional de Antropología e Historia: Fondo de Cultura Económica.

González Torres, Y. (1995–1996). The Concheros, the dancers of an ancient ritual dance in urban México. *Bulletin of the International Committee on Urgent Anthropological and Ethnological Research, 37–38*, 69–74.

González Torres, Y. (1996). The revival of mexican religions: The impact of nativism. *Numen, 43* (1), 1–31.

González Torres, Y. (2005). *Danza tu palabra: La danza de los concheros* (1st ed.). México, DF: CONACULTA-INAH : Plaza y Valdés Editores.

Grunstein, M. (Writer) & M. Grunstein (Director). (1992). Danzante. In M. Grunstein & D. Kruzic (Producer), *KNME-TV*: PBS.

Gruzinski, S. (1996). *The Conquest of Mexico: The Incorporation of Indian Societies into the Western World, 16th–18th Centuries.* Cambridge, UK: Polity Press.

Guerrera Estrella. (2010). May 26, 2010: Comment on: "Maestros" speaking for a price at a corporate-sponsored event. Accessed March 17, 2011. Retreived from <http://eagle-speaks.danza-azteca.net/2010/03/10/maestros-speaking-for-a-price-at-a-corporatesponsored-event.aspx.

Guzmán, E. (1989). *Una visión crítica de la historia de la conquista de México-Tenochtitlan* (1st ed.). Mexico City: Universidad Nacional Autónoma de México, Instituto de Investigaciones Antropológicas.

Hanna, J. L. (1979a). Movements toward understanding humans through the anthropological study of dance. *Current Anthropology, 20* (2), 313–339.

Hanna, J. L. (1979b). *To Dance Is Human: a Theory of Nonverbal Communication.* Tucson: University of Arizona.

Harner, M. (1977). The ecological basis for Aztec sacrifice. *American Ethnologist, 4* (1), 117–135.

Harris, M. (1977). *Cannibals and Kings: The Origins of Cultures.* New York: Random House.

Hassler, P. (1992a). Human sacrifice among the Aztecs? [Die Lüge des Hernan Cortes]. *Die Zeit,* (38). Retrieved from <http://www.zeit.de/1992/38/die-luege-des-hernan-cortes>.

Hassler, P. (1992b). *Menschenopfer bei den Azteken?: Eine quellen- und ideologiekritische Studie.* Bern; New York: P. Lang.

Hernández-Ávila, I. (2005). La Mesa del Santo Niño de Atocha and the conchero dance tradition of Mexico-Tenochtitilan: Religious healing in Urban Mexico and the United States. In L. L. Barnes & S. S. Sered (Eds.), *Religion and Healing in America.* New York: Oxford University Press.

Hicks, F. (1979). "Flowery War" in Aztec history. *American Ethnologist, 6* (1), 87–92.

Hicks, F. (1982). Tetzcoco in the Early 16th century: The State, the city, and the "calpolli." *American Ethnologist, 9* (2), 230–249.

Huerta, E. D. (2009). Embodied recuperations: Performance, indigeneity, and *Danza Azteca.* In O. Nájera-Ramírez, N. Cantú, & B. M. Romero (Eds.), *Dancing across Borders: Danzas y Bailes Mexicanos* (pp. 3–18). Chicago: University of Illinois Press.

Jaeger, W. W. (1943). *Paideia: The Ideals of Greek Culture: In Search of Divine Centre* (G. Highet, Trans. 2nd ed. Vol. 2). New York: Oxford University Press.

Jaeger, W. W. (1945). *Paideia: The Ideals of Greek Culture* (H. Gilbert, Trans. 2nd ed.). New York: Oxford University Press.

Kaeppler, A. L. (1978). Dance in anthropological perspective. *Annual Review of Anthroplogy, 7,* 31–49.

Kahn, R. V. (2010). *Critical Pedagogy, Ecoliteracy, & Planetary Crisis: The Ecopedagogy Movement.* New York: Peter Lang.

Keen, B. (1990). *The Aztec Image in Western Thought.* New Brunswick, NJ: Rutgers University Press.

Klor de Alva, J. J., Nicholson, H. B., & Keber, E. Q. (Eds.). (1988). *The Work of Bernardino De Sahagun: Pioneer Ethnographer of Sixteenth-Century Aztec Mexico.* Albany: State University of New York Press.

Klor de Alva, J. J., Nicholson, H. B., & Quiñones Keber, E. (1988). *The Work of Bernardino De Sahagun: Pioneer Ethnographer of Sixteenth-Century Aztec Mexico.* Albany, NY: Institute for Mesoamerican Studies, University at Albany, State University of New York: Austin, Texas.

Lane, P. (Writer) & P. Lane (Director). (1992). *The Eagle's Children* [DVD]. United States: Ethnoscope.

Larralde Sáenz, J. (1988). Reto y educación en el México prehispanico. In J. K. Josserand & K. Dakin (Eds.), *Smoke and Mist : Mesoamerican Studies in Memory of Thelma d. Sullivan* (pp. ix, 763). Oxford: B.A.R.

León Portilla, M. (1961). *Los antiguos mexicanos a través de sus crónicas y cantares* (1st ed.). México: Fondo de Cultura Económica.

León Portilla, M. (1963). *Aztec Thought and Culture.* Norman: University of Oklahoma Press.

León Portilla, M. (1980). *Toltecáyotl: Aspectos de la cultura náhuatl* (1a ed.). México: Fondo de Cultura Económica.

León Portilla, M. (1999a). *Bernardino de Sahagún: Pionero de la antropología* (1a ed.). México, DF: Universidad Nacional Autónoma de México, Instituto de Investigaciones Históricas.

León Portilla, M. (1999b). *Herencia Náhuatl* (1st ed.). México, DF: Instituto de Seguridad y Servicios Sociales de los Trabajadores del Estado.

León Portilla, M. (2001). *Rostro y corazón de Anáhuac* (1st ed.). México DF: Asociación Nacional del Libro.

Lira Montes de Oca, F. (2004). *Ciencias milenarias y aplicaciones en el continente americano: Wewehkaw ixmatilizzotl iwan iyehyecoliz itech ixachillan.* Mexico City: Instituto Politécnico Nacional.

Lockhart, J. (1999). *Los nahuas después de la conquista: Historia social y cultural de los indios del México central, del siglo XVI al XVIII.* México: Fondo de Cultura Económica.

Lopes Don, P. (2010). *Bonfires of Culture: Franciscans, Indigenous Leaders, and the Inquisition in Early Mexico, 1524–1540.* Norman: University of Oklahoma Press.

López Austin, A. (1985a). *Educación mexica: Antología de documentos sahaguntinos / Uniform Title: Historia general de las cosas de Nueva España. Selections* (1st ed.). México: Universidad Nacional Autónoma de México, Instituto de Investigaciones Antropológicas.

López Austin, A. (1985b). *La educación de los antiguos nahuas* (1a ed.). Mexico City, Mexico: Secretaría de Educación Pública.

López Luján, L., & Olivier, G. (Eds.). (2010). *El sacrificio humano en la tradición religiosa mesoamericana* (1st ed.). Mexico City: Instituto Nacional de

Antropología e Historia : Universidad Nacional Autónoma de México Instituto de Investigaciones Históricas.

Luna, Jennie M. (2011). *Danza Mexica: Indigenous Identity, Spirituality, Activism, and Performance*. (Doctoral Dissertation), University of California Davis, Davis, California.

Maestas, E. (1999). Danza Azteca: Xicana/o life-cycle ritual and autonomous culture. In M. A. Beltrán-Vocal, M. d. J. Hernández-Guitiérrez, & S. Fuentes (Eds.), *Mapping Strategies: NACCS and the Challenge of Multiple (Re)Oppressions*. Selected proceedings of the XXII Annual conference of the National Association for Chicana and Chicano Studies, held in Chicago, Illinois, March 20–23, 1996 (pp. 60–90). Chicago, Illinois: Orbis.

Maestas, E. G.-M. (1998). *Grupo Tlaloc Community Life as a Model for Alternative Pedagogy*. MA Thesis, University of Texas at Austin.

Maestas, E. G.-M. (2003). Culture and history of native American peoples of South Texas. PhD, Unpublished Doctoral Dissertation, University of Texas, Austin.

Mansfield, P. (1953). The conchero dancers of Mexico. PhD, Unpublished Dissertation + Film, New York University, New York.

Márquez Rodiles, I. (1990). *Formas de la educación en las grandes culturas precolombinas: De los orígenes al descubrimiento de América, 1492*. Santa Catarina Mártir, Puebla: Universidad de las Américas-Puebla.

Martí, S., & Prokosch Kurath, G. (1964). *Dances of Anahuac: The Choreography and Music of Precortesian Dances* (Vol. 38). Chicago: Adeline Pub. Co.

Martínez-Hunter, S. (1984). *The Development of Dance in Mexico, 1325–1910*. PhD, Texas Woman's University, Denton, Texas. WorldCat database.

McPherson, K. (2006). Protest drew as many as 125,000 police say. *San Jose Mercury News*. May 4.

Medina, J. (1970). *México: Leyendas-costumbres, trajes y danzas*. México DF: Impresa Mexico.

Mendoza "Kuauhkoatl," M. A. (2007). *Los mexicas hoy*. Mexico DF: Nekutik Editorial.

Merriam, A. P. (1972). Anthropology and the dance. *New Dimensions in Dance Research*. Proceedings of the Third Conference on Research in Dance. Tucson: University of Arizona.

Meza Gutiérrez, A. (1993). *Al otro lado de las sombras: Otra cara de los mitos en la historia*. México: Publicaciones Artesanales.

Mignolo, W. (1992). When speaking was not good enough: Illiterates, barbarians, savages, and cannibals. In R. Jara & N. Spadaccini (Eds.), *Amerindian Images and the Legacy of Columbus* (pp. 312–345). Minneapolis: University of Minnesota Press.

Milbrath, S. (2001). Aztec *Oxford Encyclopedia of Mesocamerican Cultures* (Vol. 3, pp. 68–70). New York: Oxford University Press.

Miller, M., & Taube, K. (1993). *The Gods and Symbols of Ancient Mexico and the Maya: An Illustrated Dictionary of Mesoamerican Religion*. New York: Thames and Hudson.

Montes de Oca, J. G. (1926). *Danzas Indigenas Mejicanas*. Tlaxcala: Imp. del Gobierno del Estado.

Monzón Estrada, A. (1949). *El calpulli en la organización social de los Tenochca*. México: Instituto Nacional Indigenista.

Morehart, C. T. (2011). Sustainable ecologies and unsustainable politics: Chinampa farming in ancient central Mexico. *Anthropology News, 52* (4), 9–10.

Morgan, L. H. (1964). *Ancient Society*. Cambridge, MA: Belknap Press of Harvard University Press.

Moriarty, J. R. (1969). The pre-conquest Aztec state: A comparison between progressive evolutionist and other historical interpretations. *Estudios de cultura Náhuatl, 8*, 257–270.

NCPB/KQED (Producer). (1970, September 7). Chicano Protest March. [Archival News Film] Retrieved from <http://diva.sfsu.edu/collections/sfbatv/bundles/189480>.

Nieva, M. d. C., & Nieva López, R. F. (1969). *Mexikayotl: Esencia del mexicano: Filosofía nauatl*. Mexico City: Orión.

Nutini, H. G. (1961). Clan organization in a Nahuatl-speaking village of the State of Tlaxcala, México. *American Anthropologist, 63* (1), 62–78.

Odena Güemes, L. (1984). *Movimiento Confederado Restaurador de la Cultura de Anahuac* (1st ed.). México DF: Centro de Investigaciones y Estudios Superiores en Antropología Social, CIESAS.

Odena Güemes, L. (1993). En busca de la méxicanidad. In G. Bonfil Batalla (Ed.), *Nuevas identidades culturales en México* (1st ed., p. 225). México DF: Consejo Nacional para la Cultura y las Artes.

Oltra Perales, E. (1977). *Paideia precolombina: Ideales pedagógicos de aztecas, mayas e incas*. Buenos Aires: Ediciones Castañeda.

Ordóñez, J. (1992). *La educación precolonial de Indoamérica: Su filosofía*. Heredia, Costa Rica: Secretaría del Departamento de Filosofía, Facultad de Filosofía y Letras, Universidad Nacional.

Ortiz De Montellano, B. R. (1983). Counting skulls: Comment on the Aztec cannibalism theory of Harner-Harris. *American Anthropologist, 85* (2), 403–406.

Ostrom, M. A., Foo, R., Fernandez, L., & McPherson, K. (2006). San Jose immigration rally under way. *San Jose Mercury News*. May 1.

Paideia. (2010). Accessed August 12, 2010. Retrieved from <http://www.etymonline.com/index.php?search=paideia&searchmode=none>.

Palimpsest. (2000). *American Heritage Dictionary of the English Language* (4th ed.). Boston: Houghton Mifflin.

Palimpsest (2006). *Concise Oxford English dictionary*. Soanes, C., & Stevenson, A. (Eds.) New York: Oxford University Press.

Palimpsest. (2010). *Merriam-Webster Online Dictionary*. Accessed August 17, 2010. Retrieved from <http://www.merriam-webster.com/dictionary/palimpsest>.

Perkins, S. M. (2005). Corporate community or corporate houses?: Land and society in a colonial Mesoamerican community. *Culture and Agriculture, 27* (1), 16–34.

Pohl, J. M. D., & Lyons, C. L. (2010). *The Aztec Pantheon and the Art of Empire*. Los Angeles: J. Paul Ghetty Museum.

Powell, K. A. (2003). Learning together: Practice, pleasure and identity in a taiko drumming world. PhD, Unpublished Doctoral Disseration, Stanford, California.

Price, B. J. (1978). Enriddlement, and Aztec cannibalism: A materialist rejoinder to Harner. *American Ethnologist, 5* (1), 98–115.

Programa Universitario México Nación Multicultural. (2011). Los pueblos indígenas de México: 100 preguntas 24. *¿Qué son el tequio, la gozona, la faena, la fajina, el tequil, la guelaguetza, el trabajo de en medio y la mano de vuela?* Retrieved from <http://www.nacionmulticultural.unam.mx/100preguntas/pregunta.html?num_pre=24>.

Ramírez, O. (2007). [La Educacion Mexica, el curiculo, y la danza]. April 1.

Ramírez, O. (2009). *Symbolism in the Mexica Warrior Dance/Simbolismo de la Danza Guerrera.* Paper presented at the Center for Training and Careers, San José, California.

Reagan, T. G. (2005). *Non-Western Educational Traditions: Indigenous Approaches to Educational Thought and Practice* (3rd ed.). Mahwah, NJ: Lawrence Erlbaum Associates.

Regino Montes, A. (1998). La reconstitución de los pueblos indígenas. In M. A. Bartolomé & A. M. Barbas (Eds.), *Autonomías étnicas y Estados nacionales* (pp. 415–424). Mexico City: INAH.

Regino Montes, A. (1999). Los pueblos indígenas: Diversidad negada. *Chiapas, 7,* Chapter 7. Retrieved from <http://www.ezln.org/revistachiapas/No7/ch7.html>. In English at <http://www.ezln.org/english/revistachiapas/No7/ch7.html>.

Romerovargas Yturbide, I. (1957). *Organización política de los pueblos de Anáhuac* (1st ed.). México City, México: Libros Luciernaga.

Romerovargas Yturbide, I. (1959). *El calpuli de Anáhuac: Base de nuestra organización política.* México: Romerovargas.

Romerovargas Yturbide, I. (1978). *Los gobiernos socialistas de Anáhuac.* México: Romerovargas.

Rostas, S. (1993). The Mexica's reformulation of the Concheros Dance; the popular use of autochtonous religion in Mexico City. In S. Rostas & A. T. Droogers (Eds.), *Popular Use of Popular Religion in Latin America* (pp. 211–224). Netherlands: CEDLA.

Rostas, S. (2009). *Carrying the Word: The Concheros Dance in Mexico City.* Boulder, CO: University Press of Colorado.

Rostas, S. E. (2002). "Mexicanidad": The resurgence of the indian in popular mexican nationalism. *Cambridge Anthropology, 23* (Part 1), 20–38.

Rounds, J. (1979). Lineage, class, and power in the Aztec state. *American Ethnologist, 6* (1), 73–86.

Royce, A. P. (1977). *The Anthropology of Dance.* Bloomington: Indiana University Press.

Sahagún, F. B. d. (1992). *Historia general de las cosas de Nueva Espana.* Mexico: Editorial Porrua.

Saldaña Arellano, R. d. J. (2011). El tequio o faena: ¿Práctica legal o ilegal? Retrieved from <www.ciesas.edu.mx/proyectos/relaju/documentos/Saldana_Jesus.pdf>.

Sánchez Jiménez, J. (2009). El Baile de los elotes: The corn dance. In O. Nájera-Ramírez, N. Cantú, & B. M. Romero (Eds.), *Dancing across Borders: Danzas Y Bailes Mexicanos* (pp. 165–181). Chicago: University of Illinois Press.

Soanes, C. (2006). *Oxford dictionary of English.* Oxford: Oxford University Press.

Soustelle, J. (1970). *Daily Life of the Aztecs on the Eve of the Spanish Conquest. Uniform Title: Vie Quotidienne Des Azteques: La Veille De La Conquiste Espagnole. English*. Stanford, CA: Stanford University Press.

Sten, M. (1990). *Ponte a bailar, tu que reinas: Antropologia de danza prehispanica*. Mexico City: Editorial Joaquin Mortiz.

Stevenson, R. M. (1968). *Music in Aztec & Inca Territory*. Berkeley: University of California Press.

Stone, M. (1975). *At the Sign of Midnight: the Concheros Dance Cult of Mexico*. Tucson: University of Arizona Press.

Sullivan, T. D. (1974). *The Rhetorical Orations, Or Huehuetlatolli, Collected by Sahagun*. Sl: University of New Mexico press.

Sullivan, T. D., & Knab, T. J. (1994). *a Scattering of Jades: Stories, Poems, and Prayers of the Aztecs*. New York: Simon & Schuster.

Tirquis de Oaxaca. (2011). Sucesión Triqui. Retrieved from <http://www.triquis. org/sucesion-triqui/>.

Todorov, T. (1995). *La conquista de América: El problema del otro* (p. 277: il. ed.). Mexico City: SIGLO XXI.

Toor, F. (1947). *a Treasury of Mexican Folkways*. New York: Crown.

Toriz Proenza, M. (2002). La danza entre los mexicas. In M. Ramos Smith & P. Cardona Lang (Eds.), *La danza en Mexico* (Vol. I, pp. 305–324). Mexico, DF: CONACULTA, INBA-CENIDI-danza, Escenologia.

Townsend, R. F. (2000). *The Aztecs* (Rev. ed.). New York: Thames and Hudson.

Vaillant, G. C. (1941). *Aztecs of Mexico: Origin, Rise and Fall of the Aztec Nation*. Garden City, NY: Doubleday Doran.

Valencia, M. (1994). Danza Azteca. In H. Polkinhorn, G. Trujillo Muñoz & R. Reyes (Eds.), *Bodies beyond Boders: Dance on the u.s.–Mexico Border; Curepos más allá de la fronteras: La Danza en la frontera México-Estados Unidos*. Calexico/ Mexicalli: Binational Press/Editorial Binacional.

Van Zantwijk, R. (1963). Principios organizdores de los Méxicas, Una introduccion al estudio del sistema interno del regimen Azteca. *Estudios de cultura Náhuatl, 4* (88), 292.

Vásquez Hernández, J. d. J. (1994). Nacionalismo y racismo en México, el caso de la Mexicanidad (Mexicayotli). MA, Unpublished Masters Thesis, Universidad Nacional Autonoma de Mexico, UNAM, Mexico City.

Velazco, S. (2003). *Visiones de Anáhuac: Reconstrucciones historiografías y etnicidades emergentes en el México colonial: Fernando de Alva Ixtlilxóchitl, Diego Muñoz Camargo y Hernando Alvarado Tezozómoc* (1st ed.). Guadalajara, Jalisco, México: Universidad de Guadalajara.

Velázquez Romo, D. (1998). La danza Azteca-chichimeca de los concheros: Una forma de identidad en el Estado de México. In E. A. Sandoval Forero & M. Castillo Nechar (Eds.), *Danzas tradicionales: Actualidad u obsolencia?* (1a. ed., pp. 203). México: Universidad Autónoma del Estado de México.

Vento, A. C. (1994). Aztec Conchero dance tradition: Historic, religious and cultural significance. *Wicazo Sa Review, 10* (1), 59–64. Retrieved from <http://www.jstor.org/stable/1409310>.

Vetancurt, F. A. d. (1982). *Teatro mexicano. Descripción breve de los sucesos ejemplares históricos y religiosos del Nuevo Mundo de las Indias (1682)*. México DF: Editorial Porrua.

Vogt, E. Z. (1970). *The Zinacantecos of Mexico: a Modern Maya Way of Life*. New York: Holt, Rinehart and Winston.

Warman, A. (2003). *Los indios mexicanos en el ubral de milenio*. Mexico City: Fondo de Cultura Económica.

Zepeda-Millán, Christopher. (2011). *Dignity's Revolt: Threat, Identity, and Immigrant Mass Mobilization*. Doctoral Dissertation, Cornell Univerisity, Ithaca, New York.

Zurita, A. d. (1963). *Life and Labor in Ancient Mexico: the Brief and Summary Relation of the Lords of New Spain. Uniform Title: Breve y sumaria relación de los señores de la Nueva España. English* (B. Keen, Trans.). New Brunswick, NJ: Rutgers University Press.

Index

Page numbers in italics refer to pictures, tables, and charts.

Printed in the United States of America